Healing

Healing

FRANCIS MacNUTT

HODDER AND STOUGHTON
LONDON SYDNEY AUCKLAND TORONTO

To Judith,
Rachel and David

British Library Cataloguing in Publication Data

MacNutt, Francis
    Healing.
    1. Christianity. Spiritual healing
    I. Title
    615.8'52

    ISBN 0-340-51035-8

**The Spirit
of the Lord is
on me, because he has
anointed me to preach
good news to the
poor. He has sent me to
proclaim freedom for
the prisoners and recovery
of sight for the blind,
to release the
oppressed.**

Luke 4:18

Contents

PART III
The Four Basic Kinds of Healing
And How to Pray for Each

PART IV
Special Considerations

Foreword

When Creation House told me that Francis MacNutt had revised *Healing*, his classic on divine healing, and asked if I would write its foreword, I accepted enthusiastically. Francis's original edition was one of the first books I read on healing, and it had a profound effect on me. After reading *Healing* I was more convinced than ever that God wants to heal today, and I received practical insights into how to pray for the sick.

When I wrote *Power Healing*, my book on the same topic, I relied on many of Francis's insights, especially his approach to "soaking prayer." In the *Study Guide to Power Healing* I wrote this about *Healing*: "A classic and foundational book on healing, it offers a comprehensive look into the history and the effects of worldviews on healing." This new edition only improves on a very good book.

Francis MacNutt's writing is authentic because he is a practitioner of what he writes about. Last year I had the privilege of ministering together with him at an advanced healing seminar here in Anaheim, California. Almost all of the 2,000 attendees left either healed, encouraged or inspired. We all were touched by Francis's compassion and patience as he prayed for literally hundreds of people.

The only shortcoming for me in the original edition of

Healing was its narrow denominational focus; it was written with a distinctly Catholic and sacramental orientation. As an evangelical Protestant I had to wade through some material that, though well-written, was of concern only to Catholics. My interest in divine healing was high enough to sustain my interest throughout the entire book. But I suspected many other Protestants weren't as motivated.

Well, I am happy to report that shortcoming for Protestants has been corrected in this edition. If in the past you have shied away from *Healing*, thinking it only addresses Catholic concerns, be assured that this new edition is for all Christians.

After I read *Healing* I was no longer content to talk and read about divine healing; I had to get out there and start praying for the sick. I hope that this revised edition does the same for you.

John Wimber
Yorba Linda, California
May 1988

Introduction

Since its first publication in 1974, *Healing* has reached many Christians and encouraged them to launch out in praying for the sick. Nearly a million copies were printed in the United States by Ave Maria Press and Bantam Books, and translations have been made into such diverse languages as Chinese, Swahili, Japanese and Finnish.

In spite of its success I have desired for years to write a version that would reach all Christians, and not just those of a Catholic background. Prayer for healing is so central to the gospel that it should be an integral part of the life of every community of believers. My heart cries out to see it restored to the place it had in the early Christian church.

This edition, then, is an updating and rewriting of *Healing* to reach out to all Christians who are intent upon renewal and upon bringing the riches of the gospel to all the peoples of the world today.

Francis S. MacNutt
Christian Healing Ministries
P.O. Box 9520
Jacksonville, FL 32208

Preface

In recent years an extraordinary change has been going on in the churches, all the way from the grassroots level to the most official pronouncements: The healing ministry is being renewed.

In homes and churches we are seeing prayer groups rediscovering the power of praying for the sick. This is not just a theoretical change; it is a change based on the experience of people who have seen the sick healed through prayer. At a typical conference now, when I ask for a show of hands to see who has ever prayed with a sick person that Jesus might bring healing, the majority raise their hands. Similarly, when I ask how many believe that they themselves have been healed through prayer, about half the hands go up.

Yet when I ask how many can remember their fathers ever praying for healing with them, only *three percent* lift their hands. And only *twenty percent* can remember their mothers praying with them. Clearly we have witnessed an extraordinary change in the mainline churches in one generation. My own conversion to an active belief in the healing ministry reflects this dramatic change in many churches. (The Pentecostal churches, of course, have been praying for healing since their founding at the turn of the century.)

My own involvement in the healing ministry came about

in a natural way; I never had much internal resistance to overcome—except lack of courage. My question has never really been about the reality of healing ministry, but rather about its wise use.

I was first prepared for this ministry by my desire to become a doctor, a desire which was nearly fulfilled in 1944 when I was accepted by Washington University Medical School after only two years of college pre-med. If all had gone well I would have become a doctor at the very young age of twenty-three. But that dream was shattered when I was drafted in September 1944, just ten days before entering medical school. The next two years I served in the medical department of the Army as a surgical technician, mostly working in the operating room of the hospital at Camp Crowder, Missouri.

Years later, when I entered the seminary and read accounts of so many healings performed throughout the history of the church, I couldn't help but wonder why earlier generations seemed to have so much success obtaining healing for the sick through their prayers, while we were never encouraged to pray for such things. We were given the impression that praying for healing was presumptuous—we were not worthy of extraordinary manifestations of God's power.

How clearly I remember the day in July 1956 when a friend came to me and asked me to heal his son's partial blindness. This was only a month after my ordination, and I didn't know how to respond to him. One thing I did know, however, was that I was no miracle worker, so I refused to go over to his home. I knew I was disappointing him, but I thought I would disappoint him even more if I went to his home and his son was not healed through my prayers.

Much later—when I was teaching homiletics (preaching) in the two Catholic seminaries in Dubuque, Iowa, and also trying to counsel many people—I realized that something was missing in my ministry. What kind of spiritual direction could I give to all these people coming for counseling?

Many of them were sent to me by their psychiatrists. They were depressed—some to the point of attempting suicide—some were alcoholic, some homosexual, some hopelessly confused, feeling worthless and unlovable. Their emotional problems could not be separated from their "spiritual" lives; as human beings they were being dragged down by sadness and guilt. Yet they could not overcome their problems by willpower. Among them were men and women who had dedicated their lives to Christ and to the work of the church, but found that they were not able to live happily in service to the Lord in spite of all their good will.

I could not honestly say to myself—or to those I counseled—that all this destructive suffering was redemptive. I could not sincerely tell the mentally depressed patients, who were undergoing shock therapy, that their anxiety state was God's will and was a cross specially chosen by God for them. Clearly, there was a mystery involved in this, but it was the mystery of evil, of our fallen human condition. I could not believe that it was the mystery of God's direct will for us.

One day I heard that Alfred Price, one of the founders of the Order of St. Luke (which was established to restore the healing ministry), was going to speak at the Presbyterian Seminary of Dubuque. So I took what was in those days the bold step of going over to a Protestant seminary to hear him (this was around 1960). Everything he said made sense, especially that Jesus Christ has given His apostles as much a commission to heal as to teach. On the basis of New Testament evidence, that much seemed irrefutable. So, he asked, if the church still claimed Christ's commission to teach, what had happened to the allied commission to heal and cast out demons?

After the talk a group gathered for discussion and compared

notes on how they prayed for the sick. They described some of the phenomena they had experienced, such as feeling heat in the hands, followed by swelling if the prayer went on too long. What really astonished me was that some of these ministers were not bothering to discuss a theory about whether or not healings took place; they were discussing a ministry they were sure of.

For them there was no doubt: Healings took place. For me a whole new world had opened up. But I didn't know what to do about it; no one was around to encourage me to launch out.

The next time I heard about healing was in 1966, at the annual convention of the Speech Association of America (which I was attending as executive director of the Christian Preaching Conference). There in Chicago I was introduced by some friends to Jo Kimmel, a speech professor at Manchester College (Indiana), who I was told had remarkable success in praying for the sick. Upon meeting her and finding that she really did have some unusual—and to me almost unbelievable—experiences in praying for the sick, I called a friend of mine and together we spent a whole day pumping her for information about all this prayer for healing.

I remember expressing surprise at her belief that these extraordinary healings would really take place. Her response was to ask why I thought healing should be extraordinary. She plainly considered healing an ordinary part of Christian life and said that there were hundreds of people with experiences like her own.

Where have they been? I thought. I've never met anyone like this. It's a whole new world—except that I had read about things like this in the history of earlier generations in the church.

Jo offered to introduce me to some of these people by arranging for me to attend a conference (a Camp Farthest

Out for 800 people) in Maryville, Tennessee, in August 1967. There I met two of the main speakers, Agnes Sanford and Tommy Tyson, and learned still more about praying for healing. A year later, at a School for Pastoral Care held in Whitinsville, Massachusetts, I learned still more from Agnes, Tommy and John Sandford.

These schools (really five-day workshops) were instituted by Ted Sanford and his wife, Agnes, to help convince ministers that the healing ministry should be part of the normal work of any Christian minister. Although her husband had died some years before, Agnes carried on the work of teaching and was perhaps more responsible than anyone else for renewing the healing ministry in the mainline churches. (Agnes herself died several years ago.)

Although I was the first Roman Catholic priest to attend one of these Schools of Pastoral Care, I saw immediately that the basic teachings on healing were very much in line with Scripture and with my own religious tradition. I didn't find it difficult to believe that God still heals today— occasionally. What I found difficult to believe was that healing could be an ordinary, common activity of Christian life.

When I discovered, though, that healing was common in the lives of people like Agnes Sanford, it all seemed to make sense. If it were true, it meant I would no longer have to tell people whose sicknesses were disintegrating their personalities that their illness was a God-sent cross. Instead, I could hold up the hope that God wanted them well, even when medical science could not help.

A short time after coming to believe in the reality of healing in the lives of these friends I had grown to love and respect—Jo Kimmel, Tommy Tyson and Agnes Sanford—I realized I could not treat this good news as if it were some abstract theory. I would have to put it into practice.

The first person I prayed for was a woman who had been

through shock treatment for mental depression and had been taken as far as psychiatry could take her. I knew she had nothing to lose by my praying with her. And I had nothing to lose, except a certain false humility, by offering to pray for her healing.

To my surprise (at least partly) she was healed. Somehow up until then it had been much easier to believe that God could heal the sick *through prayer* than to believe that He would heal *through my prayer*. But this healing encouraged me to believe that if *I* prayed for people they might be healed.

Since then I have seen many people healed—especially when I have prayed with a team or in a loving community. Although I travel too much to be able to follow up and estimate accurately, I would make a rough estimate that about half of those we pray for are healed (or are notably improved) of physical sickness, and about three-fourths of those we pray for are healed of emotional or spiritual problems. I say this as an encouragement for others to consider the possibility that God might use their prayers someday to heal the sick.[1]

In no way do I conceive of prayer for healing as a negation of the need for doctors, nurses, counselors, psychiatrists or pharmacists. God works in all these ways to heal the sick. The ideal is a team effort to get the sick well through every possible means.

Nevertheless, although I am aware that some prayer can have a psychological effect through the power of suggestion, I am convinced through my own experience that prayer for healing brings into play forces far beyond what our own unaided humanity contributes. The results of prayer have been extraordinary—so much so that what once would have astonished our retreat team we now take almost for granted. The extraordinary has become ordinary. Jesus Christ alone can account for the healings we now see almost every day.

That, I think, is precisely the way the healing ministry

should be: an ordinary, normal part of the life of every Christian family, church and community.

Francis S. MacNutt

PART I

The Healing Ministry—
Its Underlying Meaning
and Importance

*Someone touched me;
I know that power
has gone out from me.*

Luke 8:46

1 | Does Healing Happen?

Is it possible that God directly heals people? Does it really happen? All other questions in this ministry depend on this first question of all: Is there such a thing as healing?

In the absence of direct experiential evidence, educated Christians have tended, in recent centuries, to rely upon the opinion of theologians and Scripture scholars. On the other hand, the uneducated, in general, seem to be the ones who go to healing services. I am reminded of the words of Jesus after His disciples returned from a successful preaching and healing tour: "I praise you, Father, Lord of heaven and earth, because you have hidden these things from the wise and learned, and revealed them to little children" (Luke 10:21).

In the past hundred years, moreover, with a growing appreciation of literary forms in the Bible, some theologians and Scripture scholars have questioned whether we should accept the miracles of Jesus literally. In a similar way, the existence of Satan, as a personal entity, has been questioned. Consequently, a literal acceptance of the exorcisms of Jesus is severely called into question. (The public controversy following the opening of the film *The Exorcist* is a good example of this debate.)

Nevertheless, we are now seeing a return of the direct experience of God's healing power in such striking ways that the living tradition of Christianity—what the Spirit is helping us to experience and understand *today*—is leading us again to a more lively awareness of what Jesus did 2,000 years ago in His healing ministry. If we ourselves see miracles of healing, we no longer have difficulty in picturing the healing in the Gospels. Suddenly everywhere I travel I discover that people have experienced firsthand the healing power of God. From my own hometown of St. Louis, for example, busloads of people once traveled to attend the healing services of Kathryn Kuhlman in Pittsburgh, nearly a thousand miles away. Local church authorities heard that many Catholics, including nuns, were going on these pilgrimages and they could not understand why.

The climate is changing. People are hungering and thirsting to know God in a direct, experiential way. And the sick still need healing, just as much as they did in Christ's day. Those needs and desires are basic to our humanity. If the risen Christ is still healing the sick, then we have no problem making Christianity relevant to the needs of most people today. In fact, if we, like Jesus, could walk among the sick and heal as many as came to us, we would have some of His problems—like finding a place to hide from the pursuing multitude of sick people.

But does Jesus still heal? Next to Scripture, the most convincing argument is always experience: "Go back and report to John what you have seen and heard: The blind receive sight, the lame walk, those who have leprosy are cured, the deaf hear, the dead are raised, and the good news is preached to the poor" (Luke 7:22). The simple and the poor followed Jesus in crowds because they saw what happened, while the religious leaders tried to figure out what it all meant.

Later, when the apostles continued Christ's healing ministry, the people continued to come in crowds, while the theologians continued to question what was going on.

Remember, for example, how after the healing of the crip-
ple at the Beautiful Gate of the Temple, the high priests,
rulers, elders and scribes arrested Peter and John to question them:

> When they saw the courage of Peter and John and
> realized that they were unschooled, ordinary men,
> they were astonished and they took note that these
> men had been with Jesus. But since they could see
> the man who had been healed standing there with
> them, there was nothing they could say. So they
> ordered them to withdraw from the Sanhedrin and
> then conferred together. "What are we going to do
> with these men?" they asked.
>   "Everybody living in Jerusalem knows they have
> done an outstanding miracle, and we cannot deny
> it. But to stop this thing from spreading any further
> among the people, we must warn these men to speak
> no longer to anyone in this name" (Acts 4:13-17).

In this way the first persecution in the infant church was
occasioned not only by the apostles' preaching the resurrection, but by their power of healing in the name of Jesus. The
actual experience of seeing a crippled man healed confronted
the religious people of Jesus' day with two decisions to make:
One was theoretical: Was the healing real or not?
The other was practical: What should they do about it?
They judged that it was real. But they decided to forbid
it, because they believed that it was doctrinally unsound (being
connected with preaching the resurrection of Jesus), and that
it would undermine their authority—especially since the
preaching and healing were done by "uneducated laymen."
Consequently, these religious authorities tried to suppress
the new movement by forbidding the apostles to preach.
Today religious leaders are again being confronted, not

by theories of theologians, but by the witnessing to healing that people—many of them "uneducated laymen"—claim to have experienced. Like the Sanhedrin, they are faced with an opportunity not merely to discuss a theory, but to make a judgment: "Is this true?" and then to make a decision: "Should we do something about it?"

My own experiences have convinced me that divine healing does happen, and commonly. Having come to that judgment, I decided that I had better learn as much as I could about this phenomenon and then start praying for the sick. For me it was no longer an option: If I could help the sick by my prayers, but would not, then I would be in danger of hearing, "Whatever you did not do for one of the least of these, you did not do for me" (Matt. 25:45).

If you have not yourself experienced the ministry of healing or have not talked to a friend who has, it may seem naive to accept that God does directly touch the lives of people and heal them. But after studying philosophy and theology for seven years, I have concluded that unsophisticated people who are taken in too easily are no more mistaken than the skeptical theological world which questions whether God ever "intervenes" or "interferes" in the universe. My own experience leads me to the conclusion that healing is the most convincing demonstration to people that God is *with us*— that He is not "out there" beyond the reach of human compassion.

Many Christians today live by a practical norm of "God helps those who help themselves," and seem quite willing to limit the present Christian ministry of healing to whatever the art of medicine can achieve. Healing by prayer, they would say, was meant for a more primitive age, but now that we understand reality better, we can achieve through medicine what used to be claimed by prayer in a prescientific society open to the powers of suggestion.

Even so, I can see no point in setting medicine in opposition to healing by prayer (a point that will be developed later in this book). In fact, some doctors themselves now practice a coordinated ministry of medicine and prayer. Books such as Paul Tournier's *A Doctor's Casebook in the Light of the Bible,*[1] Dr. William Reed's *Surgery of the Soul*[2] and *Faith Healing: Finger of God or Scientific Curiosity* (subtitled "An Unexpected Medical Look at the Role of Faith in Healing")[3] are all examples of the renewed interest of doctors in the power of prayer as related to their profession.

Other individuals object to healing by asking why we should talk about healing of individuals when the great healings needed today are the healing of broken relationships, the healing of a broken society, and the healing of a world tormented by institutional injustice and the threat of war. Yet we need not set the need for the larger healing of society in opposition to individual healing. I know of no activists involved in a social justice mission who do not themselves go to doctors or dentists when they are sick, under the pretext that other, more global problems occupy their attention. The larger issues of injustice will be helped when individuals in society are themselves made whole—when they are healed emotionally so that they can enter into healthy relationships, so that they are not acting out of prejudices or ancient hurts.[4]

Recent experience with groups in Latin America indicates to me that praying for the healing of the human inner being will help as much as anything toward the creation of a just society. My friends working in the ministry of social justice have experienced the failure of so many dreams of the sixties, and they wholeheartedly agree that more is needed than mere structural changes. I find that many who have had the longest experience working with the oppressed are the most open to learn about prayer for inner healing. They themselves

27

see the widest range of its applications.

This is not an either/or question. We need to work at healing on all levels, and by all possible means: political, economic, and by prayer. Nor would I by any means put prayer last.

We are beginning to see the exciting possibility of bringing a number of previously conflicting tendencies in the church together—in particular, the drive for social justice together with the renewed concern for prayer and interior growth. The common joining point is intercessory prayer to heal the world and suffering humanity. In Bogota, Colombia, for instance, a conference was held in February 1973 for twenty-three Catholic charismatic leaders from eight countries. (The subsequent 1974 conference drew some 250 leaders.) Among their points of agreement were these: 1. The leaders share a common Latin American vision. 2. They find a tremendous thirst for God among the people. 3. They find that this is now accompanied by visible manifestations of the power of the Spirit.

In expanding on this power of the Spirit, the resume of the discussion notes that:

> Everywhere there were reports of God confirming His word and bringing people together through extraordinary manifestations of power—especially healing. In the poor barrios of Santa Cruz, Bolivia, the missionaries estimate that about eighty percent of the sick who ask for prayers in the poorest barrios are healed. The missionaries at the conference reported rediscovering the power of prayer in their own lives. Several priests had felt their lives had ended in failure in their attempts to bring Christianity to the people, until they found this new power in a simple presentation of the gospel message.

"An explosion in the church is what I see. We have been too cautious; now we have to be positive and move out among the people," said one participant.

In all this common vision there was agreement that the Holy Spirit is moving in power to do three basic things:

I. To transform *individuals* into a real personal relationship with Jesus Christ through the baptism of the Holy Spirit;

II. To heal relationships and *to build community*—especially in the family and the neighborhood community; and

III. To *transform society* by healing relationships of injustice and oppression.

In these three areas of transformation and liberation the participants found, again, certain common elements:

I. In the transformation of *individuals*:

A. Most of the participants had experienced a *personal conversion*. Commonly, the conversion was from attempting to promote works of justice through purely human, temporal and political means. These efforts in some instances were successful, in other instances, failures; but all sensed the inadequacy of these solutions trying to use purely human resources. When God's power to enlighten and heal was brought to bear on the same situation, new priorities emerged and true community began to form.

B. *Inner healing* is seen to be a principal means of bringing about this interior transformation. Justice cannot be brought to a society until there are just men; and men cannot be just until they are healed of the hurts and wounds of the past. In Latin America these wounds are prevalent as a result of widespread oppression and injustice, of "machismo," and of the wounds caused by broken families and prolonged poverty.

The missionaries, too, spoke of the need for inner healing in their own lives—of the failure and loneliness they have often suffered.

Whether or not inner healing is more needed in Latin America than in the United States is debatable; what does seem clear is that the need for it was recognized by all participants in the conference as being of key importance in building up the people of Latin America.

C. *Physical healing* was also seen as being vitally important—especially among the poor, who are almost all sick, with minimum medical care. Traditional preaching about suffering has always emphasized endurance of the Cross. This has led the people to an almost pagan view of God as handing out suffering—a God of wrath who is to be propitiated. A God of love is hard for the people to see without the kind of healing ministry Jesus Himself exercised. In Cali, Colombia, where a five-day mission at the barrio parish of San Juan Battista was begun with a healing service, attendance immediately doubled and generated a desire of the people to learn more about the gospel and to pray together.

In relation to the ministry of healing, there were also many fears on the part of the participants, because of the superstition connected with healing in the minds of the people:

i) Miracle-mongering and fraudulent healers and shrines have given this whole ministry a bad name. Just two years ago in Colombia a notorious fraud took place with a young girl healer who was exploited by her parents.

ii) Increasing a fatalistic tendency among the people to let God take action without any initiative on their part to improve their lot—to create sanitary conditions and to visit the doctor. The missionaries have had a hard time encouraging the people to take action and are not about to let them use prayer as a fatalistic dependence.

iii) Confusion in the people's minds which connects healing with witch doctors, *curanderos* and other forms of superstition.

iv) A general reaction against the old church piety which emphasizes prayer, shrines, healing and relics and other unworldly attitudes and that failed to lead the people to take action against injustice in the real world in which they lived.

Those missionaries, however, who have actually been working in Latin

America with the healing ministry
report that these problems are more
theoretical than real—that they are ob-
jections thought up by a clerical mentality and are not found among the
people once they understand a true
Christian *concept of prayer* for healing in community.[5]

In short, the opposition sometimes set up between a need
for the larger healing of society and individual healing is a
false one. It is not an either/or, but a both/and situation.

Typical of the growing discovery of the advances of join-
ing individual healing to the healing of society is this letter
(October 24, 1973) from Ralph Rogawski and Helen
Raycraft, who were then working in the poorest slums of
Bolivia. (They are now working with the Hispanic people
in McAllen, Texas.)

As you know, for the last seven years we've been
working in the marginated areas of Santa Cruz,
Bolivia. This work developed in such a way that both
of our communities now live permanently in different
areas of the city, sharing something of the life of the
people, promoting neighborhood organizations, co-
operatives, popular health and education programs,
etc. These continue, but more and more under the
leadership of the people themselves. We saw that at
the heart of the problem of social justice is the need
of a change of heart of the people themselves, a conversion to be just and to create new patterns and
values in living. Somehow this had to come about
through a personal rediscovery of Jesus Christ. So
we sought ways to bring people together in the name
of Jesus Christ. There was a need of some kind of

Christian community on a neighborhood or even a street basis.

In December of 1972 we tried something different. Using what we have learned and experienced in the charismatic renewal, we went into a neighborhood and began preaching Jesus Christ to any group of people interested enough to come. It was a simple program, preaching for a while, and then leading the people to pray spontaneously. We discovered more. People were very open to Jesus Christ and to reading the New Testament. With time, deep changes came about in their lives. They began to meet and pray regularly, and the seed of an explicit Christian community was born. And more, some spontaneously wanted to accompany us to other neighborhoods to preach with us! This experience has been repeated many times in Santa Cruz with similar results.[6]

I think, then, that we can see how a genuine correspondence can occur between healing and the aspirations of contemporary spirituality. Theology is a reflection upon Christian revelation in the light of the experience of the Christian community. The simplest, least complicated explanation of the healings of Jesus is that they happened as described, and my own recent experience, as well as that of countless other Christians, backs up that explanation. In the past twenty years I think I can safely say that I have seen thousands of healings take place through prayer.

Many of these healings taken individually are ambiguous as proof; they can be explained in a variety of ways. Who can claim that we know all the factors of a case, so that we can say with certainty, "This remission of disease took place following prayer; therefore prayer caused it to take place"? But I do believe that anyone who would come with us to conference after conference would see many of the sick healed or improved during prayer—a cumulative body of evidence all pointing in the direction of an extraordinary power being present, of a number of healings taking place well beyond the realm of chance occurrence.

Books have been written that document cases of healing[7] and, in an effort to demonstrate scientifically the power of prayer, some fascinating studies have been done on the effects of prayer upon plant growth—something that can be measured and calculated before and after prayer. For example, Franklin Loehr, a chemist, reports in his book *The Power of Prayer on Plants*[8] the results of 156 persons praying in 700 unit experiments using more than 27,000 seeds and seedlings. The experiments involved about 100,000 measurements and achieved up to a 52.71 percent growth advantage for prayer seedlings. Other experiments scientifically controlled include ''Some Biological Effects of the 'Laying on of Hands' '' by Bernard Grad,[9] in which he tested the speed with which wounds heal in mice, as well as a remarkable experiment in which the rate of growth of plants was measured when the plants (in this case, rye grass) were prayed for at a distance of 600 miles.[10]

While some of the experiments have an element of the bizarre—testing mice and rye grass—yet these were the most apt scientific controls and were perhaps necessary for a contemporary mentality seeking proof through scientific measurement. It would be a pity if scientists discovered persuasive evidence for the power of prayer at the very time when theologians were calling into question the value of the ancient Christian tradition of praying for the sick.[11]

I personally find most Christians open to discussing the possibility of praying for healing. Many have themselves been encouraged to launch out and pray for the sick with more confidence than before. They, in turn, bring back encouraging accounts of the visible renewal of their own ministry.

Priests today are discovering the power of intercessory prayers as part of their professional practice and spiritual counseling. This prayer is directed
at physical and especially inner healing. Serious
problems such as drug addiction, alcoholism, and
long-seated emotional disturbances in some cases
seem to have been helped by priests who recognize
the appropriateness of joining prayer to the equally
necessary professional counseling. They have seen
the power of Christ come through them as channels
of His love. As yet not many priests have experienced
this power, but for those who have, the problem of
discovering the relevance of their ministry has
disappeared.[12]

Seeing healing take place time after time in my own life,
I no longer have any difficulty in believing that even greater
things took place in the ministry of Christ. He said that we
would do even greater works than He did (see John 14:12),
and I suppose I would see even more healing take place in
my own ministry if I were a fitter instrument for God's healing love than I am. But even so, as noted in the preface, I
would estimate that more than half the people for whom we
pray for physical ailments are healed or are notably improved.

For me most of the battle in learning to pray for healing
was simply to conceive that God would answer my prayers
for physical needs in a human, physical way. Now I am convinced that He does. He treats us as human beings, not disem-
bodied spirits.

One of the most moving testimonies to God's healing of
physical infirmities came to me from a doctor and his patient.
The patient, Katherine Gould of Metairie, Louisiana, had
asked prayer for both an inner, emotional healing and for

the cure of various internal physical complaints, including a bladder hernia. Afterwards she wrote:

May 4, 1972

Dear Francis,

There was so much lifting for me at the Ardmore retreat that I questioned the feeling of physical (internal) lifting as perhaps being partly caused by my imagination. At the time we prayed, though, I was persuaded that healing did happen.

You remember, we also prayed for an increase of my doctor's faith. (I'm also enclosing his letter.) How I wish I could share the picture of his face after making his examination. He threw his arms up, saying, "Thank you, Jesus," because what had happened was a lifting and restoring of all the organs in my pelvic region.

According to him this kind of thing is not successfully resolved without major surgery.

After the prayer for inner healing I was so occupied with knowing Jesus in a newer, deeper, closer way that physical healing had really become secondary; I had lost the fear of surgery or of being ill. So it seems even more generous of Him to let me see His miracles.

How precious for Jesus to love us in such close and personal ways and to demonstrate for us signs and wonders of Himself.

Sincerely,
Katherine Gould

With her letter came the following enclosure from her doctor (also from Metairie, Louisiana):

May 3, 1972

Dear Francis,

This is written to testify to the glorious and magnificent power and healing grace of our Lord Jesus Christ. Mrs. Katherine Gould was seen by me, a gynecologist, for treatment of a bladder hernia—which can be corrected, as far as medical science knows, only by surgery. At the time she said she would be attending a retreat, and I suggested that she might pray for healing. This morning she returned to my office, entirely asymptomatic, without any discernible evidence of a bladder hernia. This precious grace of our Lord causes my heart and spirit to fill with joy.

In Christ,
James A. Seese, M.D., Ob/Gyn

The healing experience of Katherine Gould and countless other people has reinforced my conviction that among those signs that will be associated with believers, one will be this: "They will place their hands on sick people, and they will get well" (Mark 16:18).

Does healing happen? As you can see, I believe it does. I feel a small portion of the wonder John must have experienced when he wrote about the One who causes all this to happen:

That which was from the beginning, which we have heard, which we have seen with our eyes, which we have looked at and our hands have touched—this we proclaim concerning the Word of life. The life appeared; we have seen it and testify to it, and we proclaim to you the eternal life, which was with the Father and has appeared to us (1 John 1:1,2).

2 | Our Prejudices Against Healing

At the meeting I attended in Bogota, Colombia, in February 1973 (reported in Chapter 1), all the representatives agreed that the renewal of the Catholic Church in Latin America would be brought about through a renewal of the healing ministry. These representatives were missionaries who had long and active records in working for social justice. Yet they had discovered in prayer for healing a power for liberating people from inner problems and physical sickness that they had never known before.

At this remarkable meeting, all twenty-three leaders reported the same phenomenon: Christ is once again at work among His people just as He was 2,000 years ago, reaching out and healing the sick and wounded.[1] One missionary reported that nearly eighty percent of the poor people who prayed for healing in the barrios of Bolivia where he works were cured or notably improved. That is a remarkably high percentage, but I know the missionary (Ralph Rogawski) and trust what he says. In fact, from the reports I receive, it seems that more healing goes on among the poor (who do not have easy access to doctors and hospitals) than with those of us from more well-to-do countries.

Despite reports like these, a stout resistance remains in many Christians who have a hard time believing that such healings can take place. Although the gospels abound with accounts of healings, why is it that so many who follow Christ in our day find it hard to believe that healing can still take place? Ironically, many church leaders preach against the loss of faith among their people, yet they themselves lack a strong, active faith in Christ's power to heal the sick and wounded in their flock.

I have before me, for instance, an article from the *St. Louis Post-Dispatch* titled "Religious Education Agency Rejects Teaching That Jesus Is the Answer." How could I encourage a drug addict to turn in faith to Christ as Savior if I did not believe that Christ would actually free the victim from his bondage in answer to our prayer together? I believe that the ministry of healing is what moves the central doctrine of redemption and salvation from the realm of the abstract into the concrete reality of our lives.

One of the greatest losses Christianity has suffered has been the decline of the full heritage of healing power. This loss, this unbelief, has come about, I believe, through the growth of five basic prejudices against healing, all of which I have myself faced and seen in varying degrees in the attitudes of many Christians I know.

1) *"We want nothing to do with faith healing."*

When I encourage people to pray for healing, the first obstacle I usually meet is a stereotyped connection they have made between the healing ministry and faith healers. Because they themselves have never prayed for healing with the laying on of hands, their idea of it is conditioned by the only examples they have seen of such prayer: on television programs where revivalists shout and the people seem hysterical, or in newspaper articles which depict the Elmer Gantry type of exploitative evangelist, photographed with upraised arms and glassy eyes. These experiences are vivid enough to blot out the image we have of Jesus as He walked among the sick and touched and healed them. The popular image of "faith healer" has so completely taken over our imagination that it is hard for Christians from mainline churches to imagine healing in any other context, very much as the stereotype of "Pentecostal" makes the baptism of the Holy Spirit unacceptable to many Christians unless they are ready to shed a prejudice or two.[2]

We might well pose the question, Was Christ a faith healer? When we read the Gospels, especially Mark, we cannot help being struck by the constant references to Christ's healing ministry; about half the material of the first eight chapters of Mark is devoted to narratives of His curing the sick: "For he had healed many, so that those with diseases were pushing forward to touch him" (Mark 3:10). Can we imagine what this scene was like? Would we demean the Lord Himself by classifying Him as the kind of "faith healer" to whom we sense ourselves superior?

If He was not a faith healer, what descriptive word should we use? Whether we find the right word or not ("minister of healing," for instance), the important point is to recover the full heritage of healing that belongs to the Christian and to the church. To disparage the healing ministry because of certain excesses of snake-handling sects in the hills of Tennessee makes no more sense than to criticize modern medical practice because of the malpractice of some physicians. In either case, the fault lies in the minister or in the way the ministry is carried out and not in the validity of the ministry itself.

2) *"My sickness is a cross sent from God."*

A basic attitude that completely undercuts the idea of divine healing is the conviction that God Himself inflicts sickness upon us. In such a view, asking for healing is to oppose God's will and to refuse the cross He offers. Even granted that it is permissible to ask for relief, in this view it is far better

41

for the sick person to accept and bear his or her suffering. This endurance is more heroic, more Christ-like. "If you are going to be a saint," some claim, "you must expect suffering and sickness."

This undue emphasis on the cross and the benefits of suffering has largely displaced both the belief in and the desire for healing among many Christians of mainline churches.[3] Certainly it has affected preaching on the subject of sickness. Too often the preacher presents sickness as an effect of God's chastising love rather than as an element in the kingdom of evil. On the contrary, traditional Christian teaching insists that sickness is an effect of original sin—in other words, an ingredient of our fallen human condition which Jesus came to redeem.

Our attitude toward sickness—whether to ask God to remove it, or whether to accept it as His will—is such a key problem that an entire chapter will be devoted to it (Chapter 3). To be sure, if I believe that God sent me a sickness to test my love, I am not going to pray to be rid of it. Rather, I will embrace my cross and refuse to avail myself of any alleviation. Yet nowhere in the gospel do we see Christ encouraging the sick to live with their illness. On the contrary, He everywhere treats sickness as a manifestation of the kingdom of Satan which He has come to destroy.

3) *"It takes a saint to work a miracle, and I'm no saint."*
This is an attitude that seems to characterize Catholics in particular. Traditionally, Catholics have always believed in miracles. But these cures took place not to help the sick person primarily, but in order to point the way to a deeper truth. For instance, the healing of leprosy (which is a visible foulness) is seen as a sign of God's desire to heal the foulness of sin (which is invisible).

Or, again, if healing comes about through the prayers of a particular individual, it may be a sign that he or she is extraordinarily holy. If a number of cures take place, that might be a sign that the person is a candidate for canonization as a saint, or someone whose Christian life we should admire and imitate. Consequently, for an ordinary person like you or me, to pray for the sick would be a sign, surely, of presumption and pride.

For years this "humble" attitude totally blocked my own willingness to pray for the sick. I well remember how a Protestant friend came to visit me, just a month after my ordination in 1956 (long before Vatican II). He asked me to drive with him to his home to pray for the cure of his son who had been born partially blind.

I felt both embarrassed and challenged. I knew the gospel well enough to remember, "And these signs will accompany those who believe...they will place their hands on sick people, and they will get well" (Mark 16:17,18). But nothing in my seminary training or experience had prepared me to pray for the healing of the sick.

Through reading miracle accounts from the history of the church, I did believe in the possibility of healing. But I thought that only the holiest of saints could do such things—and that excluded me. What was I to do? I didn't think it right to build up my friend's hopes when I myself didn't believe my feeble prayers would help.

I was trapped: I didn't think my prayer could cure his son's blindness; on the other hand, I didn't want to weaken his childlike confidence in prayer. I decided to tell him how I felt: I simply couldn't drive to his home and pray for his son. The best I could do was to give him the phone numbers of two other friends who I thought were holy, who might be willing to go if I asked them. I saw his eyes drop with disappointment and knew that he would not call these other men; after all, I was his friend, the minister he knew and trusted. But that was the best I knew how to do in those days.

In the fifteen years since then, my ordinariness has not changed at all—I am still not on the roster of great saints. But my attitude about praying for the sick has certainly changed. A fear of my own unworthiness would not now keep me from getting into my friend's car and going over to pray for his son's sight. What I didn't at that time realize was the abundant goodness of God, who desires so much to heal His people that He uses ordinary people like myself. He does not limit Himself to extraordinary figures like Francis of Assisi, who seem so far removed as to be almost mythological figures.

Christ's statement, as reported in the concluding section of Mark's Gospel, is encouraging: "And these signs will accompany those who believe" (Mark 16:17). He did not say "those who are great saints," rather "those who believe."

My personal problem with healing was really a false humility. In the name of this virtue, we unwittingly have emptied our lives of the very life and power that Christ came to bring. Lowering our heads and saying, "Lord, I am not worthy," we have denied ourselves the joy of praying with sick friends in order that Christ might heal them.

4) *"We don't need signs and wonders anymore; we have faith."*

Another attitude, one of superiority toward healing, holds that miracles were needed in the early church to get it started; but now that the church is well under way and Christians understand the gospel message, there is no further need for signs or proof. This attitude is the outcome of an overemphasis on doctrine: It assumes that healing of the sick takes place, not primarily because the Father is compassionate and desires to heal broken humanity, but because He wants to make a point. Now that He has made it, it is more perfect of us to believe with naked faith, without external signs. Primitive people need props; but the mature church of today no longer needs inducements of that sort to believe.

Certain Christian groups have even made a dogma of this view ("Dispensationalism") and assert that the time for miracles has passed. Thus in this view any miracles reported today must be frauds. Meanwhile, most Roman Catholics of a traditional background are open to miracles, but tend to see them as signs of a higher truth and not to be sought in the ordinary course of events.

Certainly, healing is a sign of a higher reality, and our faith should not depend on signs and wonders—although signs and wonders certainly catch our attention and can *help* build our faith. Even so, healing the sick is in itself something to be sought. Is the point of healing merely to be a proof-factor for human intellect, or is it God's mercy reaching out to the sick? The sick *need* healing; we need healing. (More of this in Chapter 4.)

5) *"Miracles do not really take place; they only represent a primitive way of expressing reality."*

Though the first four obstacles to praying for the healing of the sick are serious, they still do not strike at the very possibility of God's moving with direct healing power. But certain current trends of thought deny even this possibility. Along with the great advances of modern biblical scholarship, a few authors tend to view everything in the gospel in purely natural, secular terms. This exaggerated demythologizing would question the possibility of a God who acts directly in history and in our personal lives. It would deny healing through any means other than that of medical science.

While not a Scripture scholar himself, a popular spiritual author, Louis Evely, reflects this attitude when he states:

> Miracles are merely a holdover from the age of pre-scientific explanation, an anachronism which persists only in those moldering ivory towers which continue

to exist in the real world.[4]

Such a view holds that primitive people can't explain the mysterious universe scientifically, and so they believe that everything they don't understand is caused by gods or spirits. Rain, for instance, is caused by a rain god, and the native shaman can cause rain by appealing to his god. But now we have grown out of such an unscientific primitive view and know that God works in the process of natural causes. A belief in healing, beyond those healing forces in the natural world, is a throwback to a kind of primitive religion that is ill-fitted for our modern world.

While it is true that primitive peoples were unduly superstitious and often ascribed mysterious phenomena to mythological forces, we need not throw out the possibility of the supernatural altogether. My own impression in visiting some so-called primitive cultures is that, while their religion is mixed with superstition, they are much more in touch with the real spiritual world than we are. For me it was quite a shock to come to this realization.

Once we begin to question whether Christ Himself really had any power over natural forces, then clearly we must ask how His own prayer could possibly work "miracles" today. Such thinking destroys the very idea of a cure taking place other than through natural, recognizable processes, and relegates divine healing to the era of primitive religion.

I have described in various discussions examples of actual healings that I have witnessed, only to hear these cures explained away as the result of psychological suggestion. Terms that prejudice the discussion from the beginning unless they are challenged would include ones like the following:

"I don't believe in an unpredictable God who intervenes in nature, who plays favorites."

"I don't believe any more in the 'God out there,' who 'zaps

in' like some pagan deity.''

Remarks like these imply that those who believe in healing believe in a kind of primitive God in the heavens. My own experience has been that a person who has known God's healing love and power senses the presence of God within, the immanent God, the God who works in and through His creation. Far from imagining God as distant, I sense Him as more present than ever before.

God has many ways of acting in our lives. To limit His power by saying that He acts only through nature does indeed make Him seem distant and impersonal. In effect, to insist that God does not heal puts Him ''out there'' and makes Him into an impersonal force even less involved in our lives than any compassionate human being would be.

The Gospels state that when Jesus sent His disciples out to preach, He instructed them to cure the sick and then to say, ''The kingdom of God is near you'' (cf. Luke 9 and 10). People respond in the same way today when a healing takes place: Christ seems closer; His kingdom is near us—now.

Nevertheless, many Christians have never seen healing occur in response to prayer, so naturally they exclude it from their spirituality. It is not surprising that such lack of confidence in the power of prayer leads people to wonder whether God has any power at all. ''If He does have power,'' they ask, ''why doesn't He exert it? Does He really care about us? If He doesn't have any power, but simply exists as part of the human process, are we sure He even exists?''

Weeds in the Wheat

At this point I am reminded of the parable of the enemy who went out and sowed weeds in the wheat field while the farmer slept.[5] Using poetic liberty, I take the farmer to represent the leaders in the church; the wheat is the good news that Christ has come to proclaim liberty to the captives and healing for the whole human being. Sometime in the night (the Dark Ages) the enemy came and sowed an interlacing network of seeds that choked out even the expectation of a harvest of wheat. Instead of the good news of healing, a multitude of interlocking arguments encourages us to return to an acceptance of sickness: the "bad news."

The arguments run rather like this:

In relation to God:

God ordinarily does not want to heal. Suffering and sickness are His will for most people; the proper attitude for a Christian is acceptance, not prayer for alleviation. "God has sent you this cross, especially tailored for you. Do not reject it, for it will lead to greater glory in the next life."

In relation to you:

1) Even if God should occasionally heal the sick, it would not be through your prayers, for you are not good enough; after all, you are not holy; you are not a saint.

2) Even if it can be shown that God does occasionally heal the sick, you should be superior to that type of spirituality.

   a) Nor do you want to be associated with an over-emotional, revivalistic type of religion associated in the popular mind with faith healers. Your approach is purer, more intellectual than that.

   b) You do not need signs and wonders to believe. Your faith does not depend on the kind of evidence a less spiritual person might need. You don't need a spiritual crutch.

   c) You can accept sickness in preference to healing. If God offers you the alternatives of healing or sickness, you will take the higher road, the royal road of the cross by choosing the higher way of suffering.

In relation to the very nature of healing:

Miracles of healing are merely a holdover from the age of prescientific explanations. It is time to forget a superstitious view of reality and get on with the real work at hand; Christianity needs to be purified of its "supernatural" element, which is irrelevant to the present state of our intellectual and spiritual development.

In short, because of a shift of our worldview about God, about ourselves and about the nature of reality, we are being shut off from the possibility of believing in healing by six interlocking prejudiced arguments against healing!

It seems to me that all the above attitudes either obscure or completely undercut the good news Christ came to bring. We are beginning to see on a wide scale a renewal of God's gift of healing in a manner not seen in the church since apostolic times. This, I believe, is the work of a personal, loving God who desires to counteract our diminishing faith. Healing is not on the periphery of Christianity; it is central.

If we deny God's active healing power, we soon lack evidence of His personal love for us. If we doubt whether God really *loves* us, does it make any difference whether we *believe* in Him or not? In the end we may wonder if, indeed, God actually exists at all.

3 | The Basic Message of Christianity: Jesus Saves

When I hear the phrase, "Jesus saves," I remember poorly lettered billboards on many a country road. I also remember an unpleasant incident when I was buttonholed by a street evangelist who asked, "Are you saved, brother?" Yet these unhappy experiences of insensitivity cannot change what is central for me, as for every Christian: Jesus does save.

But what does it really mean that Jesus saves? How does it affect my life? "Our divine Savior," "our blessed Redeemer," "Behold the Lamb of God who takes away the sins of the world" can all become such familiar phrases that the words lose their power to touch us. They can become pious cliches, empty of force.

What exactly does Jesus save *me* from? The common Christian tradition teaches that Jesus saves us from personal sin and from the effects of our fallen human condition, which include ignorance, weakness of will, disoriented emotions, physical illness and death. Some of this freedom will unfold only in the deepened life that takes place after our resurrection.

But even now the process has begun: "The kingdom of heaven is near" (Matt. 10:7). Jesus is freeing us from sin, from ignorance ("the Spirit...will guide you into all truth," John 16:13), from weakness of purpose, from disoriented emotions and from physical sickness—from all sickness, therefore, that destroys or lessens our human personality—in order to give us *new life*, a new relationship of love and union with His Father through the power of the Holy Spirit. The saving power of Jesus frees us from all those elements of evil that prevent us from entering into our new life with God.

Jesus, therefore, came to do two basic things:

1) *Positive*: to give us a new life, a loving relationship of union with His Father and with Himself, through the Holy Spirit.

2) Overcoming the *negative* by removing the obstacles to new life: Jesus heals and frees (saves) us from all those sick elements in our human personality that need to be transformed so that the new life may freely enter in.

This, of course, is the astounding message of the good news. But the danger is, and always has been, that we let this remain merely a doctrine, a truth to be believed. Too often we don't understand how to let the reality of Christ's saving power penetrate the very center of our being. But healing is simply the practical application of the basic Christian message of salvation, a belief that Jesus means to liberate us from personal sin and from emotional and physical sickness.

Yet does Jesus intend to heal us from these evils here in this life? Or does healing pertain only to a future life when God will "wipe every tear from their eyes. There will be no more death or mourning or crying or pain" (Rev. 21:4)? I believe that a full understanding of the liberating, healing, saving message of Jesus Christ demands that we investigate whether He has come to free us *even in this life* from disease and disordered emotions which, since the creation of humankind, have traditionally been considered the effects of evil—of "original sin."

To understand a Christian view of healing we must

penetrate deeper into the meaning of "Jesus saves," into the meaning of His mission—and ours.

The Name "Jesus"

The ancient Hebrews attached great significance to choosing a name for a newborn child. The name often indicated the role the child was to play in the family or in the history of the people. The son of Isaiah the prophet, for example, was named "Shear-jashub," "a remnant will return," and the very name symbolized the people who, after Isaiah's own time, would return from exile and punishment. Later, John the Baptist was named at God's command, contrary to the inclinations of his relatives, as a sign that this child's life was more than ordinary, that he was specially chosen from the moment of birth to play a unique role in the plan of salvation.

Little wonder, then, that when God came to dwell among us He chose a name that would indicate who He was and what His mission would be. Luke tells us that the angel Gabriel appeared to Mary and said: "You will be with child and give birth to a son, and you are to give him the name Jesus" (Luke 1:31).

The word "Jesus," or "Yeshua" in Aramaic, means "Yahweh is Salvation." Though it was not an uncommon name in that day, the name Jesus proclaims His very message: He who was the Messiah, the "anointed one" or "the Christ," had come to express by word and work that "Yahweh is Salvation."

His Mission

Jesus in fact conceived of His mission in precisely these terms: The time of the Messiah would be a time of healing, of liberation, of salvation. Because the Hebrews did not think of the human being as divided into body and soul, but rather as a unified, whole person, when they spoke of healing they thought not just of *saving souls* but of *healing persons*. And the human person includes our body and our feelings.

As Jesus—"Yahweh is Salvation"—began to preach, He expressed clearly why He had come. Luke describes how Jesus in His very first sermon boldly asserted His healing mission:

> He went to Nazareth, where he had been brought up, and on the Sabbath day he went into the synagogue, as was his custom. And he stood up to read. The scroll of the prophet Isaiah was handed to him. Unrolling it, he found the place where it is written: "The Spirit of the Lord is on me, because he has anointed me to preach good news to the poor. He has sent me to proclaim freedom for the prisoners and recovery of sight for the blind, to release the oppressed, to proclaim the year of the Lord's favor." Then he rolled up the scroll, gave it back to the attendant and sat down. The eyes of everyone in the synagogue were fastened on him, and he said to them, "Today this scripture is fulfilled in your hearing" (Luke 4:16-21).

Luke goes on to say that some of His listeners were critical, not of His teachings but of what He failed to do: "Do here in your home town what we have heard that you did in Capernaum" (Luke 4:23).

Later when John the Baptist sent his disciples to ask if Jesus was the Messiah, Jesus again pointed to His own healing works as *the sign that He was the Christ*:

> When the men came to Jesus, they said, "John the Baptist sent us to you to ask, 'Are you the one who was to come, or should we expect someone else?' "

At that very time Jesus cured many who had diseases, sicknesses and evil spirits, and gave sight to many who were blind. So he replied to the messengers, "Go back and report to John what you have seen and heard: The blind receive sight, the lame walk, those who have leprosy are cured, the deaf hear, the dead are raised, and the good news is preached to the poor. Blessed is the man who does not fall away on account of me" (Luke 7:20-23).

We must also note that Mark, perhaps the earliest evangelist to set the gospel into writing, devotes much of his account to the healing episodes in the ministry of Jesus, and less to the actual teaching of Jesus. Today we are coming to recognize that the miracles of Jesus are not just "proofs" of His divinity or "guarantees" that His teachings are correct and inspired by God. Rather we are seeing that the miracles were the very actions of God present in the life and works of Jesus. *The healing acts of Jesus were themselves the message that He had come to set men free*; they were not just to prove that His message was true.

In a very basic sense, Jesus' medium is His message. If people are actually being saved ("born from above," "forgiven," "set free" and "healed" are all aspects of being saved), this is not merely an outside sign that Jesus' preaching is true. His preaching is, as it were, an outside sign; He is talking about people being set free and entering the kingdom of God. People are actually saved when they are born from above, forgiven, set free and healed.

In short, I think most Christians have it backwards: Healing is not merely a sign that Jesus' teaching about salvation is true. Healing (in its fullest dimension) is *salvation actually taking place* here and now. Preaching leads up to it and explains it afterwards, but the center of it all is God's saving action.

A clear indication that Jesus Himself did not stress the miraculous but the ordinary aspect of His healing ministry is seen in the fact that Jesus calls His healings "works" rather than "miracles." They were, so to speak, the normal thing for Him to do; they formed an integral part of His mission. As Scripture scholar David Stanley explains:

> The most convincing indication that Jesus' miracles are not intended to impress the reader of the gospels with the merely prodigious is found in the vocabulary employed to designate these actions. There are but two, or at most three, instances of any usage which approximates to our word "miracle"....If there is one aspect of Jesus' acts of healing which goes unstressed in the gospels, it is their capacity for merely arousing wonder. In the synoptic gospels they are designated as "acts of power" (*dynameis*), a term which stresses their character as manifestations of the divine power, and hence their aptness, together with His words, as a vehicle of Jesus' proclamation of the coming of God's kingdom. They are presented simply as the Good News in action.[1]

Unfortunately, in our English translations of the New Testament most versions translate the Greek word for "acts of power" as "miracles," thus implying something extraordinary and rare.

The Mission of the Disciples

Since the healing of humankind—our spirit, our emotions and our body—is an essential part of the message of salvation, we can now see why Jesus gave His disciples the power to heal when He sent them out to preach. This is true both of His special group of the twelve, and of the larger group of seventy-two.

> When Jesus had called the Twelve together, he gave them power and authority to drive out all demons and to cure diseases, and he sent them out to preach the kingdom of God and to heal the sick (Luke 9:1,2).
>
> After this the Lord appointed seventy-two others and sent them two by two ahead of him to every town and place where he was about to go...."When you enter a town and are welcomed, eat what is set before you. Heal the sick who are there and tell them, 'The kingdom of God is near you' " (Luke 10:1,8,9).

Jesus was simply giving them the power to preach the same message of good news that He Himself preached. That message was not merely a doctrine; it contained the very power of God to liberate people from the wretched state they were in. They were preaching as their Master preached: Jesus, after making the crowds welcome, "spoke to them about the kingdom of God, and healed those who needed healing" (Luke 9:11).

The Early Church

The inspired account of the early church's activity is of course the Acts of the Apostles. Certainly this title does not refer merely to the acts of the twelve apostles, for this book tells far more about Paul's activities than about any of the original twelve, except for Peter. What is meant in the title, then, is not *Apostles* but *apostles*—Stephen and Philip (both deacons), Barnabas, Silas and all the other early Christians who were sent out to preach the gospel and to heal.

Knowing that the synoptic Gospels usually speak about Jesus' healings as "acts of power" rather than as miracles helps us understand the basic theme of Acts, which is to show that the early church, the early Christians, had the same power to preach, to heal and to cast out demons that Jesus had. The church is the continuation of Jesus' saving power in history. The Jerusalem church (Peter) and the Gentile churches (Paul) all carry on the same preaching and healing as Jesus Himself did, because Jesus is the one who is still doing it. Now He is multiplied in the apostles, who can be His witnesses to the end of the world.

Just as Jesus connected preaching and healing in His presentation of the gospel, the early apostles carried on that tradition with no diminution of power. When these early Christians were persecuted, listen to how they prayed for help:

> Now, Lord, consider their threats and enable your servants to speak your word with great boldness. Stretch out your hand to heal and perform miraculous signs and wonders through the name of your holy servant Jesus (Acts 4:29,30).

Notice that they did not pray to preach *and* to heal, but to preach *by* healing. They preached the message of salvation by actually continuing the works of Jesus. Preaching a doctrine of God's salvation without salvation actually taking place, or preaching about healing without healing taking place, is empty rhetoric. Perhaps this is why so much of today's preaching impresses people as abstract and irrelevant.

As we read through Acts, we realize that the same Spirit who empowered Jesus in His life and work is meant to empower the mission of the church. A thoughtful reading of the text shows that there are definite parallels between the work of Peter and Paul (not, as is far too often emphasized, just conflict and controversy). Both are representatives of the Christian community which continues the saving mission of Jesus.

ACTS OF PETER	ACTS OF PAUL
Peter and John heal a lame man at the Gate Beautiful (3:1 ff.), saying, "In the name of Jesus Christ of Nazareth, walk."	Paul cures a man, lame from birth, at Lystra (14:8 ff.), saying, "Stand up on your feet!"
Peter cures Aeneas, the paralytic who had been bedridden for eight years (9:32 ff.).	Paul cures the father of Publius, who was in bed suffering from fever and dysentery (28:7 ff.).
Even Peter's shadow cures the sick (5:12a ff.).	Even handkerchiefs or aprons which had touched Paul cure the sick (19:11 ff.).
Crowds come and they are healed (5:16).	"The rest of the sick on the island came and were cured" (28:9).
At Jaffa Peter revives the dead woman Dorcas (9:36 ff.).	At Troas Paul raises the dead boy, Eutychus, to life (20:7 ff.).

The ordinary expectation of the apostles is shown by their direct form of prayer: "Walk" (3:6), "Stand up" (14:10), "Get up and take care of your mat" (9:34), "Get up" (9:40). The apostles use the same form of prayer that Jesus had used: a prayer that expects something to happen because the authority of God is behind the prayer.

Here, healing does not seem extraordinary but is the ordinary answer to prayer. Not only do we read of healings worked through the apostles Peter and Paul, but also through Philip, Stephen and Ananias of Damascus. The clear implication is that healing and liberation are part of the mission of the church.

Consequently, a better translation for the Acts of the Apostles would be "Acts of Apostles," to indicate that the book contains only *some* of the noteworthy activities of *some* of the apostles. The work of the church is not yet complete but is meant to continue with modern apostles, contemporary Christians who preach and perform the same acts of power that Jesus—and Peter, Paul, Barnabas, Agabus, Ananias, Philip and Stephen—performed.

The Saving Mission of Jesus Today

We must conclude, then, that unless we hold that healing was only meant for the early Christian community as a special grace to get the church established, the healings characteristic of the early church should somehow continue happening in our day. We still have the sick with us and we still need to be made whole. All around us in the pews on Sunday morning we see broken persons. And sometimes those in the pulpit or at the altar are broken, too. Since the church is made up of people, we still need healing as much as ever.

Significantly, Augustine in his early writings claimed that healing had ceased in the church and was no longer necessary. But his own experiences broke down his prejudice. After he was made bishop he found out about seventy miracles that took place in just two years' time. In 427, just three years before he died, in his book of *Retractions* Augustine took back what he had said in one of his early writings (*De Vera Religione*) about the age of miracles being past. Instead, he described the miraculous cures which he had seen and which had caused him to change his mind.[2]

The ending of the Gospel of Mark[3] indicates that a share in Christ's mission is extended to *all* believers:

> Go into all the world and preach the good news to
> all creation….And these signs will accompany those
> who believe: In my name they will drive out demons;
> they will speak in new tongues; they will pick up
> snakes with their hands; and when they drink deadly
> poison, it will not hurt them at all; they will place
> their hands on sick people, and they will get well
> (Mark 16:15,17,18).

We find no indication here that at some future time the
charismatic dimension of the church will cease, or that its
main purpose is to build up the institution to such a point
that the structured elements can carry on under their own
power.

If the work of the Christian is to carry on the same mission as Christ, we must recapture the essential elements of
that mission. Here is how Peter, in a thumbnail sketch,
describes Jesus' public ministry:

> You know what has happened throughout Judea,
> beginning in Galilee after the baptism that John
> preached—how God anointed Jesus of Nazareth with
> the Holy Spirit and power, and how he went around
> doing good and healing all who were under the power
> of the devil, because God was with him (Acts
> 10:37,38).

Here the emphasis is on what Jesus *did*, rather than on what
He said; for what He did was the message of the gospel. He
preached salvation and healing by actually healing people
and freeing them from evil.

Think of what it might mean if we could, in all honesty,
describe how we had fully entered into the life of Christ,
saying truthfully: "God has anointed me with the Holy Spirit
and with power; and because God is with me, I go around

doing good and curing all who are under the power of the devil.''

Then think of what it might mean if the entire church could make the claim to those who honestly inquire about her credentials: ''Go back and tell the doubters what you have seen and heard: the blind see again, the lame walk, lepers are cleansed, and the deaf hear, the dead are raised to life, the Good News is proclaimed to the poor; and happy is the man who does not lose faith in me'' (a paraphrase of Luke 7:22,23).

The test of orthodoxy is not doctrine alone, for doctrine remains incomplete unless it is accompanied by the power to make the doctrine come true in our lives:

> I tell you the truth, anyone who has faith in me will do what I have been doing. He will do even greater things than these, because I am going to the Father (John 14:12).

4 | Wholeness Is Holiness

If Jesus comes to save and to heal, what is it that He saves and heals? Did He come just to save souls? Are pastors meant to concentrate only on the "care of souls"? Is the Divine Physician interested only in our spirits?

I think it is only honest to say that most pastors and preachers have emphasized Christ's desire to save souls and to take away sin, the sickness of the soul; but there has been no corresponding emphasis on Christ's desire to heal the sickness of the body. In fact, quite the contrary: sickness has often been presented not as evil, but as a blessing desired by God because of the great good that comes to a person's soul as a result of a suffering body.

How then are we to regard sickness? Is God's ordinary will sickness—or is it health? If it is health, does God heal our bodies with a power beyond the natural resources of medicine and health care?

Personally, I believe that the attitude of most Christians today in regard to healing is shaped more by pagan thought than by Christianity. Most sermons on sickness and suffering reflect more the influence of Roman Stoicism than the doctrine of the church's founder.

The Attitude of Christ Toward Sickness

I think it is also fair to say that every time Jesus met with evil, spiritual or physical, He treated it as an enemy. Every time a sick person came to Him in faith, Jesus healed that person. He did not divide people, as we so often do, into a soul to be saved and healed and a body that is to suffer and remain unhealed. He came to heal suffering humanity in whatever way it was sick. Sickness of the body was part of that kingdom of Satan He had come to destroy.

No—*we* are the ones who talk about "saving souls." Nowhere in the New Testament does it say that Christ came to "save souls." He came to save human beings—body and soul.

Jesus healed those whose spirits were sick and needed deliverance or forgiveness. He also healed those whose bodies were lame, blind and leprous. In fact, there are many more accounts of how He healed the physically sick than of how He forgave sins.

We remember how, when the paralytic was brought in by his friends (Matt. 9:1 ff.), Jesus forgave his sins. Since the scribes thought He was blaspheming, Jesus replied, "Which is easier: to say, 'Your sins are forgiven,' or to say, 'Get up and walk'? But so that you may know that the Son of Man has authority on earth to forgive sins….Then he said to the paralytic, 'Get up, take your mat and go home' " (Matt. 9:5,6).

The authority Jesus exercises over both these forms of evil seems to be the same. But which is easier *for us* to say: "Your sins are forgiven" or "You are healed"? Why do we have such faith in the words, "Your sins are forgiven," but have so little faith in stating, "You are healed"?

The early church, as we have seen in Acts, acted as Christ did: The apostles proclaimed the gospel and healed the sick.

At the same time, the epistle of James, traditionally used as the scriptural foundation for the anointing of the sick, moves back and forth between forgiveness of sins and physical healing with no discernible change of assurance or emphasis:

> Is any one of you sick? He should call the elders of the church to pray over him and anoint him with oil in the name of the Lord. And the prayer offered in faith will make the sick person well; the Lord will raise him up. If he has sinned, he will be forgiven. Therefore confess your sins to each other and pray for each other so that you may be healed. The prayer of a righteous man is powerful and effective. Elijah was a man just like us. He prayed earnestly that it would not rain, and it did not rain on the land for three and a half years. Again he prayed, and the heavens gave rain, and the earth produced its crops (James 5:14-18).[1]

Here James seems to give the example of Elijah to increase our readiness to pray for material needs—such as rain—and not just spiritual needs. He doesn't point out what a great prophet Elijah was, but only that he was as frail as we are. James also emphasizes that our prayer must be *heartfelt*; apparently, if we don't have faith in this kind of prayer it will not work very powerfully.

A Later Christian Tradition: the Body Should Suffer

What happened to the simple gospel view of Christ healing the whole human being? We can trace the historical development of a changing viewpoint as the early fathers of the church moved gradually from a wholehearted belief in healing (Justin Martyr and Irenaeus in the second century) to the idea that the body's suffering is preferable for the sake of the soul (Gregory the Great in the fifth century).[2] What happened throughout all those centuries to lessen the church's belief in Christ's healing ministry is complex; but certainly one of the main factors was that pagan thought (Platonic, Stoic and Manichean) all influenced and infected Christian spirituality. These philosophies, dominant in the world of early Christianity, tended to view a person's body as a prison that confines the spirit and hinders our spiritual growth.

Under the influence of some of the Desert Fathers, severe asceticism was held up as the model of Christian perfection: The human body is to be distrusted and not just tamed; it is to be put to death through various mortifications and penances. The Christian then looks forward to a time when the soul will be released from the confines of the flesh. Such an exaggerated model of the flesh warring against the spirit, the Spiritual Combat, tends to make us see the body as an enemy to be subdued through punishment rather than as a wounded friend that needs to be healed.

Today a book on spiritual growth is likely to treat of the "Art of Becoming Human," and a seminarian's room may well be filled with the finest hi-fi equipment and colorful fine art reproductions. But I can remember my own training when, for years, we were even forbidden to read *Time* magazine in our starkly simple cells. For nearly 1,500 years traditional Christian spirituality emphasized severe mortification and distrust of the body. Seeing a recent rerun of *The Nun's Story*, with its world of black habits and the putting to death of "worldly" desires, made me realize how much times have changed. That film now seems almost unreal, as if it came from another century.

Nevertheless, the effects, hidden perhaps, of that older spirituality are still with many Christians. There is much to be said for its discipline, and in some ways we may have lost something. But it did reflect, in part, a Stoic, unchristian view of the body that still affects many Christians. Recently, for example, I was asked to pray for an elderly lady who is losing her eyesight through glaucoma. She told me she felt guilty about praying for healing because she felt that maybe God wanted her to endure failing sight to prepare her soul for its last passage. Even so, she had no qualms about trying to get help from a doctor. It was only in direct relation to God, in prayer, that she felt she maybe ought to go blind.

She, and many other Christians like her, are affected by a basically pagan view of the universe—stemming from Platonic, Stoic and Manichean sources which they have probably never even heard about. In these, the body is seen at the very least as an encumbrance if not as an enemy to the spirit. The lady I mentioned had formed her thinking from the sermons she had heard which stressed penance and reflected an attitude of contempt for the body.

A fascinating example of this kind of spirituality that treats the body as an enemy to be subdued is Henry Suso's autobiography. (In this writing Suso refers to himself in the third person.)

> Having learned that true love for Christ Crucified demands imitation, he decided to conquer his ease-loving nature by chastising the flesh so that the soul might go free; for this purpose he wore for a long time a hair shirt and an iron chain around his body so tightly as to draw blood.
>
> He had someone make him a half-length, tight-fitting, coarse undergarment, equipped with 150 sharp brass nails, the points facing the flesh. This was his night shirt for sixteen years.
>
> On simmering summer nights when the heat was

almost unbearable and he was half-dead from the day's fatigue or from blood-letting, he would fret and squirm sleeplessly from side to side like a worm being pricked with sharp needles. Then there was the annoyance caused by insects....

But no matter how long the nights were in winter or how hot in summer, he refused to yield an inch to the Flesh's craving for comfort, even though his hands and arms became afflicted with a nervous trembling.

In order to prevent himself from obtaining any relief from the pests, he fastened his belt around his neck and tied his hands in such a way that he could not move them in his sleep. He was so securely confined in this manacle that if a fire had broken out, he would have been as helpless as a handcuffed prisoner.

After some time he discarded this instrument, only to encase his hands in a pair of leather gloves which he had instructed a tinsmith to stud with sharp iron nails. The purpose of this new instrument was to tear his flesh every time he tried to obtain relief from the plaguing insects. More than once when he unlocked his voluntary prison...his bruised and bloody body looked as if it had come out the loser in a fight with a bear....

After sixteen years of these torturous practices when his whole nature was tamed and withered, an angel appeared to him on Pentecost Sunday with the welcome whisper that God wanted him to discontinue this manner of life. He lost no time in throwing his Flagella into the Rhine.[3]

Certainly, Suso's example is extreme, even for the fourteenth century in which he lived. But his basic attitude was typical of a spirituality that formed the backdrop for the lives of some saints who strongly influenced the ideal of Christian perfection in some churches until quite recently.

According to this model of Christian perfection we were regarded as weak if we failed to punish our bodies, but especially if we failed to accept those sufferings that were seen as coming from the hand of God. Sickness was generally regarded as a gift from God to help Christians grow spiritually. To pray for healing, in such a case, would be a sign of weakness and a concession to the flesh. Consequently, we would ordinarily expect God to say no to a prayer asking for healing.

The pervasiveness of this basic contempt for the body is perhaps most clearly evident in the negative attitude toward human love and the beauty of the physical aspects of marriage which marked much of the thinking in the Roman Catholic Church until the 1960s (Vatican II). In this view, human love and its physical, sexual aspects ("the relief of concupiscence") were regarded as entirely secondary to the procreation of children. Several of the important "Fathers of the Church" such as Gregory the Great (pope from 590 to 604) even went so far as to consider that any bodily pleasure taken in marriage itself was sinful:

> In his *Pastoral Rule*, Gregory provided a chapter on "How the Married and the Celibate Are to Be Admonished." The married were to be admonished that they might copulate only to produce children. This was merely Augustine. But Gregory went further. Not only is pleasure an unlawful purpose in intercourse, but if any pleasure is "mixed" with the act of intercourse, the married have "transgressed the law of marriage." Their sin, to be sure, is as small

a one as the nonprocreative purpose in Augustine; it may be remitted by "frequent prayers." But sin has been committed. The guilty married have "befouled" their intercourse by their "pleasures" (*Pastoral Rule* 3.27, *PL* 77:102)....Miraculously a man might have intercourse without sin, as one might be in a fire without burning. But miracles did not usually attend marital intercourse; sin was to be expected.[4]

At first it might seem that these stern attitudes toward marriage had little to do with Christ's healing message. Yet they exemplify in dramatic fashion a harsh attitude toward the body and "the world."

In this view, only the human spirit is truly worthy of unconditional prayer. Prayer to heal the broken human body, like prayer for all other material benefits, was considered of questionable spiritual benefit. Christians were taught to pray with confidence only for spiritual gifts. Since this harsh attitude toward the body (and consequently a dim view of God's desire to heal our suffering bodies) prevailed for hundreds of years, most mainline Christian denominations have been influenced by a prejudice against physical healing.

Today we no longer regard the body as an enemy, but celebrate its goodness. Scores of books are written to celebrate the Christian dimensions of marriage. Yet our spirituality of sickness seems relatively untouched.

A contemporary Roman Catholic catechism, for example, in its brief treatment of illness and the anointing of the sick, repeats none of the medieval praise of sickness as an imitation of the cross, nor does it treat the body as an enemy; yet it has very little to say about illness that is practically helpful. All that this well-known compendium of contemporary Catholic faith has to say is that: 1) people often feel abandoned by God in times of sickness; 2) this can lead to a new perspective on reality and a deepened relationship with God; 3) Christians should visit the sick. There is no suggestion that a Christian might consider praying for healing.[5]

The Anointing of the Sick

Most Protestants know little about the sacrament of anointing of the sick, but it has nevertheless affected the practice of most churches. So it's helpful to understand something of its 1,900-year history in order to see where we now stand in relation to healing.

The anointing of the sick has, in its history, closely patterned itself on the changes in attitude toward healing. Originally, it was regarded basically as a sacrament intended for *physical healing*. Its model was the epistle of James, which instructs the elders to gather around the sick person and pray for forgiveness of sins and for healing.

Later, as the attitude toward sickness changed so that it was seen more as a blessing than a curse, the purpose of the sacrament shifted until its primary effect was spiritual: to prepare a soul in danger of death for immediate entrance to glory. Physical healing was still prominently mentioned in the words of the sacrament (faithfully passed down and representing an earlier tradition), but this was now regarded as a secondary purpose of the sacrament, while its primary effect had to do with the soul. In time, its name became "extreme unction" (last anointing). Originally this name, "last anointing," only referred to the fact that it was the last in the list of the sacraments that used anointing with oil as part of its ritual.[6]

Later, in popular understanding, "last" came to mean the last act the church performed to prepare a person for death. Furthermore, regulations were made insuring that this sacrament was to be administered *only in danger of death*. All this emphasized that the only sure effect of extreme unction was a purely spiritual one: that the person was being prepared to meet God at the moment of death. The tradition that Christ also worked physical cures through this sacrament endured as well—but that was regarded as a secondary effect.

Many priests can tell remarkable stories about how the sick either got well or noticeably improved after being anointed. They did believe in the possibility of an occasional physical healing, but their faith was directed almost exclusively to the spiritual preparation for death, especially since the sacrament was not to be ministered unless there was an immediate danger of death. As a result, the sight of a priest in the sickroom was often regarded by the patient as a harbinger of death.

I remember being asked by a Protestant friend to visit a Catholic relative who was in the hospital to undergo an operation. I promised to go, but an hour later the friend called back, embarrassed, to say that the Catholic relatives had asked that I not come: The sick man might be frightened by the appearance of a priest and might worry before surgery that his condition was worse than it actually was.

In short, rather than signifying healing, my appearance to that family signaled the approach of death. I could not but reflect that, while the sick hastened in crowds to see and touch Christ, here was a sick man who was afraid to see someone who desired to act as Christ's ambassador. This family had been conditioned to expect the priest to prepare a patient for death—not to pray with him for life.

Happily, the name "extreme unction" has now been changed back to the original name, "anointing of the sick." Again authors are emphasizing the healing effect of the sacrament as today Christians return to a deeper sense of Christ's mission of healing the sick.

The Religious Sense of Ordinary People

Despite changes in the "official" attitudes of the church, however, the people—especially the simple people— continued to pray with great faith for the sick through their various popular devotions. But since praying for healing was no longer performed by the priests, the people turned to the saints to pray for their ailments. Mary in particular was sought for healing at Lourdes and at the other shrines, which were really centers of healing.

Such popularity of shrines and devotions among Catholics in preference to the official liturgy was often ascribed to the fact that these offered a better emotional outlet than the simplicity and austerity of the Latin Mass. But a deeper reason for their popularity, I think, was that these devotions met a basic human need of people who wanted to pray for their real material concerns. If God seemed distant, if it was His will to permit sickness, Mary at least seemed approachable. Although the official leaders did not themselves ordinarily pray for healing among the people, the healing ministry for hundreds of years was preserved through these shrines and devotions.

Similarly, among Protestant groups popular evangelists such as Oral Roberts and Kathryn Kuhlman preserved the healing tradition when it was not promoted in the official church worship services. The notable exceptions, of course, were Pentecostal churches and certain ministers, particularly Anglicans, who instituted healing services in their churches.

These shrines and popular evangelistic services drew the same kind of crowds that Jesus attracted in His lifetime: wounded people crying out along the roadside and asking to be healed. They remind us of blind Bartimaeus, the woman with the issue of blood, the epileptic boy—the kind of people Jesus always attracted. Admittedly, some devotions have sometimes been superstitious and frequently embarrassingly commercialized.[7] But I believe this all came about because the prayers for material and physical needs were moved from the center of the life of the church and shunted aside into the area of popular devotion. It was as if theologians moved off in one direction, while the simple people with their basic needs moved off in another.[8]

The crowds of people traveling to shrines, to tent meetings and healing services have been portrayed as having a religiosity that appeals to the heart and emotions; "they need this kind of prop." But the matter goes deeper than that. These people are simply looking for help in their real human, material needs. If a modern American woman finds she has inoperable cancer, where is she most likely to find prayer for healing? From her priest or from John Wimber? From her minister or from the Pentecostal church at the other end of town?

A Contemporary View of Our Humanity

Today we find that psychology has effected a return to the Hebrew view of the human person—not separated into body and soul, but as a whole individual whose emotions and body very much affect the mind and spirit. Once again we see our souls not as imprisoned in the body but at home in the body: The resurrection of the body answers our deepest desires.

This means that our view of the human person today is perhaps closer than ever before to the view that Jesus held. Pagan (Platonic, Stoic, Gnostic and Manichean) views of our humanity have all touched the post-apostolic Christian spirituality; these views all stress a dualism with spirit and mind being seen as noble while the body is, at best, regarded as a necessary evil. But we are now returning to a glorious sense of celebrating God's creation with a realization that God does care for us—not just our souls, but all of us!

The reason we have not prayed for healing in the past is not just because we have lacked the faith. It goes back to this "body as enemy" spirituality that has been with us for more than 1,500 years. But we are now recovering the full proclamation of the good news, that salvation is for the whole person and that Jesus came to bring us the fullness of life in every possible dimension. The Gospel of Matthew explicitly reflects this fullness; after describing how

> Jesus cured a leper,
> healed the centurion's servant
> and restored Peter's mother-in-law to health,

the Gospel states:

> When evening came, many who were demon-possessed were brought to him, and he drove out the spirits with a word and healed all the sick. This was to fulfill what was spoken through the prophet Isaiah: "He took up our infirmities and carried our diseases" (Matt. 8:16,17).

My hope is that we are now returning to the biblical view of our humanity, to God's view of us: that holiness is wholeness. As a friend of mine once remarked when I was looking physically worn down, "even God cannot play on a broken violin."

5 | Let Him Carry His Cross Daily

Admittedly God cannot play on a broken violin. Yet many people—good Christian people—are broken. How can God use them? Of course, all people suffer a certain kind of brokenness on their way to wholeness. But unfortunately, too many Christians are broken in a destructive way—so badly broken that they cannot carry out the great commandment of loving God and neighbor. Their inner turmoil *prevents* them from carrying out God's will, and yet, paradoxically, they may still believe that such a sickness is God's will. Therefore, they feel no inclination to ask for release from what they think God evidently wants of them.

Take, for example, those persons suffering from mental depression who find it hard to believe in God's love for them. How can they in turn love God? Typically, such sufferers are too wrapped up in sadness to relate to others in a loving way or to become active members of a functioning Christian community. They are too broken to fulfill even the very basics of a Christian life. Moreover, their wounds probably stem from such deep childhood scars that they can do little to change themselves, even with the help of a psychiatrist. Yet how many priests or ministers are ready to pray for a person like this, sure that God does not will such a state and will bring peace of soul if only it is sought?

If God has come to save the human race, why are there so many Christians broken in body and spirit? One key reason is the remarkable shift from the days of the early church when Christians looked at health and healing as the ordinary response of a loving Father to His children. Today that attitude has changed 180 degrees in many Christian churches to the point where suffering is often regarded as a sign of God's special benediction.

A Misunderstood Emphasis: "Carry Your Cross"

One familiar attitude toward suffering which has influenced many, myself included, is that those whom God loves most will have to suffer most. This view has been reinforced in a number of ways with familiar sentiments like this: "If you suffer the cross nobly in this life, you will be rewarded by a glorious crown in heaven."

A picture at the beginning of the book *Ascent of Mount Carmel* by John of the Cross makes the same point. It depicts a steep mountain with a narrow, painful way leading to the top, while winding, pleasant side paths portray all the temptations that lead us astray from God. Older biographies of the great saints (such as Henry Suso, quoted in the last chapter) usually emphasized the penances and sufferings these spiritual heroes had to endure. The ordinary untaught reader of these books comes away with the conviction that union with God is serious business (which it is) and demands great suffering if we wish to reach the heights of union to which God is calling us. The natural tendency of the less valiant is to shrink back and say, "I leave it to the great saints."

Traditional popular spirituality has also taught the importance of suffering and penance—especially suffering that is *not self-chosen*—by claiming that it offers several benefits:

1) For *the individual*: "It purges me of self-seeking and

selfishness. If I can kill my excessive desire for pleasure by accepting suffering, I can then advance in detachment and purely unselfish love of God and neighbor."

2) For *the world*: "I can unite my sufferings with those of Jesus upon the cross and ask Him to use them redemptively to help other people. Like Paul, I can ask Jesus to make up in my body what is still lacking in the sufferings of Christ for the salvation of the world."

Thus in this view, in my desire for suffering my chief aim would be to imitate Christ as perfectly as I might, to walk in His bloodstained footsteps so that I might become like Him and share in His mission of redeeming humankind through suffering. Hasn't Christ explicitly stated that the person who does not take up his cross daily and follow Him is not worthy to be His disciple?

Many priests and ministers visit hospitals and encourage the patients by telling them that they are especially loved since God has singled them out to share more deeply in His crucified life. This ideal of living a crucified life is starkly heroic: It is reflected graphically in the handmade crucifixes brought from Spain and Latin America that sometimes find their way into gift shops and hang on the walls of convents and monasteries. With glistening drops of blood and pain etched into the face of Christ, viewers feel guilty looking into His face, realizing how comfortable and unmortified their own life is.

How could a person with a "cross-centered" spirituality like this ask for relief from pain? A healing would take away our opportunity to imitate Jesus and help redeem the world. Would we prefer to surrender to weakness rather than aspire to holiness? We might ask for spiritual blessings but would hesitate to ask for material ones for fear they deprive us of the merits of suffering.

Unconsciously affected by this kind of doctrine, most

Christians, certainly most Catholics, have seldom thought about praying for a cure of their ailments, even though they knew that Christ (and after Him, His apostles) prayed to make people well. My thought used to be that I had better hang on to the cross that God had given to me rather than to ask for a lighter one: To ask for healing might be cowardice.

What Is the Correct View of Suffering?

The Bible teaches an apparent contradiction: Jesus tells His followers to bear their cross. Yet, whenever He meets people who are sick, He reaches out and cures them. Was He inconsistent, or have His words been misunderstood?

I think we can solve this problem by making an important distinction between two kinds of suffering:

1) The cross that Jesus carried was the cross of *persecution*, the kind of suffering that comes *from outside* because of the wickedness of evil people. He suffered deeply within Himself, too, but the source of His anguish was outside Himself. Jesus wept over Jerusalem; He was reviled and mocked; He was nailed to the cross and died.

2) The suffering that Jesus did not Himself endure, and which He took away from those who approached Him in faith, was that of *sickness*, the suffering that tears us apart *from within*. I think it is fascinating that some doctors are now saying that much physical sickness comes about because we are spiritually sick within.

The Life of Jesus

This twofold distinction seems clear in the life of Jesus. Precisely because He was good, He drew down upon Himself the wrath of the authorities of this world. He endured calumnies, insults and most painful torture and death at the hands of His enemies who were infuriated by His life and teachings.

But nowhere do the Gospels recount that Jesus was ever physically ill. The long Christian tradition has recognized that Jesus probably did not suffer from leprosy, epilepsy, schizophrenia or any of the other diseases and emotional disturbances that plague mankind. We intuitively sense that these sicknesses result from a corruption of our inner being and are not in accord with our nobility as children of God. Sickness shows that, in one area at least, the sick person is being attacked from within. Consequently, we instinctively believe that Jesus must have been an emotionally balanced and healthy man.

In His words and actions as well, Jesus distinguishes between sickness (attacking our life and wholeness from within) and persecution (attacking us from without). For instance, He warns His disciples that they will be persecuted, hauled before magistrates and judges, thrown out of synagogues; that their enemies will be their own brothers and sisters; and that they are to rejoice when all manner of evil is spoken about them (Matt. 10:17 ff.).

But contrast the rejoicing of Jesus at persecution to His reaction to sickness and demonic possession. The evangelists never show Him counseling a sick man to rejoice or to be patient because disease is helpful or redemptive[1]; instead, Jesus "healed all their sick" (for example, Matt. 12:15).[2] While we, by and large, have encouraged the sick to accept their illness as the will of God, Jesus, in the Gospels, seems to reveal a very different attitude. Once when a leper came up to Jesus and said, "Lord, if you are willing, you can make me clean," Jesus replied, "I am willing. Be clean!" (Matt. 8:2,3).

As a friend of mine once said, "Every time you meet Jesus in the Gospels, He is either healing someone, or has just come from healing someone, or is on His way to heal someone."

The Attitude of the Disciples and Apostles

Clearly, Jesus taught His disciples to take the same uncompromising stand toward sickness. When He commissioned the twelve to preach (for example, in Luke 9), and when He sent out the seventy-two (Luke 10), He also gave them the commission to heal the sick and to drive out evil spirits. (The close association of the command to heal the sick and to drive out evil spirits reiterates the attitude of the early church that disease is an evil—not a blessing sent by God.) Moreover, the mandate to all believers to preach the gospel (at the end of Mark) promises healing as a sign of belief: "They will place their hands on sick people, and they will get well" (Mark 16:18).

Paul, who makes such a point of telling people to imitate him as he imitates Christ, and who adds that his desire is to "know...the fellowship of sharing in his sufferings, becoming like him in his death" (Phil. 3:10), sees no contradiction in healing sickness: "God did extraordinary miracles through Paul. Handkerchiefs and aprons that had touched him were taken to the sick, and their illnesses were cured and the evil spirits left them" (Acts 19:11,12). By his actions, Paul, even with his emphasis on the cross, does not encourage the sick to bear their illness as though it were willed by God.

Paul himself once fell sick ("Even though my illness was a trial to you, you did not treat me with contempt or scorn," Gal. 4:14). But when it came time for him to boast of his sufferings for Christ, he did not mention his sickness. Rather he boasted about the kind of suffering that comes from persecution, and the labors inherent in his vocation:

> I have worked much harder, been in prison more frequently, been flogged more severely, and been exposed to death again and again. Five times I received from the Jews the forty lashes minus one.

Three times I was beaten with rods, once I was stoned, three times I was shipwrecked, I spent a night and a day in the open sea, I have been constantly on the move. I have been in danger from rivers, in danger from bandits, in danger from my own countrymen, in danger from Gentiles; in danger in the city, in danger in the country, in danger at sea; and in danger from false brothers. I have labored and toiled and have often gone without sleep; I have known hunger and thirst and have often gone without food; I have been cold and naked. Besides everything else, I face daily the pressure of my concern for all the churches. Who is weak, and I do not feel weak? Who is led into sin, and I do not inwardly burn? (2 Cor. 11:23-29).

To say, then, that God ordinarily desires that we be healed of our sickness does not mean that we believe in a Christianity without a cross. I speak of the kind of Christianity preached by Christ Himself and His apostles, where suffering is seen as an evil[3]: either an evil to be overcome when it appears to overwhelm and destroy our inner life, or an evil to be endured and rejoiced in when it comes from the persecution of evil men or from the fatigue of apostolic labors. Although good can result from it, suffering is in itself the result of sin; it is only to be endured *for the sake of the kingdom*, not for its own sake.

In discussions about suffering, a problem nearly always comes up: What is the meaning of Paul's celebrated "thorn in the flesh" and of his inability to get rid of it even when he prayed? Paul says:

To keep me from becoming conceited because of these surpassingly great revelations, there was given me a thorn in my flesh, a messenger of Satan, to torment me.

Three times I pleaded with the Lord to take it away from me. But he said to me, "My grace is sufficient for you, for my power is made perfect in weakness" (2 Cor. 12:7-9).

The exact nature of this "thorn in the flesh" is obscure. Various commentators have suggested that it could have been a person, a sickness, a persecution or a sexual temptation. Whatever the case, certainly no one can use this text to bolster one point of view. What can be said is that Paul's initial response was to pray that the "thorn" leave him. He only ceased praying when he learned that there was a purpose to it and that it was for the sake of the kingdom (lest his exalted revelations make him proud). Moreover, he calls it "a messenger of Satan," and not a blessing sent by God.

On the other hand, the story of the epileptic demoniac (Mark 9:14-29; Matt. 17:14-21; Luke 9:37-41) does seem to make two realities clear. First, *Jesus* expected His disciples to be able to cure the boy. Second, the *disciples* themselves expected to be able to cure the boy. They were embarrassed by their failure.

As Mark describes the incident, a crowd has gathered around to watch the disciples try to cast out of the epileptic boy "a spirit that has robbed him of speech." Yet the boy's father must report to Jesus when He returns to His disciples, "I asked your disciples to drive out the spirit, but they could not." Jesus, instead of giving a calm reply (He might have said, "Now that I am here, just bring him to me"), says, "O unbelieving generation, how long shall I stay with you? How long shall I put up with you?" Apparently, He expected the disciples to be able to cure the boy themselves.

Then Jesus talks to the boy's father to learn what is wrong. The latter concludes the pathetic story of his son's long-endured convulsions with a very human prayer: "But if you can do anything, take pity on us and help us."

Again Jesus reacts strongly. Mark reports that Jesus said, " 'If you can?' Everything is possible for him who believes." Jesus is telling the father that he or anyone else should be able to do what He is being asked to do. The problem is not outside themselves; there is no "if" about it. The question is whether or not they have faith.

Next Jesus proceeds to cure the boy. Then the embarrassed disciples wait until they can speak to Him privately to ask, "Why couldn't we drive it out?"

"This kind," He answers, "can come out only by prayer."[4]

Nothing in this episode gives the impression that Jesus is setting Himself up as unique in the work of healing. Rather it is as if He were training His disciples to cure people as part of their ordinary ministry. He is blaming them precisely because they are still not ready to do the work to which He has called them.

The attitude of the early church seems to have been that not only Jesus, but His followers as well, were to call upon God's power to cure sickness. They were guilty of shoddy work if they failed to cure the sick and drive out demons.

The New Testament record leaves no doubt that, in the mind of Jesus and His disciples, health is God's normal will for human beings. As Irenaeus wrote: "The glory of God is man fully alive." Accordingly, the reaction of the people to Jesus' cures was to glorify God and praise Him, as with the blind man who recovered his sight and then followed Jesus, "praising God. When all the people saw it, they also praised God" (Luke 18:43).

What Meaning, Then, Does Suffering Have?

Suffering is a mystery that all of us have had to wrestle

with in some form or other. If God can put a stop to suffering, why doesn't He? I have talked to people who have suffered greatly, who have seen the innocent suffer, and who said they were now atheists because they could not believe in a God who would want people to suffer.

What is the answer? Certainly, there is no simple one. But there are several key ideas I believe are biblical and represent a balanced point of view that may help answer many of the questions we ask:

1) "The glory of God is man fully alive." God has revealed Himself as being on the side of life (He *is* life), of wholeness, of health in spirit, mind and body. *In general, it is God's desire that we be healthy* rather than sick. And since He has the power to do all things, He will respond to prayer for healing unless there is some obstacle, or unless the sickness is sent or permitted for some greater reason.

2) *Sickness is in itself an evil*, although good may result from it. Sickness is ordinarily not directly willed by God, but as a result of our fallen human condition, it is permitted. Through the power of the resurrection, God's life is breaking into our wounded world, and He gives us the power to cooperate with Him by healing and reconciling the human race and all of creation, "that the creation itself will be liberated from its bondage to decay and brought into the glorious freedom of the children of God" (Rom. 8:21).

3) There inevitably comes *a time for a person to die*. This reality, of course, is obvious; but people do ask whether they should pray for elderly people who are ill with a terminal disease. The answer is that we should pray for light about when to ask God to take away the sickness and when to pray for a happy death—which is a passing to a deeper life with God and not a tragedy at all.

Agnes Sanford describes the need for guidance in praying for the elderly in her autobiography. Here she recounts the poignancy of making a decision about the sickness of her husband, Ted:

> But complete healing did not come. So I asked for guidance. There is a time for everyone to depart, that I know, and he was approaching seventy. I said, "Lord, how long does he have?" And the answer came, "Three years."
>
> His days were lengthened a little bit by continual prayer. He had three years and six months. But the last year and a half, after he was threescore years and ten, were truly, as Solomon said they would be, labor and sorrow. He had a massive stroke....I did not pray for healing this time, for I knew that if Ted's life were prolonged it would be only labor and sorrow. I prayed only for whatever was best, trusting God to take him at the right time.
>
> However, others—all his people who loved him— did not consider these matters, but prayed definitely for healing. In all my books I counsel people to ask guidance before leaping into healing prayers, but few pay any attention. Ted did make a recovery, but indeed and truly he was not himself.[5]

It is normal for an apple to drop to the ground in the autumn after it has spent the summer ripening to its full richness and growth. But if a green apple falls off the tree in July because a worm has gotten into it, something has gone wrong. Similarly, we can ordinarily assume that we should pray for desperately sick young people (for example, a young mother apparently dying of leukemia) that they might live.

4) Some sickness may have *a higher purpose*. Sometimes it serves to chastise us or to bring us to our senses. At other times, it may turn us around and redirect our lives into a better course. A striking example was Paul, who was blinded

on his way to Damascus and, consequently, found the Lord, who completely changed Paul's life. His blindness lasted three days until he was healed by the prayer of Ananias. At a later time he fell sick in Galatia, but this provided the occasion upon which he was enabled to evangelize the Galatians.

Furthermore, the church has a long tradition of *redemptive* suffering among the saints who have asked Christ to be allowed to share in His cross as a special privilege. This tradition is too long to be lightly dismissed by those persons who like to see things in simple terms of black and white—of the devil and sickness completely on one side and God and health on the other side. Nevertheless, at times so much has been made of the redemptive value of suffering that it has all but obscured the good news of the gospel.

All too often the hospital chaplain tells the patients indiscriminately, "God is offering you this cross to accept." By New Testament standards, it should be *normative* for the Christian to pray for the removal of sickness rather than its acceptance. Redemptive sickness is the exception, not the rule.

The Reverse Side of the Cross

The basic question, then, comes down to whether the healing effects of Christ's suffering, as far as our bodies and broken hearts are concerned, are meant for this life or whether they are only reserved for a time after death. Popular spirituality has suggested that our bodies are meant to suffer in this life, and that this is what it means to carry our cross in imitation of Jesus. But the renewed focus on healing coincides with today's realization that the resurrection is the central mystery of the redemption.

The Spirit dwelling in Christ's body is leading more and more Christians to claim the victory that Jesus has won. They no longer confine this victory to their spiritual lives, but apply it as a power and strength for the whole human person. This new awareness of the resurrected life available to us even now is beautifully exemplified in a vision described by Rufus Mosely (Rufus Mosely was an educator from Georgia who had various unusual experiences with God and was known in certain Protestant circles in the 1930s and 1940s as a remarkable retreat master):

> Suddenly and unexpectedly, a Presence, Power, and Glory, not of me, descended upon me and apparently had possession and full use of me. The whole body, as well as mind and soul, shared in the wonder....My arms began to go out and my body began slowly to rise, and while I did not realize it at first my body was becoming or taking the form of a cross, a cross of life, of honor, of bliss, and of glory. The higher I arose the greater the bliss and glory....When my body was apparently in the form of a perfect cross the glorified Jesus manifested Himself immediately in front of me...quickly He inbreathed or infused Himself within. I...said to myself, this is the fulfillment of John 14:20, "At that day (when He gives the other Comforter) you shall know that I am in the Father and you in me and I in you."...It was made known that the kind of union that Jesus has with the Father is precisely the kind of union that He is seeking for us to have with Him....I had asked for the truth about the Cross....It was apparent that there was a glory side to the Cross that had been almost unseen in most of Christian history. In this experience in answer to my question, I was put upon a cross of life, while He went to a cross of shame. I had been put upon a cross of bliss, while He had been put upon

a cross of agony. I had been put upon a cross of heavenly manifestation....He was put upon a cross of desertion, where it appeared that even God Himself did not care, or had forsaken Him....The Cross is a way of life; the way of love meeting all hate with Love, all evil with good, all negatives with positives.[6]

6 | Miracles— A Proof?

The real problem for anyone who adopts an exclusively cross-centered spirituality, who embraces all suffering as God's will, is what to make of the Gospels, where over and over we read that Jesus "healed all their sick" (for example, Matt. 12:15). How do we account for the fact that everywhere in the Gospels Jesus treated sickness as an enemy? Today, why do so many followers of Jesus always encourage the sick to accept their sickness as God's will? Once when a leper came to Jesus and asked if He wanted to cure him, Jesus replied, "I am willing" (Matt. 8:3). In contrast, we tend to say to the twentieth-century leper, "Jesus probably doesn't want to cure you physically. Learn to accept your leprosy, for it is the cross He wants you to carry."

The previous chapters have mentioned some of the reasons for the radical shift of attitude from treating sickness as an enemy to welcoming it as a friend. But I believe the principal reason for this shift has been that we have tended to emphasize *doctrine* rather than experience, as if right knowledge coupled with willpower were enough to produce Christians.

In many ways the Roman Catholic Church is discovering the inadequacy of such an approach. The parochial school system, for example, financed with great sacrifice by the people, is in itself insufficient to create enthusiastic Christians. In some Catholic colleges no more than twenty percent of the students still participate in the Sunday liturgy; yet they have sat through years of courses in religion and theology. The general discouragement felt over the failure to discover a successful method of teaching Christianity to the rising generation is all part of the same sad situation: An intellectual approach is in itself not enough to Christianize a generation—or a nation.

How often I meet young people who say, "I used to be a Catholic, but now I'm a Christian." What they seem to be saying is that their training merely made them conscious of rules and doctrines. They claim that it was only after they began to move outside Catholic circles that they found a personal relationship with Jesus and a new life.

I have met a goodly number of graduates of Catholic colleges who tell me they were not convinced of the reality of Christ's presence until they were converted at a Jesus rally—this in spite of years of training by concerned parents and dedicated teachers. Admittedly, this "turning on" to Christ can sputter and die out; it is only a beginning, but it is a beginning—this personal experience of Christ's presence which is so needed for a living faith.

As a consequence of an overemphasis on doctrine, we also seem to have lost a lively sense of Christ's healing presence and power. In general Christ's cures have been presented mainly as signs of the *truth* of His message. From this perspective, since faith is beyond the direct argument of reason, the best way Jesus had of showing He was the Messiah was indirectly, by working miracles. ("Tell John the Baptist what you hear and see.") Jesus cured people to show that what He said was true—that He and the Father were one.

Healing, therefore, came to be seen primarily as a sign of the truth of a doctrine, of a message, or as a proof of holiness. Seen from this viewpoint, healings came to have a threefold purpose:

1) They were worked *by Christ* to show that He was the Messiah and that He was divine.

2) They were worked *in the early church* to show that the church was carrying out the work of Christ and was now the chosen people. Once this fact was clearly established, the need for miracles subsided. After the first century, miracles still occurred occasionally—at Lourdes, for instance—to show a skeptical world that Christ was still with the church. Textbooks (including those I studied in the seminary) taught that true miracles could not occur in the Protestant churches because God would not want to signify that these were true churches.

3) They were worked *by certain holy persons*—the great saints—who could perform exceptional miracles to show precisely that they were great saints. Ordinary Christians, according to this view, would never expect God to heal people in response to their own prayers, for they would be presumptuous to regard themselves as such spiritual heroes.

There is much to be said, of course, for seeing healing as a sign of proof. After all, Christ told His critics that, if they didn't believe Him because of His words, they should believe because of His works. What I see as harmful, however, is an *overemphasis* on the proof aspect of healing, which tends to distort its true place in Christian living. Consider, for instance, each of the areas mentioned above—the life of Christ, of the church and of the great saints. Even in each of these regards, healing has deeper significance than being a mere proof of doctrine or of holiness.

Jesus' Own Motivation for Healing

Christ's motivation for healing was clearly something more than a desire to prove His messianic mission. In the first place, He frequently healed on the Sabbath, a practice that defied the teaching of the scribes and Pharisees. Far from convincing these men that He was the one sent from God, His cures convinced them that He was an imposter who should be done away with: "The Pharisees and the teachers of the law were looking for a reason to accuse Jesus, so they watched him closely to see if he would heal on the Sabbath" (Luke 6:7).

Certainly, if Jesus had been primarily concerned about convincing people that He was the Messiah, He could easily have confined His healing ministry to the other six days of the week. But His willingness to violate the tradition of His contemporaries shows the strength of His compassion for the sick. Compassion was a stronger motivation for His actions than trying to prove His mission to the religious leaders.

Furthermore, after healing people Jesus often commanded them not to speak about their cures. He was not looking for publicity, but He was constrained by His own overwhelming love to help the sick even to the extent of jeopardizing His own life.

> Instead [the healed man] went out and began to talk freely, spreading the news. As a result, Jesus could no longer enter a town openly but stayed outside in lonely places. Yet the people still came to him from everywhere (Mark 1:45).

The picture we get of Jesus—especially in Mark, perhaps the earliest Gospel—is that of a man trying, if anything, to conceal His messianic identity. He is not trying to prove anything and even seeks to escape the crowds who have come to be healed:

> Because of the crowd he told his disciples to have
> a small boat ready for him, to keep the people from
> crowding him. For he had healed many, so that those
> with diseases were pushing forward to touch him
> (Mark 3:9,10).

Miracles as a Proof of the Truth of a Church or of Heroic Sanctity

The theory that healings take place in only one church to prove that it is the true church simply goes against the facts. Healings apparently have been taking place in many of the churches—and even outside the established churches, such as was the case in the sixties among the "Jesus people." The main thing, evidently, that God wants to show people by these healings is that He is real, that He loves ordinary people and that He wants them to draw near to Him. Christ appears more anxious to bring people to Himself than He is to validate any one church. (That is a question of priorities and does not mean, of course, that it is unimportant for a person to belong to a church.)

Finally, we find no New Testament backing for the view that healings take place to show that a person is a great, exceptionally holy, saint. On the contrary, Jesus seems to assume that extraordinary actions will be performed by ordinary—or even evil—human beings.

> Many will say to me on that day, "Lord, Lord, did
> we not prophesy in your name, and in your name
> drive out demons and perform many miracles?"
> Then I will tell them plainly, "I never knew you.
> Away from me, you evildoers!" (Matt. 7:22,23).

Moreover, He said that one of the signs that will follow those who *believe*—not necessarily those who are holy—will be that they will lay hands on the sick, and they will recover

(Mark 16:17,18). The rebuking of the disciples who failed to heal the epileptic demoniac indicates that Jesus wanted to bring His disciples to a point where they could cure even the most difficult cases.

Destructiveness of the Proof Emphasis

All these theoretical considerations are vital, for they affect our lives in important ways. The "proof" mentality seems to keep Christians from praying for healing. If I believe that healings are extraordinary events in the Christian life, proofs of holiness rather than ordinary Christian works, I certainly will be hesitant to pray for the sick for fear of elevating myself to a level of activity appropriate only to the great saints.

Because of this overemphasis on proof, many church leaders hold that we need not pray for healing today because Christianity has sufficiently proved itself throughout history. In their view only the sensation seekers pant after the miraculous. In keeping with this attitude, church leaders, generally speaking, neither encourage healing services nor urge ministers and lay people to visit the hospital to pray for healing.[1]

Most important of all, if healing has meaning only as a sign and has no value in its own right, then healing must be extrinsic to the gospel message—an external proof pointing to the key thing: the gospel itself. But this viewpoint fails to see that healing is an integral part of the gospel message: If the good news is that Christ came to save us, then the *power* to save has to be there. If the power to save us extends to the whole person, part of the very message of salvation is that Christ came to heal us—spirit, mind, emotions and body.

To deny or minimize the healing ministry is thus to take away much of the power of the gospel and to leave in its stead a body of truths devoid of life. As Paul wrote:

> Then I will find out not only how these arrogant peo-
> ple are talking, but what power they have. For the
> kingdom of God is not a matter of talk but of power
> (1 Cor. 4:19b,20).

Christianity is more than doctrine; it is power. It is power
to transform our lives, to destroy the evil that prevents us
from loving God and our neighbor. Jesus came to bring us
a new life, a share in God's own life. We have always believed these things, but where is the reality of it? Where is
the power truly to change lives?

All too frequently we have taken the good news and
changed it into good advice. The good news is that Christ
has come to help us enter into the very life of His Father
and to transform us by His power into new persons who can
love and rejoice and help the poor in a way far beyond our
own capabilities. Good advice, on the other hand, is to hold
up a Christian ideal of life and service and then to say in
effect: "Here's the ideal; now use your willpower to achieve
it."

A good test of our Christian attitude would be the response
to this question: What would you do if a drug addict came
to you and asked for help? Would you merely give the addict
all kinds of helpful advice and then try to encourage him or
her to use willpower to stay off drugs? Would you then call
a local agency and help the addict enroll in a special drug
program or be committed to a federal hospital?

These measures may prove necessary, but would you, first
of all, as a Christian, pray with the addict, asking the Lord
to free him or her from addiction? If you believe that prayer
can accomplish that person's deliverance, then you really have
good news to offer—of freedom for the captive. Jesus not
only holds up an ideal, but He gives us the power to reach
it. Christianity would be dreaming the impossible dream if

it were only words without the transforming power that frees us from bondage.

David Wilkerson is a minister of the Assemblies of God, a church which emphasizes Christ's power to heal. He has founded Teen Challenge centers all across the country because he believes in Christ's power to cure the drug addict. More than that, Wilkerson has evidence: More than seventy percent of the addicts who have submitted to his program of prayer have come off drugs and stayed off—compared to the less than five percent rate of cure in federal hospitals.[2]

Is the gospel just a talking game preparing for the hereafter, or does Jesus aid a desperate person who needs help right now? For the drug addict or the alcoholic, healing is not simply a matter for academic discussion; it is a matter of life and death. And it is not just physical life and death; it is spiritual life and death as well. What willpower cannot accomplish, Christ's healing power can and does.[3]

Why, then, weren't more organizations like Teen Challenge and Alcoholics Anonymous, which are based on a belief in the power of prayer and the need for a community of love, formed within the institution of the church? I think it is because we have stressed only that sinners use their willpower, that they "take the pledge," as it were. But many of us never learned to pray with confidence that Jesus would free addicts from their habit; nor did we form that close community to support alcoholics or addicts and prevent their falling again.

Christians have always believed in the need for prayer and community. But when it comes right down to the practical order, do we really believe that Jesus has come to free and transform people? Do we have only good advice to offer, or do we believe in the power of Jesus to change what we ourselves cannot?

With faith, we can begin to pray with alcoholics that the

Lord take away their inordinate craving for drink. We can begin to pray with drug addicts that the Lord might help them kick their drug habit "cold turkey." We can even dare pray for the lame man that he might walk again.

Then we will come to learn from our own experience what Jesus meant when He said: "I tell you the truth, anyone who has faith in me will do what I have been doing. He will do even greater things than these, because I am going to the Father" (John 14:12).

7 | God Is Love

Because of all the conditioning which makes Christians believe that suffering is sent by God, they are likely to feel guilty if they ask for healing, to feel cowardly if they ask for alleviation. As Christians, not only do they feel that they should be able to endure their cross; they think they should be able to run out and embrace it.

So many Christians feel they must have an excuse, an unselfish reason for asking God for a cure. Typically, a mother will say something like: "I want to get well so I won't be a burden to my family." Or a professional may well say, "I want to be cured, so I can go to work again."

In contrast, if either of these persons went to a doctor, they would not feel they had to make up such excuses. The man would go to an orthopedic surgeon simply because he had injured his spine and wanted to get well. He would not need to justify his presence in the doctor's office by proving to the doctor that his getting better would help his family or enable him to do his work better. Reason enough that he is sick and wants to get well.

Why is it, then, that so many of us feel we have to justify our asking God to make us well? It is as if we cannot believe that God loves us; He values us only for our work. How different we are from little children asking a loving father or mother for a very natural favor.

As one British housewife, reflecting on the spirituality she learned, described her feelings:

> Despite all the formal instruction we received on the Fatherhood of God, the lesson we really learnt was that our relation to God is as little like the normal relation of a child to its father as can be imagined. Picture your own child jumping nervously when it hears your voice; unwilling to play with others in case it gets dirty; always a little anxious because, even though you *say* nothing, you may be inwardly critical and disapproving; fearful of getting on your wrong side; uncertain of asking you for anything it wants because it thinks you will say it is too much trouble or too expensive or not good for it or too good for it—anything but a simple, affectionate "Yes"; obscurely convinced that the root of the trouble is that you don't like children, and its only chance of approval is to be as little like a child as possible.... We *know* He loves us...; we *feel* that His love is the dubious kind that used to result for us in spinach and the thwarting of natural impulse. We daren't formulate these feelings, because we know obscurely that if we did, we should have another set of concepts framed something like this: God is horrid...God is always trying to trip you up—and so on. These feelings are kept well out of sight and are only *consciously* present in the form of certain implicit expectations.[1]

Part of the reason ordinary Christians have such a fearful relationship with God is that they have exchanged Christ's revelation of a Father who brings healing for their own more or less pagan conception of God as one who sends suffering as a punishment or a penance. Healing is essential to the gospel message and carries us all the way back to our very idea of God.

What kind of a being is God? If we truly believe that God is love, then it should be easy to believe that healing is an ordinary, not extraordinary, sign of His compassion. Any other attitude toward healing robs the gospel of the reality of God's revelation of Himself as a loving father: "If you, then, though you are evil, know how to give good gifts to your children, how much more will your Father in heaven give good gifts to those who ask him!" (Matt. 7:11).

What is at stake here is not something out on the periphery, but something right at the heart of Christianity: When I speak of God's love for me, do I speak of it in terms that I, a human being, can understand? Or am I talking about some unreal concept of "divine love" or "charity" that does not touch my real life?

I know what real human love is. I am certain that, if I am in pain, if I am sick, my family and friends will do everything they can to get me well. They will take me to the doctor, buy me medicine, put me in a hospital; they may even help me pay thousands of dollars in hospital bills. Their actions show a love and concern that I can understand.

But if, while I am lying in my hospital bed, the hospital chaplain tries to cheer me up with small talk and then tells me that God probably does not want to heal me, I become confused. The chaplain is not portraying the love of God in any human way that I can grasp. Either Jesus meant something very definite when He said, "Ask and you shall receive," or the gospel has to be reinterpreted in such a way that ordinary people find it hard to understand in terms of their everyday lives.

C.S. Lewis, in *The Problem of Pain*, set forth all the understanding his brilliant mind could focus on the mystery and anguish of suffering. Some time after writing the book, his wife died. Faced with this terrible loss, Lewis's reasoned reflections were of no comfort; he began to rage against God for taking his wife.

In his uncontrollable grief, he took a writer's way out of his pain: He wrote a journal describing his day-to-day battle with despair. When at last he regained his senses and emerged again into the light, he decided to publish his journal. Yet realizing that his treatment of pain endured was very different from his previous reasoning about it, he did not attach his real name to the work but chose a pseudonym. (The book was later published under his real name.) Because of C.S. Lewis's reputation as an intellectual defender of Christianity, it is especially revealing to read his human reactions to personal suffering and temptations against faith:

> But go to Him when your need is desperate, when all other help is vain, and what do you find? A door slammed in your face, and a sound of bolting and double bolting on the inside. After that, silence. You may as well turn away. The longer you wait, the more emphatic the silence will become.
>
> There are no lights in the windows.[2]
>
> Not that I am (I think) in much danger of ceasing to believe in God. The real danger is of coming to believe such dreadful things about Him. The conclusion I dread is not "So there's no God after all," but "So this is what God's really like. Deceive yourself no longer."[3]
>
> There is no answer. Only the locked door, the iron curtain, the vacuum, absolute zero. "Them as asks don't get." I was a fool to ask.[4]
>
> An overdose of sleeping pills would do it. I am... afraid that we are really rats in a trap, or, worse still,

rats in a laboratory. Someone said, I believe, "God always geometrizes." Supposing the truth were "God always vivisects"?

Sooner or later I must face the question in plain language. What reason have we, except our own desperate wishes, to believe that God is, by any standard we can conceive, "good"? Doesn't all the *prima facie* evidence suggest exactly the opposite?

We set Christ against it. But how if He were mistaken? Almost His last words may have a perfectly clear meaning. He had found that the Being He called Father was horribly and infinitely different from what He had supposed. The trap, so long and carefully prepared and so subtly baited, was at last sprung, on the cross. The vile practical joke had succeeded.[5]

I wrote that last night. It was a yell rather than a thought. Let me try it over again. Is it rational to believe in a bad God? Anyway, in a God so bad as all that? The Cosmic Sadist, the spiteful imbecile?[6]

The terrible thing is that a perfectly good God is in this matter hardly less formidable than a Cosmic Sadist. The more we believe that God hurts only to heal, the less we can believe that there is any use in begging for tenderness. A cruel man might be bribed—might grow tired of his vile sport—might have a temporary fit of mercy, as alcoholics have fits of sobriety. But suppose that what you are up against is a surgeon whose intentions are wholly good. The kinder and more conscientious he is, the more inexorably he will go on cutting. If he yielded to your entreaties, if he stopped before the operation was complete, all the pain up to that point would have been useless. But is it credible that such extremities of torture should be necessary for us? Well, take your choice. The tortures occur. If they are unnecessary, then there is no God or a bad one.[7]

In these passages C.S. Lewis provides a striking example of what happens to the human heart when it is confronted with a tradition that God, rather than evil forces, brings suffering. He describes the human heart as crying out, unable to conceive how a loving God could be without compassion. Intuitively, he and all Christians know that God's love cannot be so different from human love as to be a complete mystery.

While in Peru, I was surprised to find that the most popular Christian feast of the year is that of *El Senor de los Milagros*— Our Lord of the Miracles. This feast, established by the people, is more popular than Easter or Christmas in spite of all official teaching, for the people look to God for help, for healing, for miracles. The month of October is spent much like Lent in other countries, preparing for the procession of Our Lord of the Miracles. The Peruvian people in their simple faith look to God and their church for help—not just for a doctrine of acceptance of suffering.

It is the devotion of simple people that has built most of the great Christian shrines. Expectant pilgrims continue to go to Lourdes in search of healing. Catholics go to Mary as to a compassionate and loving mother, approachable and reaching out to heal, but often they are afraid to approach Jesus or God the Father. Yet Jesus told us that the love of His Father for us is greater than the love of a human father (Matt. 7:9-11), and God spoke through the prophet Isaiah: "Can a mother forget the baby at her breast and have no compassion on the child she has borne? Though she may forget, I will not forget you!" (Is. 49:15).

In question here is our very notion of God. Against a God

who desires us to suffer here on earth, we may be tempted
to rage as did Ivan in *The Brothers Karamazov*:

> "Tell me yourself, I challenge you—answer. Imagine
> that you are creating a fabric of human destiny with
> the object of making men happy in the end, giving
> them peace and rest at last. Imagine that you are
> doing this but that it is essential and inevitable to
> torture to death only one tiny creature—that child
> beating its breast with its fist, for instance—in order
> to found that edifice on its unavenged tears. Would
> you consent to be the architect on those conditions?
> Tell me. Tell the truth."
>
> "No, I wouldn't consent," said Alyosha softly.[8]

But the revelation of God in Jesus Christ is that we have
a merciful Lord who saves and heals. Jesus, as the visible
manifestation of the invisible God, shows us that God is a
loving Father.

Repeatedly, Jesus asks us for confidence: "Whatever you
ask in my name will be granted." It is time to return to this
childlike trust in prayer, to a confidence that God really loves
us. For the most tangible sign that God loves is that He stoops,
as Jesus did, to heal the wounded.

If God has the *power* to help people, yet refuses to do so,
we naturally ask several questions:

1) Does God really *care*? If I have the power to help a
friend when I see him hurt, I use all my powers to help. If
God has power to help me, but doesn't, I don't know what
it means to say, "God loves me." This is a very real question asked many times, especially by despairing people. "My
condition," they say, "proves that God doesn't care. Maybe
He cares for you; but look at me, and you know why I'm
convinced that God doesn't care about me."

2) If God cares, but lets people remain in their suffering,

He seems to *lack the power* to help. He is irrelevant to my real life, to my real needs.

In either case, the very idea of God's goodness and love can be deeply shaken when we deny that He heals through prayer. Part of the present crisis of faith is, I think, related to a basic lack of confidence in prayer. Some preaching, emphasizing caution and stressing that God often says no, has contributed to this lack of hope and faith.

If God does not ordinarily answer prayer but only wants us to accept and endure suffering, what is the *good* news? If someone says he is my friend, but then lets me suffer when he has the power to help, how can I help but question whether he really cares?[9] A mother's love, a father's love, a friend's love, I understand. But what about God's love?

God has said in Scripture that His love surpasses that of a mother (Is. 49:15) or of a father (Matt. 7:11). The marvelous revelation is that He is not a God on the mountaintop of Sinai whom we dare not approach, but that He has become a human being like us in everything but sin. The mission of Jesus was to share our suffering and then to transform it into new life, to heal us in body and mind.

Inspired by Christ, we have built hospitals with the assumption that it is God's will that we should do everything humanly possible to care for the sick and help them get well. Only certain non-Christian religions believe in letting people die on the streets, believing it to be fate, or karma, that brought them there where passersby should let them suffer it out. Christians should be proud that the Red Cross was founded through the compassion of Camillus, and that Christian nurses and doctors are ready to give their lives to cure the sick.

Why is it, then, that those who give spiritual advice usually counsel patients to accept their suffering as God's will for them, while everyone else in the hospital labors to restore the person to health? No wonder many people fear God when it comes time to die, for God does not seem to show love by healing as the patient's friends and relatives show their love by wanting to see us well.

Reflected in these attitudes is a kind of spiritual schizophrenia: Christian doctors and nurses work to make the patient well, obeying Christ's injunctions to help the sick and needy. On the contrary, preachers sometimes persuade the patient that acceptance of the cross is Christ's basic message. If the patient recovers through human ministration, fine; but God is somehow portrayed as mysteriously desiring us to suffer in a redemptive way.

Little wonder, then, that in many parts of Latin America when disaster or sickness strikes, the people say, "It is God's will." To regain health they go, not to God, but to a *curandero*, a witch doctor, to pray for recovery. The roles have thus been reversed: The people treat God as if He were a pagan deity to be appeased by suffering. But for healing, they turn to the world of spirits and demons.

We desperately need to return to the vision of God revealed in and by Jesus Christ: a tender, loving and compassionate God who raises us up and makes us whole wherever we have been cast down by the world of evil—whether we have sinned and need forgiveness, or are sick and need physical healing. Even now the kingdom of God is among us, saving and healing and destroying the kingdom of evil.

In short, the nature of God as manifested visibly in Jesus Christ is love. Jesus' compassion impelled Him to reach out whenever He saw a sick person, even when it was against His own best interests in His relationship to the authorities. The healing works of Jesus were so important in Peter's mind that when, in preaching to the household of Cornelius, he summed up the ministry of Jesus, he said nothing about the content of His preaching. Instead, he reported:

You know what has happened throughout Judea, beginning in Galilee after the baptism that John preached—*how God anointed Jesus of Nazareth with the Holy Spirit and power*, and how he went around *doing good and healing all who were under the power of the devil*, because God was with him. We are witnesses of everything he did in the country of the Jews and in Jerusalem (Acts 10:37-39, italics added).

After this, Peter speaks of Jesus' crucifixion, death and resurrection; but he sums up the entire public ministry of Jesus in terms of what He did rather than what He said, for Jesus established the kingdom of God through the power of healing as well as through preaching.

The healing of Jesus, then, is central to the doctrine of the gospel. To deny this is, in effect, to deny the gospel—to change it from good news into good advice, which lacks the power to transform us into a new creation.[10] In short, Jesus did not heal people to prove that He was God; He healed them *because He was God*.

PART II

Faith, Hope and Charity As They Touch Upon the Healing Ministry

*Faith, hope and love.
But the greatest
of these is love.*

1 Cor. 13:13

8 | The Faith To Be Healed

All the books on healing—including *the* book on healing, the New Testament—emphasize the role that faith plays in healing. "Go in peace, your faith has made you whole" is a constant saying of Jesus. Jesus asks of us the strongest kind of faith—a faith that admits of no doubt or hesitation:

> "Have faith in God," Jesus answered. "I will tell you the truth, if anyone says to this mountain, 'Go, throw yourself into the sea,' and *does not doubt in his heart* but believes that what he says will happen, it will be done for him. Therefore I tell you, whatever you ask for in prayer, *believe that you have received it*, and it will be yours" (Mark 11:22-24, italics added).

This is a nearly unbelievable statement! Nevertheless, we are asked to believe it; we are to have no hesitation in believing that we have already received whatever we ask for. (Later we will say more about how to pray "the prayer of faith" for healing, but for now, just notice the strong emphasis Jesus Himself places upon faith.) Such strong statements are not rare in the Gospels, as even the most cursory reading will show. On the contrary, faith in asking God for our needs is one of the common New Testament themes.

In consequence, many evangelists stress faith as a condition

113

necessary for healing. "Have faith," they say, "and you will be healed. 'By His stripes you are healed.' Can you believe those words of Scripture? If so, lay hold of that promise and you will be healed."

With absolute faith, all Christians accept another aspect of the healing ministry, the forgiveness of sins, provided the person meets the necessary condition: repentance. With a faith equally strong, some evangelists stress that physical healing will always take place, provided the person meets the necessary condition: faith. In both cases—the healing of sin and the healing of disease—preachers stress the same basic principle: Christ has already won these blessings for us through the cross; all we have to do is apply the fruits of redemption to our own lives. "He took up our infirmities and carried our diseases" (Matt. 8:17).

But there is a problem. While all Christians believe that forgiveness of sins always takes place, they can see that physical healing does not always occur. Forgiveness is not something our eyes can see, but healing is. The blind either see, or they do not; the lame either walk, or they remain in their wheelchairs. Since not all the lame walk following our prayers for their healing, how can we have the same certainty of faith that we have when we pray for forgiveness of sin? What are we supposed to believe will happen? What kind of faith do we need?

What Kind of Faith Do We Need?

In order to talk about this entire matter of faith intelligently and to avoid some of the oversimplification that has harmed people's faith instead of helping it, it may be good to describe four basic faith attitudes toward healing:

1) *Healing is simply our human responsibility.* There are many members of Christian churches who do not believe in

the possibility of God's direct healing power, though they admit the use of natural means and secondary causes (including the power of suggestion).

Take for example the scorn for healing miracles evinced in the writings of a spiritual author, Louis Evely:

> It seems that Jesus Himself placed miracles beyond the pale of religion. Man left to himself would hope to better his condition through all sorts of wealth and power; but God has taught us to better it through love, by accepting it willingly, as He accepted His death on the cross. Nothing is more foreign to God than miraculous *tours de force*, phenomena which excite in man only fear or curiosity.
>
> With the acceptance of the theory of human evolution, with the development of scientific method and technical resources, it becomes more and more evident that the religion revealed by Christ is one that is fully human and fully divine—not an archaic religion of miracles and contradiction to human nature, but a religion of patient love and responsibility.
>
> If there are miracles to be worked, then it is we who must work them. Man, being man, has unlimited resources at his disposal.[1]

Certainly, such an attitude of self-sufficiency sees no need for a ministry of prayer for healing, which only prolongs an illusion that prevents us from accepting responsibility for our own destiny.

2) *Healing is possible but extraordinary.* This attitude toward healing represents the belief of many Christians (Roman Catholics, in particular). Here is faith, certainly in God's *power* to perform miracles of healing; but there is doubt as to God's *desire* to perform such healing as a matter of course. Miracles are the exception—they prove something

(for example, the holiness of a saint); they are rare occurrences. In fact, if miracles should become common, they would lose their value as exceptional signs.

The ordinary will of God, according to this view, is that sick persons should raise their sufferings to the level of the cross; at that level they must learn to accept pain and not try to escape it. People should pray only for what will bring them spiritual advancement. Since suffering has redemptive value, we should not pray to be freed from pain but rather seek the royal road of the cross.

The result is that the sick are not strongly encouraged to pray for healing, lest they lose the merits of the cross. The situation is something like a football game; play as long as you can with an injury for the sake of the team, unless the pain becomes unbearable. A sick person asking for an end to pain may feel guilty, like the player—a quitter—asking to be taken out of the game.

Frequently, I meet people unwilling to pray for the cure of small sicknesses and hurts because they feel it is unworthy to ask for relief from such small ailments as, for example, an infected toe. Yet the same people will go to a doctor seeking a cure for the same ailment. If persons with such an attitude do pray, they generally doubt whether God will condescend to answer their prayers, which they fear are contaminated by self-interest.

Experience leads them to believe in the truth of the self-fulfilling prophecy: Blessed are those who expect nothing, for they shall not be disappointed.

3) *Healing is ordinary and normative, but does not always take place.* It is this author's belief that the ordinary will of God is that we should be whole. Usually, we glorify God more mightily when we are healthy than when we are sick. Therefore, we can and should pray to God with confidence for healing.

Even so, there are exceptions; sometimes sickness is directed toward a higher good, for the kingdom of God. (There are other reasons, too, enumerated in the chapter on "Eleven Reasons Why People Are Not Healed.") Consequently, healing does not always take place, even where there is faith.

4) *Healing always takes place if there is faith.* This kind of absolute belief is, I think, more strongly exemplified by persons who present a very simple doctrine of healing. Such persons favor the writings of evangelists like Kenneth Hagin, who has written a number of booklets on faith as a precondition for healing. Typical of this teaching is the following:

> There are those who are especially anointed with the ministry of healing, but every believer ought to have a ministry of healing. I don't mean every believer ought to be anointed of the Spirit to minister in certain ways, but I mean every believer ought to be able to take the Word of God to a sick person and open that Word to them and give them what the scripture says on it.
>
> If those folks are receptive to the Word of God, then faith will come into their hearts. When you open the Word up to people, then they will see that the Word says, "By his stripes we are healed...." Open the Word to the sick, and if their minds are open, that Word, through their mind, will get down into their spirits.
>
> As they meditate upon it, they will come to see that by His stripes, according to the Word, I am healed.
>
> If that person acts upon the Word of God, they will ignore what this outward man tells them. The body may tell them that the symptoms are still there,

even the pain or the misery, or whatever it is. But instead of walking by natural, human faith, you walk by Bible faith. I have seen people with conditions that the doctors said could never be cured, but as I opened the Word to them, I have seen them with every symptom still present say, "I'm healed."

I asked them, "How do you know you are?" They said, "Because the Word says, 'Himself took my infirmities and bare my sicknesses.' " Those people are alive and well. Not just one of them, but many of them. They are alive and well today with no symptoms of the disease whatsoever. Yet, when they acted in faith and made their confession, they had every symptom they had ever had. As far as medical science was concerned, their condition was still incurable. What happened? They believed in their hearts.[2]

This is, no doubt, a powerful statement on faith, a real challenge. Yet questions remain. For those who still exhibit the symptoms of sickness, is the *only* answer their need for more faith? One young couple, for instance, is trying to live up to this most stringent belief in healing, but they are having problems:

Pat and I have a few questions that we thought you might have the answers to:

We do not allow sickness in our new home because we know that faith and scriptures can drive it away, and Jesus bore our diseases for us. Why then do Spirit-filled Christians sometimes get really sick? X Y's singer,[3] the last I heard, was in a hospital, not allowed to move so that a blood clot could hopefully pass through without killing her. She does not believe in sickness. So why or how can this happen? We cannot teach healing positively and then end by say-ing, "If it is the Lord's will this time." That is not faith. I thought the Bible had laws that were obeyed in faith, and that there were no "perhaps." Are there shades of gray in the Bible?

Also, do we have dominion over animals? Our cat has coughing spells that really irritate us. We've prayed and laid hands on her, cast off bad spirits, etc. Veterinary bills are expensive and since we will not allow sickness in our lives, why allow it in our cat's life?

Of such problems is life made up. Such real difficulties with the theory of the faith required for healing do lead to anxiety—or, in some cases, to a rejection of the whole idea of healing as incredible and contrary to the reality of a suffering mankind. So it is necessary to make important distinctions in order to render credible the glorious ministry of healing to people who dare to ask questions. It is not just a matter of rendering this ministry credible to someone else; it is also a question of the reality itself: How do we explain the sickness of Christians?

I do not pretend to have all the answers. Far from it, I bow down, like Job, before the mystery of healing in its con-nection with suffering: "And now let us proclaim the *mystery* of our faith." But there are some distinctions we can make that will help us know the kind of faith, which is often—but not always—a precondition for healing.

1) *My faith is in God—not in my faith.*

My faith is not in my faith, but *in God*. This sounds obvious. Perhaps it is obvious. But if every person who prayed for healing really understood these words, we could clarify many problems that we now find in the healing ministry.

My faith is in God—in His faithfulness to His promises, in His wisdom, in His power and in His goodness:

In His faithfulness to His promises to hear and to answer my prayers. I have absolute confidence that God answers my prayers, whether I see the results or not.

In His wisdom. Because of His wisdom, which so far surpasses mine, I trust that He understands, even when I do not, every motive, every circumstance involved in my praying for the healing of this particular person. Because of my ignorance I sometimes pray for a mistaken thing, or in a mistaken way, and so I do not see the results turn out as I think they should. But these will turn out as God in His wisdom sees best.

In His power. I believe that everything is possible with God. Nothing then is impossible to the prayer of the Christian, even a resurrection from the dead.

In His goodness. Because I believe in God's goodness I try to see everything as reflecting His love. Whatever is ultimately the most loving thing will happen in response to my prayer for healing.

But my faith is not *in my faith*. My faith opens up doubts once I begin to look at its quality. When a blind person, one who has no eyes whatsoever in the sockets, comes forward to ask for prayer, I wonder if I have the faith required for such a healing. Most of us would have to admit our doubts.

Once we look at our faith, however, rather than at God, we concentrate on our own inadequacy. Those who claim to have no doubts sometimes seem more in need of healing than those they pray for. Instead of examining their own ministry and asking realistic questions about why they are not always successful, they simply project the guilt of sickness onto those they pray for.

In short, my faith has no doubt about God's power to heal and about His desire to heal (contrary to those who feel God does not heal at all, or only in extraordinary circumstances). But I can doubt whether I know all the circumstances required to pray rightly for a given person. Is there something I do not understand in this situation? More often than not, I am at least partly in the dark. Consequently, I don't always know whether the person I pray for will get well. Unless the Lord reveals to me all the necessary details of the situation, I simply do not know whether healing will take place at this time.

Does this mean I lack faith? No, I don't think so; it simply means I am human. My faith is in God, not in my own powers—not even in my own faith.

Even so, many people I have met, who do believe in healing, feel guilty about their human doubts. They turn inward when they hear the challenge, "Do you have the faith to be healed?" Instead of trusting absolutely in God's power and goodness, they probe within themselves to examine whether they are entirely free of doubt; and nine times out of ten, their answer is no.

Then there ensues a painful conflict, in which they begin to feel guilty. The more they examine their doubt, the bigger it grows. In the struggle to pass beyond the point of doubt, they end up by suppressing their real feelings. The more they wrestle, the deeper their anguish.

They may finally manage to surmount the doubt by a strong act of will, moving beyond the doubt that still swirls around underneath. But faith is a gift that cannot be attained by our own efforts. As Bogart Van Dunne, a Methodist Scripture scholar, once said in a seminar: "Protestants began by rejecting Catholicism for what they conceived was its reliance on works for salvation. But now, for some Protestants, *faith has become the works* they struggle to achieve."

This struggle to "achieve" faith reminds me of what often happens when I begin to lose a tennis game. I start overstraining; I hit the ball harder, trying to make winning shots in order to regain my confidence; I smash my serve harder to win a few quick, impressive aces. But all that really happens is that I hit the ball out of court more often, and I start missing my first serve. My straining efforts worsen my game. So I try still harder. I talk to my partner, or myself, to generate a little more enthusiasm; I try running faster to refresh my drooping spirits. But I only end up beating myself. My efforts cannot cover up my lack of coordination.

Similarly, I see people in prayer groups, in the face of defeat (when the person they are praying for does not seem to be changed), pray louder and faster. They press the person with stronger and stronger exhortation to have faith. But they do not increase the sick person's faith. Instead, they only add to the tension. Their efforts cannot cover up the fact that the object of their faith is off center.

This anxious approach can do great harm. Persons who are not healed go away with the impression that they lack the faith they should have, or that God does not love them as He so obviously loves those who have been healed. They identify with the man born blind in John's Gospel who was being argued over by the disciples (not the Pharisees): "Who sinned, this man or his parents, that he was born blind?" (John 9:2).

I remember a woman at a large prayer meeting who had been encouraged not to see a doctor, rather to disregard her symptoms (seizures similar to epilepsy). During the meeting, she had an attack. The advice she had been receiving now only resulted in greater anxiety and sleepless nights, which, in turn, led to lower resistance and more frequent seizures. Far from increasing her faith, the advice she received only led her to condemn herself for lacking the faith to resist the attacks of Satan.

If we really believe that only God is responsible for answering our prayers, then we can do our part, which is to pray, and leave the results to God. Glenn Clark, founder of the Camps Farthest Out, used to compare asking God for a favor with a hen hatching an egg. You put the egg under the hen and leave it for twenty-one days. If you keep taking the egg out to look at it, you inhibit the whole process; you may be helping your own anxiety, but you may also kill the egg. Why, he asked, can't we put as much trust in God as we do in an old hen?

Clark used another analogy as well:

> When you take a pair of shoes to the shoemaker to be half-soled, you go off and leave them, don't you? How otherwise would the shoemaker be able to mend them? Likewise, how can God get at our problems if we continue to hug them to ourselves? Yes, the biggest problem in prayer is how to "let go and let God."[4]

When I try to suppress my doubts and have faith in my faith, I become human-centered rather than God-centered. I scrutinize my own doubts and my own fears and feel guilty about them; then I try to get rid of them by my own will-power. I may *seem* to myself to be getting out of myself and centering myself on God. In reality, though, I am doing the very opposite: I am trying to create faith in myself, forgetting that faith is a gift from God.

So often this kind of approach, far from creating confidence and trust in God, ends in a sense of fear and worthlessness. A good example of this confusion appears in a letter I once received:

> When I'm used as an instrument in a big physical healing I'm *scared to death*. There's no other way to describe it. Two examples have taken place in our community. I feel that a certain child remained in

braces partly because of my lack of faith; then last Wednesday a blind man came in great faith to our meeting. We prayed over him and, though I believed that the Lord could heal him, at the same time I was afraid that he would not. I can't help but feel that our lack of faith as a community prevented this man from seeing. I prayed about this and I felt led to 1 John 5, so I know the Lord wants my fear to go away. How do I strengthen my faith in this matter? It's not lack of faith in Jesus' power but in His using me as an instrument. I have no qualms about being used for prophecy, but this doesn't frighten me like healing. Why?

I would suggest that the teaching this writer has had on healing has been faulty. She believes she should be able to say, "This man will be healed at this time." Because she cannot do that—in all honesty she cannot—she feels guilty. This leads her to avoid prayer for healing.

If I cannot force myself to believe that this particular blind man will be healed right now, does that mean that I do not have faith in God's promises? No, it simply means that I am willing to admit I do not know all the factors involved in this situation unless God chooses to reveal them to me. To admit this does not mean that I lack faith.

Faith, after all, is not in my faith, but my faith is in God—in His goodness and wisdom, in His unfailing listening to my prayers and answering them. To claim more than this, unless it has been specifically revealed that a given person is going to get well, is to make ourselves into a counterfeit trying to play God.

The way, then, to pray in faith is this:

a) to turn *to God* in the complete trust that He knows what is best, that He loves us more than anyone else and that He has the power to accomplish whatever we need;

b) to accept as normal *our doubts* about our own adequacy and about what is going to happen after we pray;

c) to see that the faith-*action* we need to take is to *pray for the sick* (when our guidance in prayer indicates this);

d) to *leave the results up to God*. Ordinarily we need not keep after the person we have prayed for to prove results.[5]

2) *"The gift of faith" is not the same as the virtue of faith.*
To every Christian faith is given—the *virtue* of faith which, in my opinion, implies the kind of confidence mentioned earlier: a belief in God's faithfulness, His wisdom, His power and His love. It seems to me that this kind of faith should include a belief in healing. This faith is a gift. But though it is a gift, this is not the "gift of faith" enumerated by Paul among those gifts given only to *some* members of the community:

> To one there is given through the Spirit the message of wisdom, to another the message of knowledge by means of the same Spirit, to another *faith* by the same Spirit, to another *gifts of healing* by that one Spirit (1 Cor. 12:8,9, italics added).

In the next chapter Paul again mentions many of these special gifts and adds, "If I have a faith that can move mountains, but have not love, I am nothing" (1 Cor. 13:2b). The faith to move mountains is an obvious reference to Jesus' statement: "If anyone says to this mountain, 'Go, throw yourself into the sea,' *and does not doubt in his heart* but believes that what he says will happen, it will be done for him" (Mark 11:23, italics added).

This "gift of faith," or fullness of faith, is given to some, but not to all, Christians. As I understand it, the "gift of faith" is a ministry-gift which God imparts to help us pray with confidence and "no hesitation in our hearts" for a given intention. Since this confidence can come only by God's revealing His will at a given moment, the gift of the "word of knowledge" is closely connected with the "gift of faith." Through the word of knowledge, God intimates to the person(s) praying that His will is to heal a particular person at a particular time. Through this gift God may inspire us to know:

a) That the one we are praying for or have prayed for will be healed. The gift of faith then lies in accepting this inspiration without hesitation and praying with absolute trust, believing that this person will be healed.

b) That the one we are praying for should stop taking medication or disregard symptoms. In this case, the rules for testing the spirit certainly hold true, because the effects of false inspiration can be so harmful. If someone else tells a sick person to stop taking medication or to disregard symptoms, the one who is or has been sick should obey this instruction only if the person himself feels inspired to do so.

The distinction between the faith in healing that all Christians should have and the special "gift of faith" is of particular practical importance. It explains why some Christians who believe in healing can always say: "I believe that God does heal, that He loves you and has the power to heal you. Let's pray for healing, but I can't predict exactly what will happen." Meanwhile, others can, upon occasion, pray with far more confidence: "God loves you and will heal you now if we just ask Him to do so." It explains why evangelists like Kenneth Hagin can pray the prayer of command, "Be healed," with assurance. (God does not inspire him to pray for everyone; but he has, upon occasion, been interiorly prevented from praying for some of the sick who asked for healing.) Without discernment, which is a gift from God to know when to pray and when not to pray, we are bound to have some doubts when we pray—not doubts about God but about our own knowledge of God's will in a particular situation.

Praying in the Name of Jesus

Consequently, only when we pray "in the name of Jesus" can we have absolute assurance and faith in prayer. For praying in the name of Jesus means much more than just using a formula of words (praying to the Father "in the name of Jesus Christ"). In Hebrew thought, the name of a person stood for the entire person: to pray in the name of Jesus means to pray *in the person of Jesus*—as Jesus Himself would pray. To pray in the name of Jesus means that we must put on "that mind which was in Christ Jesus," that we see people and situations as Jesus does, and then speak with the power and authority of Jesus.

To see people and situations in this way is a gift. But it is only then that we can pray the prayer of command— commanding sickness to leave in the name of Jesus, commanding people to rise up and walk. The apostles prayed in this way, for they were inspired more directly by God than most Christians today. They could say without hesitation, "In the name of Jesus Christ of Nazareth, walk" (Acts 3:6b). They spoke with the authority of Jesus because they had the mind of Jesus.

In brief, I see two models of praying for healing. Each is perfectly valid. But one is deeper and better than the other; and it cannot be forced, for it is a gift.

a) For the ordinary Christian in ordinary circumstances: The prayer of healing is a *prayer of petition*, asking the Father to heal the person in the name of Jesus Christ (in the unity of the Holy Spirit).

b) For the person with the gift of healing: At those times of true inspiration, the prayer of healing is more like a *prayer of command*, "Be healed." Or if our prayer is one of petition, it is far stronger than the ordinary prayer of petition, for it contains no element of doubt in it: "Amen. I see it being done. Thank You, Lord." It is a prayer in the name of Jesus, in the fullest sense of the word, where the person praying already knows in some mysterious way the mind of God and so can speak in His person. It is as if the person praying were standing *with* God and speaking for Him.

A diagram may be helpful in understanding these two styles of prayer:

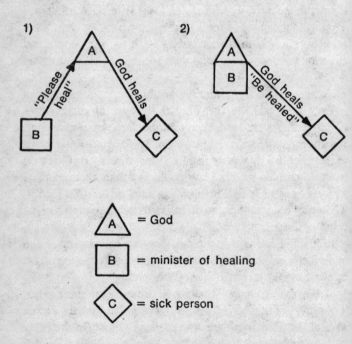

The trouble with this diagram, of course, is that it makes

God appear "out there," whereas God lives within us (see John 14:20) and heals from within. But the diagram is primarily meant to illustrate the difference between two cases: In one, the person(s) praying is not altogether sure what God's will is in asking for the healing of this sick person at this time. Thus he or she is, as it were, speaking *to* God, asking Him to heal the person. In the second case, God in one way or another has revealed His will to heal at this time; therefore, the minister of healing is not only praying to God but is speaking *for* God to the sick person.

These two styles, both based on faith, are quite different. Many of the problems in the healing ministry are caused by persons who imitate the style of others with gifts they themselves do not possess. The healer who does not really have the gifts of knowledge and faith may easily develop an empty and pretentious style of prayer. We can harm the sick by imposing guilt upon them, when, for instance, we tell people they have been healed, not because God has revealed this to us, but because we are imitating the prayers and actions of others who do have the gifts necessary to pray the prayer of command.

Each of us must search out where we really are and learn to pray in a style that suits the reality of our own healing ministry. We can learn from others, but we should not imitate them unless our own inner spiritual reality corresponds to their style. Do not pretend to be better than you are! Develop your own style, as the Spirit leads you.

Even if we have no exceptional gifts of knowledge, discernment or faith, it should not stop us from praying for the sick, provided we are aware of our limitations. Furthermore, we should realize that we can *grow* in these gifts. Use what God gives you and you will see that God will use you more and more as His instrument.

Agnes Sanford recommends that beginners pray for the

cure of minor ailments, such as colds, that seem more amenable to healing than chronic and deep-seated ones like cancer, arthritis and blindness. Even here, though, I would not want to set up hard and fast rules: I have seen people new in the healing ministry whose prayers God has used in marvelous ways never experienced by others who have been praying for the sick for many years.

As you exercise your faith and see God heal people through your prayers, you will find your own faith and courage growing. Use whatever gifts you have. Learn to pray the prayer of faith which will be described in a later chapter. Above all, love people, and you may yet see miracles.

3) *The faith needed for healing can be in anyone—or no one.*

We should be comforted to know that God can work through our weakness to accomplish the things He wants. "My power is made perfect in weakness" (2 Cor. 12:9).

Whose faith is needed?

a) The faith can be in the *person praying* for the healing; or

b) it can be in the *sick person* asking, even when the minister of healing has little or no faith; or

c) sometimes it just seems that God wants to manifest His goodness when *no one in particular* seems to have faith.

I remember, for instance, a creative preacher once telling me about a sermon he thought had backfired on him. This preacher used to work out clever introductions for his sermons to capture the audience's attention. On one occasion, he had what for him was a difficult audience: a college group. He wanted to speak to them about faith, about how important it is to hold on to the faith, in spite of appearances or emotions.

To emphasize that they should not look for emotional highs or for proofs but should be willing to endure suffering and dryness, he decided to introduce his sermon on faith with a spiel on faith healing (in which he did not believe). So when the time came for him to give his sermon on faith, he told the students that he had the gift of healing. Then he exhorted them to come forward to the altar railing and be healed.

When he had finished giving his fake altar call, he was happy to see some thirty students come forward. His plan was to pray for them; then, when they were not healed, he could say, "You see! You were fooled. You are looking for miracles. Our faith is not like that; it is a belief in God's revealed word simply because He has spoken it. You are not to be seeking signs and wonders."

As the preacher went along the line, praying for the sick, he copied what he had once seen Oral Roberts do on television. With absolutely no thought that anything would happen, he prayed for the students by imposing his hands on their heads with great force, proclaiming loudly, "In the name of Jesus, be healed!" "Then," he said to me, "you know what happened? They were all healed—or seemed to be.

"The headaches I can explain; they were cured by the power of suggestion. But there was one boy with his arm in a sling who went back to his pew waving his arm and claiming he was cured; that bothered me. I was really glad the next day when one student did come back to say she still had swelling in her sprained ankle which she had thought was cured. But all those other students acted as if they were healed. It spoiled the whole point of my sermon."

Who had the faith for healing in this case? Certainly it was not the preacher who was faking the healing service and did not want any healing to take place. Was it the students? Perhaps. Or was it the power in the words of the prayer, "In the name of Jesus Christ, be healed"? Perhaps it was that, too.

Kathryn Kuhlman and other ministers of healing have seen

that sick persons who lacked faith were nevertheless healed. We too have seen sick persons without faith in their own prayer who were healed through the prayers of another person (such as their minister). Perhaps such healings are meant by God to help people receive the faith they do not yet have.

Faith is important for healing; but if we, in our weakness, do all we can, God will bless us far beyond our own merits. *Our faith lies in the obedience of praying for the sick*, despite our weakness, doing the best we can to show forth the mercy of Christ. We need to take ourselves less seriously—and God more seriously.

> I am not in the least inferior to the "super-apostles," even though I am nothing. The things that mark an apostle—signs, wonders and miracles—were done among you with great perseverance (2 Cor. 12:11b,12).

This is something that we must each discover: In spite of our weakness, when we step forward and pray the prayer of healing, doing the best we can according to the faith that God has given us, God blesses us in abundance, beyond our merits—even beyond the power of our faith.

4) *Faith means showing "chutzpah."*

Recently I learned a whole new understanding of faith that has been freeing! It came from Bob Lindsey, who was pastor of the Narkiss Street Baptist Church, the largest English-speaking church in Jerusalem. He had become involved in the healing ministry and had himself been cured of diabetes through prayer. Bob has been studying the Gospel of Mark in the original Greek for years and knows the culture in which Jesus lived. So when Bob was visiting the States I thought he would be the perfect person to ask: "What is the meaning of 'faith,' as Jesus Himself would have understood it?"

Without hesitation Bob said, "Chutzpah." Now, chutzpah is a Yiddish slang term meaning something like "nerve" or "brass," "extreme confidence in action." In today's terms a person with chutzpah is someone who "goes for it." A classic Jewish illustration of chutzpah tells of a boy who murdered his mother and father, then threw himself on the mercy of the judge on the grounds that he was an orphan. Now *that's* chutzpah!

The Gospel example of chutzpah that Bob used is the story of the woman with an issue of blood who decides that she is going to sneak around in the crowd until she can touch the hem of Jesus' garment (Luke 8:43-48). According to the Law she is unclean because of her flowing blood, so she is breaking the Law in touching Jesus. Yet she decides to touch His garment secretly—to "go for it"—so that she can be healed.

When Jesus finds out what she has done, He encourages her by saying, "Your faith has healed you" (v. 48). Her faith was a determination to act, legally or illegally—to reach out for healing at all costs. And that, said Bob, is what faith usually means in the Gospels.

This explanation of faith, very different from anything I expected him to answer, helped explain something confusing that had happened to me. In 1977 I asked the Thomas Merton Foundation (of which I was director) to share with a Christian film company the risk of putting up $50,000 to shoot a movie, *The Power of Healing Prayer*. The purpose of this thirty-minute film was to let people *see* the wonderful healings that take place when we pray for the sick.

To do this we arranged with St. Vincent Hospital in Toledo, Ohio, to pray with twenty-four patients under medical supervision. We wanted to be scrupulously honest in showing a genuine cross-section of what we ordinarily see: some people being healed, others improved and others for whom nothing much external seems to happen. The remarkable end of the film is when the physician who was chief-of-staff reported that, of the twenty-four patients, twenty reported that they felt a change. Of those twenty, a change was medically verified in fifteen. One of the patients, in fact, with whom I was able to stay in touch, was totally healed of lupus erythmatosis.

Now for me the confusing part was that some of my friends thought I showed an extraordinary faith in being ready to risk so much money on a film that might prove a failure. "Suppose nobody gets healed!" they suggested. On the other hand, I was surprised that they thought I had extraordinary faith, because I think that my faith is very ordinary. When I pray I usually have no special sense whether or not the person I am praying for is going to be healed; in my own eyes I lack the special "gift of faith," connected so often with the healing ministry.

What they were actually saying, though, was that I had chutzpah: I believed that we should risk all the finances we had and "go for it," assuming that God wants to show people of good faith the kinds of healing that I ordinarily see.

Seeing faith as chutzpah will set you free. In this view, faith isn't an extraordinary version of *what* you believe, such as, "I know that you are going to be healed tonight when we pray," but rather has to do with the courage to pray for a sick person. Like Abraham we set out for an *unknown* promised land. The faith lies in setting out on the journey, not in being sure of exactly where we are going. We believe that God is faithful, provided we do what is in our power—and that is to pray for the sick. Discovering this reality was liberating: to know that faith is simply obedience and the willingness to risk; not an absolute certainty about what is going to happen on the journey!

9 | The Mystery Of Faith

As I experience the paradoxes of the healing ministry, I become more and more aware of the mystery involved. Those who want simple answers and absolute clarity are bound to be disappointed. They will never have the beautiful experience that I have almost every day, of seeing a person touched and healed by God's merciful love.

Read these words from a letter I once received:

> A thousand thanks for the spiritual healing. It was complete. Courage, joy and strength filled my heart at your prayer. God spoke through it to assure me of His love. It was the greatest consolation to know that you could understand my sorrow. After the prayer I went to chapel and there felt such a release! It seemed as if all the bitter memories were gone. From that moment I was filled with joy as the burden of years disappeared.

We will always face a mystery, and anyone who tries to over-simplify will only end by causing confusion. Paul wrote, "Now I know in part" (1 Cor. 13:12b); surely we should not be ashamed to admit that our own knowledge is less than perfect.

Reliable authority has informed me that about ten percent

135

of those who have sought healing at meetings by a famous healing evangelist were cured or improved. The ten percent is cause for rejoicing, but what happened to the other ninety percent who asked for health? (My own experience indicates that a much larger percentage of persons obtain healing in our retreats.)

If the only factor the evangelist stresses is, Do you have the faith to be healed? then people accept the converse, If I am not healed it is because my faith is weak. Simplistic preaching causes guilt in those who are not healed and increases resistance in those who are skeptical about the very possibility of healing. Most people like simple solutions; they flee complexity which annoys them.

As Dr. Paul Tournier wisely observed:

> It is the common experience of all, that humanity moves between these two poles of simplicity and complexity. People who have the sort of mind that sees only one side to every question tend toward vigorous action. They succeed in everything they do because they do not stop to split hairs and have abounding confidence in their own abilities. Your successful journalist, for instance, is inclined to simplify every problem and condense it into an arresting phrase. On the other hand, those with subtle and cultivated minds tend to get lost in a maze of fine distinctions. They always see how complicated things really are, so that their powers of persuasion are nil. That is why the world is led by those who are least suited to raising its cultural and moral standards. It is only very few who manage to combine both tendencies, and in my view a lively Christian faith is the best precondition for the accomplishment of this miracle, because it gives both profound

understanding and simplicity of heart.[1]

As Tournier suggests, the popular preacher or evangelist may therefore simplify in order to make a point: "If you have faith, you will be healed." Meanwhile, most of my educated friends are appalled by such approaches.

Many ministers of healing (those who launch into action without many doubts) are probably the least capable of explaining what they do. On the other hand, those who might best understand the complexity of this ministry are so immobilized by their doubts and speculations (for instance, on the traditional place given to the value of redemptive suffering in the church) that they seldom launch out and pray for the sick themselves. Prayer for healing is consequently more associated with tents than with theological seminaries.[2] Not surprisingly, then, the world of healing "is led by those who are least suited to raising its cultural and moral standards."

To preserve the sense of mystery in a way that experience has convinced me is realistic and helpful, I suggest two basic principles:

1) Do not expand any one method or experience into a universal method.

2) Ask God to meet your needs with confidence, but don't tell Him when or how to do it.

Let me explain these two principles more fully:

1) *Do not expand any one method or experience into a universal method.*

Something in us makes us want to find the right technique for every task, the right formula of prayer for every need. We still seek the alchemist's stone—a magic way of controlling what God does. But God teaches us over and over again that He is beyond our limitations and will not be boxed into our neat compartments.

An example of this very human tendency has already been

given: those who say that all you need for healing is "to lay claim to God's promises in faith." Another example would be those who feel comfortable with the concept of healing only in a sacramental context. Like the disciples, some people today, too, are always seeking the perfect answer: "Who sinned, this man or his parents, that he was born blind?" (John 9:2). But Jesus, as He did with the disciples, must take us completely out of the either/or of our thought patterns: "Neither this man nor his parents sinned...but this happened so that the work of God might be displayed in his life" (John 9:3).

So often we try to apply to all situations a technique we have found successful in one set of circumstances. We may even have enough successes with such a technique to encourage us to claim that our experience proves we are right. But we also selectively ignore our failures and find reasons to defend our customary way of proceeding.

Consider a few examples to illustrate this problem, all of which apply to the healing ministry as practiced in the United States. First, we see the tendency of some persons to treat all illnesses as cases of demonic oppression and to treat them by casting out the demons. In certain instances this may work. Such successes then encourage the exorcists to continue their work even though some of the people they pray for may be badly harmed by the approach, and intelligent onlookers may be so horrified by what they see that they are permanently prejudiced against any form of healing or deliverance ministry.

We see a second example in the practice of "claiming your victory"—that is, accepting the fact that you have been healed once you have prayed for healing. From my own experience, this sometimes is the right thing to do, *if* it is what the Lord wants and if the sick person has been truly inspired by God to accept his or her healing as an accomplished fact despite remaining symptoms. I especially remember one woman who was suffering from endometriosis. She asked the entire group at the meeting to pray for her. The next day she wrote about her experience:

> To tell you more about the second healing, the physical healing [she had earlier experienced a psychological healing], I've had no pain since the prayers for me, not one pain. Yet for the last month and a half I have been intermittently plagued, especially after a meal. (But now I've had four meals and no pain.)
>
> The next part is funny. When I asked the group to pray, my thought was that I would continue taking the medication every two weeks until it was depleted in May [the retreat was held in February]. Then I'd see if I was cured. The Lord had other plans. To give me a hint as to what He wanted, He stopped the pains that had been present for three hours. Then—and this is the crucial point—He asked me quietly if I could prove my faith by not taking the shots anymore. I was struggling with this while everyone was praying, because after three-and-a-half years of getting no relief these shots were a tremendous help in keeping me from becoming desperately ill. How could I stop taking them?
>
> The Lord didn't make me think of not taking them until the plunge was made. Finally I said, "Yes, Lord; I'll go all the way. Now You will be put to the test to really heal me."
>
> That I received the courage to respond in complete faith is in itself a healing, for there is no cure for endometriosis but surgery. Wow, that's faith!
>
> To express how joyous I've been these days is

impossible. For me a totally new life has begun.

Clearly, this woman was inspired by God to take the risk of faith and to trust that she had been healed—a healing that has now lasted for more than ten years. This she did without the advice of others, moved solely by an interior urging.

Just as a minister of healing may receive a "gift of faith" to trust in a private revelation and to pray the prayer of command, so a sick person may receive a genuine inspiration to believe that he or she has been healed—sometimes in spite of remaining symptoms. For such a person, obedience to the inner prompting seems to be the condition for healing to take place. The danger, however, comes about when this special but rather common experience is elevated into a general principle—the claim of the healer that this is precisely what should happen in all cases, that everyone who lays claim upon the promise will be healed.

I was once present, for example, when leaders of a prayer group told a man in a wheelchair whose spine was severed in an accident that they were confident he would be healed if he had faith. They had been praying and fasting for him and some had promised not to break the fast until he was healed.[3]

As these good people gathered around him in all sincerity to pray for his healing, it was clear that the man was suffering from considerable pressure and anxiety. He was doing the best he could with his parents and friends around him, for they all knew that it would require a true miracle for the severed nerves to be reattached. As they prayed and encouraged him to get out of the wheelchair and walk, tension in the room mounted. As a matter of fact, however, in the end he did not leave the wheelchair, and his last state of discouragement was worse than the first.

This incident—and I know of many similar ones—is painful

to relate in a book designed to encourage healing. But such sad happenings do occur with harm both to the sick person and to the prayer group; and they do much to spoil the good image of the healing ministry in general. Through erroneously deducing universal laws from particular inspirations, we turn grace into law all over again. In consequence, the ministry of healing, which should be one of the most glorious, most uplifting and most consoling in the church of Jesus Christ, has been turned by some well-intentioned but unwise practitioners into a ministry of wounding and condemnation.

We can safely say that for *some*, "claiming their healing" is what releases in them the current of God's healing power. But to say that this method is for *all* sick persons leads, I believe, to grave pastoral harm.

To turn again to Dr. Paul Tournier:

> It is easy to build theories, to pursue one's adversities with implacable logic, and to collect enthusiastic followers when one develops a corpus of doctrine that is coherent and intransigent. But when it comes to daily practice, how many impenetrable mysteries, how many paradoxes, how many failures and equally unexpected successes! I am always discovering more of the complexity, the subtlety, and the delicacy of the human mind. One makes a few experiments, but as soon as one tries to build a theory upon them, one finds that life refuses to be bound by them, and the same results cannot be obtained again. On the other hand, it is often just when one feels helpless, perplexed, and in despair when faced with the disaster of a person's life, that there takes place suddenly, one does not know how, a living "experiment."
> ...Thus each of us deduces from his personal experiences a system of thought, which he sets up as

the truth against all other systems of thought.

Each of us calls to witness his personal experience in support of the system to which he considers it to be due. Each maintains the truths which the system he favors has revealed to him, and concludes that those who disagree with him are in error....

Each of us hides his secret weaknesses, and the painful failures which still persist in his life, for fear that to admit them might call in question the system he holds to be true. And each points to the errors of others, and uses their inconsistencies and wrong-doing as a demonstration of the worthlessness of their teaching....

In Leibnitz's celebrated words, all systems are right in what they affirm, and wrong in what they deny.[4]

2) *Ask God to meet your needs, but do not tell Him when or how to do it.*

This is a helpful principle distilled from experience. God has certainly encouraged His children to ask for *what* they need—and to ask with insistence. Yet in His wisdom, God knows far better than we the time and place for healing to take place.

Repeatedly I have seen an interval between the time of prayer and that of the actual healing. Once I was with a group who prayed for a woman whose arm had been permanently immobilized through cancer and the consequent radiation treatment. According to her doctors, the impairment was permanent and would not improve with physical therapy. The group prayed with her on a Saturday night; several received a distinct impression that she had been healed, although she experienced no visible change. But on the following Monday morning, she found upon awakening that her arm had been restored to full mobility.

Oral Roberts, in his book *The Miracle of Seed Faith*,[5] describes how he made the same discovery—not in relation to healing, but to praying for financial needs. He suggested praying for *what* we need, but not trying to determine the *time* or *way* God would meet that need. Even though we may be tempted to pray, "Lord, inspire my wealthy cousin to help me in my need," we would do better simply to name our need and leave the rest to God. Three times when I have had immediate financial needs, I myself have found this to be true. People I would never have expected to help me were prompted *in prayer* to put a check in the mail or to appear at the door and offer help.

If a person seems not to be healed after we pray, we need not be anxious, provided we have done all that we can to seek God's guidance and wisdom. I have seen so many process healings (that is, those that take place over a period of time) and so many delayed healings that now I just pray and entrust the results to God. "Maybe now," we should conclude, "is not the time. Maybe someone else's prayer will bring the final healing. Perhaps this prayer has begun a process which will, after a time, produce the long-desired outcome."

I still remember one beautiful example of how God meets His creatures' needs when they ask but does so with a wisdom far beyond human planning in His choice of the time and the manner in which He will work. A woman had asked for an inner healing to repair the effects of a poor childhood relationship with her father which had badly affected her self-image as a lovable, worthwhile human being. She wrote:

> This letter comes to you so that you may know the beautiful way that the Lord worked during the conference this past weekend to help me.

143

When I signed up to see you I wasn't really sure why. All the beautiful healings that I have received this past year flashed through my mind: I have been prayed over for a healing of what happened when I was only a few days old; another person prayed for childhood guilt feelings regarding sex; one of my friends prayed for hurts of past years in my community. All these healings were real and powerful, so I questioned whether I had a right again. Yet I knew I was still unsure of myself as a person.

Saturday after being prayed for by you two things struck me. First, the beautiful gift of discernment that the Lord gave you regarding my need. I was amazed at how within a few minutes you could bring up two points of hurt of which I was unaware: my appearance and my father.

Secondly, I felt absolutely no release after you prayed for me. My past experiences with inner healing led me to believe firmly in its power, yet this time I felt absolutely nothing. Each time before there had always been a release accompanied by a great peace, usually following a flow of tears. So I returned to my room and prayed prayers of trust in the healing, believing it had already begun, yet feeling like a pressure cooker ready for release.

...Gradually I experienced the first healing. I began to feel pretty, not unrealistically so. Yet I could actually look in the mirror and smile at myself without feeling like someone to be shunned.

Then Monday afternoon during prayer I became convinced that the second healing would take place when I felt my father's arms around me. He loves me greatly and has always given generously to me of his wealth, but now I knew I needed him to express his love.

Wednesday evening when I returned to my home I knew I had to speak to my father and felt sick and teary. God is so good! I sat in front of my dad after Mom had gone to bed and just began to cry and cry. He hugged me and asked what was the matter. I told him, so he embraced me while I cried and then we were both able to express our love for each other for the first time. It was beautiful and the Lord gave me the gift of tears for about a half hour, which gave me great peace and security in Him. Praise God, our Father, for His love, which I know so clearly now. My return to my mission will be joyful, secure in His love—free finally to let Jesus flow through me to the people I love so dearly.

This case is also an example of another process I see so often: The Lord does not answer prayer on a superficial level; He wants people to work back to the source of the problem. How much more beautiful it was that a relationship between father and daughter was worked out and deepened in real life and not just in some imaginary way. The perfect, immediate outcome of prayer for this woman was an unsatisfied, "pressure-cooker" feeling, which proved to be the preparation for the final healing which took place four days later. Had I personally been overly concerned about the lack of immediate response to my prayer, I probably would have hindered its eventual success.

Mrs. Bob Cavnar of Dallas offers still another example of how one must be open to healing in whatever fashion God chooses. For many years Mrs. Cavnar had suffered from a painful back condition. On this particular occasion, she was present at a meeting at which a man was praying with people in a way which she felt was ridiculous—namely, the so-called "leg-lengthening" type of prayer (more about this in a later chapter).

Nevertheless, something within her prompted her to join the praying group. She found that the prayer did not repel her in the way she had imagined it would. A gentle interior urging persuaded her to ask for prayer. She did so and was immediately healed—by a method that she had earlier rejected as completely inappropriate.

Still another example of the unexpected ways God works was the healing of Avina Michels. Our group had prayed previously for Avina, who was confined to her wheelchair after she had been badly injured in an automobile crash in which two other women had been killed. In this earlier prayer her arm had been completely healed; consequently, with far greater confidence, several months later, Avina asked for a healing of her knees in order that she might leave her wheelchair and walk. The retreat team gathered around her wheelchair and, following the principle that it is good to be specific when making a petition in prayer, we asked for the healing of her knees.

Suddenly, she put her hands to her face. As we watched the change of expression on her face, we saw her being healed of a facial paralysis and neuralgia that she had not even mentioned to us. In short, we prayed for her knees and the healing took place in her face. Later, she received complete healing and is now able to walk without difficulty.

I have witnessed similar unanticipated cures a number of times. Apparently, the Lord wants to make sure that we have faith in Him alone, and not in our own planned methods. These experiences have also shown me that God has a sense of humor, and that He uses it to shake us out of our preconceived notions about how we think things ought to take place. Time and again we rediscover the complexity of the healing process; we are forced to seek God's wisdom on how to proceed. Then, without anxiety, we can leave the results to Him.

One of the most celebrated ministers of healing in the mid-twentieth century was Kathryn Kuhlman, who often had to ask herself why some people were healed in her services and others were not. In her long experience, she came to the same conclusions set forth in this chapter. In an interview she shared what she had learned:

"I have decided that God doesn't have preferences in theology," she told me with a chuckle. "We are the ones who try to put a fence around God, to bring Him down to our level. But it doesn't work; God is too big for us to confine.

"I've never written a book on the how and why of divine healing—even though I've been besieged with requests to do so—simply because I *don't know* the how and why. You see, just about the time the book was about to be published, the Holy Spirit would do something absolutely contrary to what I said. I'm still learning the mysterious ways in which God moves. I'll tell you one thing—I'm sure God has a sense of humor!"

Some of her own theological presuppositions have been shattered, the evangelist allows:

"There was a day, when I was very young and knew a great deal more than I do now, that I said, 'You must do thus and so, to be healed. There are certain conditions to be met.' I thought, for example, that faith on the part of the seeker was absolutely necessary.

"Then one day I got the shock of my life. A man said his deaf ear had just been opened in a service, but he had no faith at all. 'I don't believe it,' he said.

'I never go to church.' Well, there went my theology out the window....

"Take another example. Twenty years ago I believed that absolutely, come hell or high water, it was God's will for everybody, without exception, to be healed.

"But I've watched this thing very carefully. Now I see that we can't demand or command that God do anything.

"In general, I definitely believe that it is God's will to heal. But I can't say absolutely what is or is not His will in a particular case. There are some things I've learned just not to touch."[6]

In her younger days, Kathryn Kuhlman had seen many people hurt at evangelistic services by being made to feel guilty when they were not healed. So in all the services in which I heard her preach, she made an explicit announcement. She admitted that she did not know why some people were healed while others were not, why some who came to a service with complete faith went away not healed, while others who were quite skeptical were healed at the same service.

Healing is mysterious. The best that we can do is to bow down before the mystery that is God. When God chooses to reveal His mind, we can act with assurance. At other times, when we are in doubt about a particular case, the most honest thing to do is to admit our doubt and bow down before the awesome mystery of God's will.

This was the humble response Job finally gave to God:

I know that you can do all things; no plan of yours can be thwarted. You asked, "Who is this that obscures my counsel without knowledge?" Surely I spoke of things I did not understand, things too wonderful for me to know (Job 42:2,3).

10 | "But the Greatest Of These Is Charity"

Faith is a requisite for healing, both in the sick person and in the person praying for a healing. But the primary disposition needed by the ministry of healing is love. Even so, I seldom hear a sermon on the foremost place of love in the healing process.

Glenn Clark once wrote about how important a loving climate is in a healing situation. This loving presence he found characteristic of the ministry of Agnes Sanford:

> That "something besides" which Agnes Sanford possesses more than anyone I have met is hard to catch and put into words; it is something as evanescent and indefinable as the air we breathe. For want of a better word I shall call it the "climate" necessary for healing....
>
> Anyone who steps into the presence of Agnes steps into the right kind of climate for healing. When I looked over the manuscript of this book I had only a secondary interest in seeing whether she had the "technique" of healing because I knew she had that. I knew that thousands of people who had never healed anyone in their lives also have the technique. My primary interest was in seeing whether this book

(prepared for a world where the spiritual temperature is so far below zero) could furnish a "climate" that would make healing a living reality. To my great joy I found that this is exactly what it does do....

This book shows how this boy and scores of others like him were healed through simple exposure to the climate of faith and love. If to this faith and love there is added the warm sunshine of enthusiasm, humor and good cheer there is nothing more to be asked.[1]

Whatever else we do, it is absolutely essential that in praying for healing we establish an atmosphere of faith and love. When love is present, I have never seen a person hurt in any way by the healing ministry.

The minister of healing prayer in some way represents God; he or she stands for the very person of Jesus. Therefore, the sick person looking upon us should be able to sense to some degree what God is like. This is no doubt embarrassing because we know our weakness; it may even be frightening to think that people actually expect to find Jesus in us. But they do.

If we shout and demand that the sick accept their healing, then the representation of God which people see in us is a God angry with His people, at times harsh and peremptory. But if the love of God shows through our face and in the tone of our voice, the sick person sees the compassion and tender love of Jesus incarnate in a fellow human being. This is one piece with what we said earlier about what kind of God we believe in. Jesus cured not just to prove He was God, but because He was God abounding in love and compassion; sinners and sick came flocking to Him because He reached out to touch every one of them. What we unconsciously *think God is like* affects not only our ideas about what to emphasize in the healing ministry, but also the way we pray with people.

Emphasis on Power

In healing, we can concentrate on either of two attributes: the power of God or the love of God. In every healing, both are manifested. But because of human limitation, we tend to concentrate on one of these and to make the other subordinate.

Those who emphasize God's power in healing hold up the promises of God's mighty works and miracles to those who believe. They stress the faith that sick people need to receive these promises. For them, God's promise is offered; then the sick person accepts and claims that promise in faith; and finally God honors that faith by acting in power and love to heal.

The prayer of those who emphasize God's power is authoritative. It is usually uttered in a loud voice and accompanied by a forceful laying on of hands. This is a valid approach in its reflection of God's authority and power, but as I mentioned earlier, it can place an undue accent on our efforts to achieve faith and upon the legal elements of the Bible.

The preacher who emphasizes power is much like a lawyer pleading his case. He holds up the Book and says, "There are certain promises here. We have a written contract. God on His part is absolutely faithful to what He says. If you can accept these promises, then you will be healed. If you cannot accept these promises, cannot accept this contract, you will not be healed."

I heard one evangelist say, "All you people out there—are you standing on the promises, or are you resting on the premises?" Now, while it is true that one should stand on promises, the very metaphor conjures up the picture of a little man standing on his Bible, vehemently shaking his fist, as it were, and saying to God, "You must pay attention to me and honor Your promise."

Nevertheless, if we know that God is our loving Father and that we are gifted with the Holy Spirit who enables us to cry, "Abba, Father," we do not have to shout. Children in their own home need not claim the promises of their father. They can simply rest on the promises, certain that they have a loving father who will give them everything they ask for and need.

I believe it is a greater proof of faith to think of ourselves as "resting" on the promises rather than as "standing" on them. These are only figures of speech, of course, but they do reveal a person's conception of God. I cannot imagine, for instance, in my own home ever talking to my father the way some people talk to God. I cannot picture myself as a child sitting down at the dinner table and having to claim loudly to my father to send food down to my end of the table. Rather, I quietly ask him to pass the chicken.

Serenity is a sign of trust and sureness; loud claiming indicates a deep insecurity. Some of the prayers I hear, proclaiming deep faith and trust in the promises, sound to me anxious and uncertain—like the words of people who speak loudly to mask their own deep fears about being accepted.

Emphasis on Love

Another way of teaching about healing accentuates God's love, which of course includes His power. In proclaiming the mystery of God's love, we dwell on God's willingness to save and to heal all those who come to Him with open and contrite hearts. Such preaching emphasizes our receptiveness to God's love and the casting out of everything opposed to this love, especially hatred and lack of forgiveness. The answer to prayer is then left to God. What matters is that God loves us so much that He always hears and answers our prayers—sometimes in unexpected ways, sometimes by deferring an answer, but always by answering.

Personally I prefer to concentrate on the love of God made visible in Jesus, from which flows His healing power. The more we are centered on Jesus, the less desire we have for effect, and the less anxious and more peaceful we are. Then we find it easy to be honest.

When we focus on God's love, we can admit that not everybody is healed, and that this is a mystery hidden from our understanding. But we can nevertheless affirm that we do believe God heals and that His ordinary will is for everyone to be healed. People generally feel more comfortable with this approach than with one which tells people they have been healed, even though their symptoms do not reveal it; or which tells people to claim their healing and orders them to stop taking their pills.

Personally, I find it easier to be myself when I pray if I am thinking only of God's love. I find no need to raise my voice, no need to assume an authoritative posture. I can just be myself, knowing that anything good which results is accomplished through God's will, His power and His love, and not through any efforts of my own to generate a faith that the sick person does not have. In short, we must take God seriously but we must not take ourselves too seriously. Healing is not so much a test of faith as it is the natural response to God's generous love.

How to Pray for Healing

Clearly, then, our ideas about healing will influence the very way we pray for it. If we want to show God's love as well as His power we will speak gently. We will "put on the mind that was in Christ Jesus." Our tone of voice will reflect our union with Jesus. Our eyes will reveal Jesus' searching look of compassion. We will uncover whatever should be brought to light, but we will do this out of love and not out of condemnation.

We must be free of the need to prove anything, free of any personal desire for achieving results. To be cast down when our prayers have failed to effect a cure means it is time to examine our motives to see how much our own fear of failure is mixed into our ministry. I may think I am defending the honor of God by demanding faith; but perhaps what I am really defending is my own self-image as a successful minister of healing.

I must call to mind over and over again that the gift of healing is a manifestation of God's Spirit working *through* me. It is not "a thing" I have in my possession, which I can turn on or off at will. It is rather a transient grace, a passing movement of God's Spirit working through me to help someone else.

In most healings three persons are involved: God, the sick person and the minister of healing. My part, as the minister of healing, is to pray the prayer of faith and then to move out of the way. In fact, the sick person is capable all alone of asking for God's help without anyone else being there at all. The key persons are God, who is love, and the sick person, whose sickness elicits God's loving compassion. I am simply the human channel of God's love, and I should be humble about that. At times I am used; at times I am not used.

I feel uncomfortable when someone calls me a healer. The connotation is much like putting on a label of certification, a star on your epaulets, a kind of rank—a something which you possess permanently and over which you have control. But that notion simply is not true.

Sometimes God uses my prayers and touch in order to heal; at other times, He does not. Why this is so, I do not know. What I do know is that this inability to control keeps me humble; it helps me realize where the healing power comes from.

So all we have to do is simply to pray as best we can and, above all, to love all the sick and wounded who come to us.

I have seen extraordinary things happen when a climate of love was present. Sometimes cures have taken place without explicit prayers for them. I remember, for example, how within a short period of time I was twice asked by married couples to pray for an increase of their love for each other. In one instance, our team prayed for a couple named Chuck and Alice that their love would increase. As we prayed, however, a cyst on Alice's shoulder that had bothered her for some time began to go down and then disappeared altogether with a sensation of heat.

Shortly afterwards a similar incident took place. Several of us were praying for a missionary and his wife. Again, their prayer request was for an increase of the bond of love between them. After we had finished praying, the man was clearly surprised when he felt his abdomen; he kept saying, "It's gone! It's gone!" We were confused about what was happening until he told us that he had just been healed of a hernia that had afflicted him for several years.

Time after time we find people healed, not only through direct prayer, but simply because of their love for each other. God seems pleased to work in a climate of love, to reach and heal people who love Him and each other so much.

The attitude on the part of the person praying for healing is in itself part of the healing process. As Paul Tournier says, it all depends on the spirit:

> You give a child advice. Your state of mind is far more important than the advice itself. You may be inspired by fear—the fear that he is "turning out badly."
>
> In this case you will suggest the fear to him, even without formulating it. And your advice, however

proper it may be, by turning his thoughts toward evil, gives power to evil. If, however, you are inspired by prudent and trusting wisdom, this same advice will be useful.[2]

Tournier's cautions have direct application to the healing ministry. I have seen people who exercise a genuine gift of healing, who have prayed for many people with astonishing results, and yet who seem, at the same time, to engender a certain anxiety and fear. While they effect lasting healings, they also hurt some people by making them more anxious and more fearful. I believe that every healing should bring the person cured to a closer awareness of the presence of God, of His power and His love; no one should ever be hurt.

This seems to be the one reason for the success of Kathryn Kuhlman's celebrated healing services:

> In the miracle services a community of love and acceptance is created. People feel secure enough to lay aside the barriers of fear, distrust and egotism that have shut them off not only from fruitful contact with their fellowmen but from their own deeper selves. There is a yielding up of self-isolation. The individual loses himself in the group, the symbol of the loving family where one is accepted in spite of his faults and sins. He identifies with the needs of others. He sometimes forgets his own illness, his own needs, in praying for someone else whose need is greater. In this self-forgetfulness, as it happens, he is healed.[3]

In every prayer for healing, both God's power and His love should be invoked, but first place should be given to His love. The display of power and authority and the claiming of promises may be fine for evangelists mature in the healing ministry. But for simple persons, who are servants instead of masters, the way of love has far less danger of self-deception. Furthermore, it brings peace, not anxiety, to the sick person asking for help. "If I have a faith that can move mountains, but have not love, I am nothing" (1 Cor. 13:2).

PART III

The Four Basic Kinds of Healing and How to Pray for Each

O Lord,
truly I am
your servant;
...you have freed me
from my chains.

Psalm 116:16

11 | The Four Basic Kinds Of Healing

We have already noted that one problem in the ministry of healing is a problem we find in every area of human activity: a tendency to oversimplify. We tend to take what we know from our limited experience and then apply it to every situation.

For a long time, for example, most priests and ministers were trained to treat most problems as though they were moral problems that could be solved by *willpower*—with God's grace and help, of course. The alcoholic was given sermons and told to repent. Some were helped. But it took Alcoholics Anonymous to show that a community of support was needed for most alcoholics to make a comeback. Now, beyond even that approach, we are finding that even those persons whom AA has not been able to help can be cured instantaneously through prayer.

In our ministry we have come to recognize four different kinds of basic healing, differentiated by the kinds of sickness that afflict us and the basic causes of those sicknesses. Unless we know these differences, we will not be able to help most people. In fact, we may harm them by insisting on one particular diagnosis and one particular method of prayer when a different diagnosis and a different type of treatment and prayer are needed.

Someone, for instance, who has had experience only with deliverance and exorcism—who has no knowledge or experience of the value of inner healing ("healing of the memories")—can do untold damage by insisting on casting out devils every time he or she tries to help a person with a psychological problem. Some psychological problems seem to be caused by demonic infestation, but in my experience, most problems can be explained by the past hurts and rejections in a person's life. Still other psychological problems are caused by such physical causes as chemical and enzyme imbalances in the bloodstream (for example, postpartum depression).

Anyone, then, who hopes to pray for the sick should be aware of three basic kinds of sickness, each requiring a different kind of prayer:

1) Sickness of our spirit, caused by our own personal sin.

2) Emotional sickness and problems (for example, anxiety) caused by the emotional hurts of our past.

3) Physical sickness in our bodies, caused by disease or accidents.

In addition, any of the above—sin, emotional problems or physical sickness—can be caused by demonic oppression, a fourth and different cause that requires a different prayer approach: prayer for exorcism.

Consequently, we must understand at least *four basic prayer methods* in order to exercise a complete healing ministry:

1) prayer for *repentance* for personal sin;

2) prayer for *inner healing* ("healing of memories") for emotional problems;

3) prayer for *physical healing* for physical sickness;

4) prayer for *deliverance* (exorcism) for demonic oppression.

Not all of us will have a deep ministry in each of these

areas, so we should recognize our own limitations and be ready to refer a person to someone else who has more experience than we in one or the other area. In fact, I look forward to a time when Christians in every locality will be able to join their gifts to work as a team, much as doctors work together in any hospital or clinic. Most of us lack the time or God-given gifts to work in all these areas of healing. But each of us can develop some discernment to evaluate the problem and to choose an appropriate type of prayer to use.

Such cooperation becomes even more important when we meet people who seem to need *all* these forms of prayer. For example, a middle-aged woman may ask for prayer to be cured of arthritis (physical healing). Then, upon talking to her, you find she was deeply hurt by her father when she was young (inner healing), and that she was never able to forgive him (repentance); nor has she been able as a woman to relate to her husband (inner healing, probably). In her search for a way out of her predicament she has attended seances where she has supposedly met a "spirit-guide" from the dead who gives her guidance through automatic writing (a need for deliverance is here indicated).

Medicine

Ordinarily, of course, God works through doctors, psychiatrists, counselors and nurses to facilitate nature's healing process. This may seem so obvious as to go without saying, except that some evangelists set up an artificial opposition between prayer and medicine—as if God's way of healing is through prayer, while the medical profession is a secular means of healing, somehow unworthy of Christians who have real faith. Consequently, they encourage people to pray and not to see their doctors.

On the contrary, God works to heal through doctors as well as through prayer; the doctor, the counselor and the nurse are all ministers of healing. All these different professions, with their different competencies, go to make up God's healing team. Any time we disparage any person who helps bring about healing we are destroying the kind of cooperative healing ministry that the Christian community might have, and we are setting up false divisions between divine and human healing methods.

As evidence of such harmful division we have already seen too many:

- faith healers who tell the sick they have no need to see a doctor;
- doctors who disparage the ministry of healing as a nonscientific appeal to the credulous;
- persons who believe in healing but who prefer to ignore the ministry of exorcism;
- exorcists who disparage the ministry of inner healing.

These unhappy divisions and misunderstandings are sad and totally unnecessary. The ones who suffer are the sick who may be dissuaded from the means of healing they most need because of the ignorance of the very ministers of healing who should be helping them.

We need to learn to work as a team, rather than as competitors, to bring God's healing power to the entire Christian body. Anyone who prays for healing should have a healthy respect for all four types of healing prayer as well as all the other legitimate methods of bringing about healing.[1] We must also be aware of our gifts and of our limitations. Where we are limited we should be ready to defer to the ministry of someone else more gifted, wiser or more experienced than we are.

I prefer now to give conferences with a team, for I experience a definite advantage when working with a team of persons who can pray effectively for inner healing as well as for physical healing, who can lead those who need it to personal repentance, as well as those who know how to counsel.

Still, I look forward to a time when we will do even more of this teamwork, when all over the world there will be a collaboration of doctors, nurses and hospitals with persons who have been given charisms for inner healing, physical healing and deliverance, working together with ministers who understand God's healing power. When that time finally comes, I think we will be approaching a renewal of Christianity such as we have not seen since the times of the apostles.

All the pertinent information we have given in this chapter on these four types of healing, based on the four kinds of sickness we experience, can be summed up in the following diagram.

SICKNESS	CAUSE	PRAYER REMEDY	ORDINARY HUMAN REMEDY
1. ...of the *spirit* • often contributing to emotional sickness • sometimes contributing to bodily sickness	*Personal sin*	*Repentance*	
2. ...of the *emotions* • often contributing to *spiritual* sickness • often contributing to *bodily* sickness	*The fallen human condition* (i.e., the person has been hurt by the sins of *others*)	Prayer for *inner healing*	Counseling
3. ...of the body • often contributing to *emotional* sickness • sometimes contributing to *spiritual* sickness	Disease, accidents, psychological stress leading to psychosomatic illness	Prayer of faith for *physical healing*	Medical care
4. ...any, or all, of the above can, upon occasion, be	*Demonic* in its cause	Prayer for *deliverance* (Exorcism)	

The following chapters will be based on these basic kinds of healing and their appropriate remedies (including medicine).

In summary we can say that the most basic questions we should ask before praying for healing are these:

1) What is the *basic sickness*, the basic problem?

2) What is its *basic cause*?

3) What *kind of prayer*, or what kind of other remedy, should we use?

12 | Forgiveness Of Sin

The first and deepest kind of healing that Christ brings is the forgiveness of sins. Our repentance and God's forgiveness are emphasized by every Christian denomination. No one doubts that Jesus died for our sins and took them away, provided we do our part and repent. This is salvation and healing at the deepest level.

What I have come to see, though, is how intimately the forgiveness of sins is connected with bodily and emotional healing. They are not separate. In fact, far from being a sign of God's blessing, much physical sickness is a direct sign that we are not right with God or our neighbor:

> For anyone who eats and drinks without recognizing the body of the Lord eats and drinks judgment on himself. That is why many among you are weak and sick, and a number of you have fallen asleep. But if we judged ourselves, we would not come under judgment. When we are judged by the Lord, we are being disciplined so that we will not be condemned with the world (1 Cor. 11:29-32).

Here Paul ascribes some of the sickness and death affecting the early community at Corinth to the effects of sin; here, sickness is no blessing, but a punishment.

This connection between sin and sickness is now being brought to our attention again remarkably—not by the church, but by psychologists and doctors who recognize that much, if not most, physical sickness has an emotional component:

> Even cancer has recently been linked to emotion. Researchers are finding that cancer victims are often people who have long felt hopeless, who have believed that their lives are doomed to despair. The onset of the disease in many cases is associated with a series of overwhelming losses that make the person finally give up entirely.[1]

Although we risk playing amateur psychologist and reading too much into a person's physical sickness, these findings do show how appropriate was the angry reaction of Jesus to sickness ("He rebuked the fever")—much more appropriate than the reaction of some later Christian writers who saw most sickness as redemptive. Far from being redemptive it is often a sign precisely that we are not redeemed, that we are falling apart at a deeper level:

> Ulcerative colitis is thought to develop when a predisposed person fails to express chronic resentment and anger. On an unconscious level, the mucous membrane of his colon *does* respond to these repressed emotions. The ensuing engorgement and hyperactivity produces bleeding....
>
> Ulcerative colitis is often accompanied by severe depression and feelings of hopelessness and despair. The typical victim is immature and dependent, particularly on his mother. He often is perfectionistic and rigid and tends to be wary of other people.[2]

We have good evidence, then, for a natural connection between much of our sickness and our spiritual and emotional health. For very human reasons we can see why physical sickness can symbolize a deeper sickness of the human person. This profound realization caused Dr. Paul Tournier, a physician, to abandon the merely physical treatment of his patients. He began as well to deepen his prayer life and to study psychology so that he could help heal the entire human person who was sick at all levels of his or her being.

The same kind of realization changed the medical career of Dr. Bernie Siegel, who decided to concentrate on the inner changes that needed to take place in himself and in his cancer patients in order to help them get well: "I feel that all doctors should be required, as part of their training, to attend healing services, at which people with so-called incurable diseases appear. The physicians should be told they are not allowed to prescribe medications nor consider operations for these people, but simply told to go out and help them. Then doctors would learn that they can help by touching, praying or simply sharing on an emotional level."[3]

Because of these relationships between all types of healing I have found it often helpful—sometimes essential—to consider a prayer for repentance or a prayer for inner healing first before praying for physical healing.

We might remember here the story of the paralytic who was let down through the roof by his friends and then forgiven his sins by Jesus before Jesus told him to pick up his cot and walk. This account is often used to show that the physical cure was a sign to the unbelieving Pharisees of Jesus' real power to forgive sins. That it was. But I also believe that Jesus was proceeding to heal the paralytic by stages in both areas of his life where he needed healing. Perhaps the sin and the paralysis were interconnected.

In my own ministry I have seen this connection borne out in striking ways. Once while giving a conference in

Aylesford, Illinois, our team conducted a service in which I stressed the need to forgive enemies and then gave the people (some 200 were making the retreat) the time to forgive anyone who had ever hurt them. We followed this repentance with a prayer for inner healing.

Nowhere in the service did I mention physical healing. Yet two persons testified immediately afterward that they had received physical cures. One was a man who had suffered constant chest pain since undergoing open-heart surgery. During the repentance/forgiveness time when he was asked to think of someone who had hurt him, he thought of his boss, a man he regarded as mean and cruel. At first, he wasn't going to forgive him, but then with all the time allowed, his heart softened and he entered into a prayer of forgiveness. At that moment all the painful effects of the open-heart surgery left him.

A similar healing took place in July 1973, when I conducted a repentance service at the West Virginia Camp Farthest Out. Afterward a young woman came up to me and said that a pylonidal cyst had instantly disappeared at the moment she was able to repent of a long-standing grudge.

Forgiving Enemies

These examples indicate that the key form of repentance we need is to forgive our enemies. I have found few sins that block God's healing power as stubbornly as a lack of forgiveness. I understand better than I used to why Jesus laid such a heavy stress on forgiving enemies when He talked about prayer. He does not talk nearly as much about drunkenness and lust as He does about being unforgiving.

Furthermore, He often seems to connect forgiving enemies with His Father's answering our prayers:

Therefore I tell you, whatever you ask for in prayer,

believe that you have received it, and it will be yours.
And when you stand praying, if you hold anything
against anyone, forgive him, so that your Father in
heaven may forgive you your sins (Mark 11:24,25).

I used to consider such passages as a kind of jumping from
one subject to another: In one sentence Jesus encourages us
to have faith in prayer; in the next He tells us to forgive our
enemies. But now I see that the two ideas are intimately
connected.

Evidently, God's saving, healing, forgiving love cannot
flow into us unless we are ready to let it flow out to others.
If we deny forgiveness and healing to others, God's love cannot flow into us. In the great commandment, after all, loving our neighbor is included with loving God. As someone
once said, "I love God only as much as I love my worst
enemy."

Not surprisingly, then, the healing ministry is directly
related to our willingness to love others:

Be merciful, just as your Father is merciful. Do not
judge, and you will not be judged. Do not condemn,
and you will not be condemned. Forgive, and you
will be forgiven. Give, and it will be given to you.
A good measure, pressed down, shaken together and
running over, will be poured into your lap. For with
the measure you use, it will be measured to you (Luke
6:36-38).

To paraphrase: If you forgive, you will be forgiven; if you
are willing to heal all others, including your enemies, you
will be healed. If we seek healing, the first condition is to
cast out our sin, especially the roots of bitterness.

Nevertheless, for some reason we seem to be insensi-
tive to our worst sins: bitterness and resentment. Sins of

drunkenness we detect with the same sensitivity with which the non-smoker sniffs cigarette fumes lingering from last night's party. But we may not be nearly so sensitive to our bitterness and anger.

Illustrative of the bitterness that often wracks Christian churches so sensitive on such issues as smoking and drinking is a section of history I was just reading today:

> All went well with the "Tomlinson Church of God" until the death of its founder in 1943 when a power struggle developed between his two sons, Milton and Homer, for control of the church. In a bewildering set of moves and countermoves, the younger brother Milton, who was not a minister but a printer, was elected as "General Overseer." After Milton's accession to power, Homer was inexplicably expelled from the church. Following this development, Homer went to New York City where he founded a third denomination which he christened "The Church of God, World Headquarters." In March 1953, the former "Tomlinson" Church of God with Milton as Bishop and General Overseer changed its name to "The Church of God of Prophecy," which, it is claimed, designates it as the one, true "Church of God."[4]

We feel we have a right not to forgive; in justice let there be an eye for an eye, a tooth for a tooth. We have a good reason for exacting the vengeance we feel is only fair for wrongdoers.

Yet we have these words of the Lord: "You have heard that it was said, 'Eye for eye, and tooth for tooth.' But I tell you, Do not resist an evil person" (Matt. 5:38,39). Upon this command John L. McKenzie comments:

The law of revenge was an ancient custom of the Near East that protected individuals by obliging the next of kin to avenge injury or murder....The laws of the Pentateuch are actually restrictions that limit the injury inflicted by the avenger to injury proportionate to the damage done by the aggressor. The customary principle of self-defense is rejected by this saying of Jesus; and the customary principle is not replaced by another principle of self-defense. This saying is probably the most paradoxical of all the sayings of the passage and has certainly been the object of more rationalization than any other....It is difficult to see how the principle of non-resistance and yielding could be more clearly stated. The rationalizations of the words of Jesus do not show that His words are impractical or exaggerated, but simply that the Christian world has never been ready and is not ready now to live according to this ethic.[5]

In praying for healing the most common phenomenon we experience is the sensation of heat, which we ordinarily associate with human love, with the warmth of friendship. On the contrary, cold is associated with the presence of evil.

One sensation recurs frequently, both in accounts of demoniacal possession and in those of metaphysical experiences. The subjects and the assistants experience a sudden feeling of glacial cold, which often seems to emanate from the walls. At a Sabbath, the devil's arrival is signalized by an icy chill and a sensation of freezing physical contact. Cold hands close about the neck of the possessed; a cold wind blows suddenly. Fear, making the flesh creep, and the chill of the extremities, partly explain this sensation of cold; but sometimes it seems inexplicable. It is generally accompanied by sexual frigidity.[6]

Heat and cold, symbolizing love and hate, are not, I believe, accidental concomitants of God's total healing and its opposite, the death wish of the devil. Life and death are here in conflict. Too often, though, we ourselves block physical healing through our own coldness, our own resentment and lack of forgiveness. I can see more clearly now why James in his passage on praying for the sick with anointing, also encourages confession of sins: "Therefore confess your sins to each other and pray for each other so that you may be healed" (James 5:16).

I remember being asked by a woman to pray for an inner healing. When we talked about her childhood, she indicated that her deepest problem, an unreasoning hatred of men, including her husband, went back to harsh treatment and derision that her brothers had heaped upon her as a little girl. Before praying for that healing, I asked her to forgive her brothers. This she refused to do.

I told her that her unforgiving attitude would block any healing. She still refused. When I asked her why she hung on to her resentment, even if she was being destroyed by it, she thought for a while and then replied that, if she forgave her brothers, it would take away her last excuse for being the kind of person she was (she could no longer blame them). After praying a short time more she realized how contrary this was to her Christian commitment and to her professed desire to be whole. With tears she forgave her brothers as best she could. She then received the deep healing she was seeking.

To sum it all up: The more I pray with people for healing, the more I discover the close interrelation between all forms of healing. The churches have long known the power of Christ to forgive sins, but I realize with increased intensity that we need to recognize as well these realities:

1) Our physical sickness, far from being a redemptive blessing, is often a sign that we are not totally redeemed, not whole at a spiritual level.

2) Physical healing often *requires first a forgiveness of sin* or an inner healing.

3) The most important repentance is of *bitterness or resentment*, sins which Christians often do not recognize as sins in themselves.

4) Again, *love* is the best remedy to break through the coldness, the hurt and bitterness that block God's healing power from flowing into us.

Knowing this we can see what Jesus was getting at when He pointed to the woman who had poured ointment all over His feet at Simon's banquet:

> Then he...said to Simon, "Do you see this woman? I came into your house. You did not give me any water for my feet, but she wet my feet with her tears and wiped them with her hair. You did not give me a kiss, but this woman, from the time I entered, has not stopped kissing my feet. You did not put oil on my head, but she has poured perfume on my feet. Therefore, I tell you, her many sins have been forgiven—for she loved much. But he who has been forgiven little loves little." Then Jesus said to her, "Your sins are forgiven." The other guests began to say among themselves, "Who is this who even forgives sins?" Jesus said to the woman, "Your faith has saved you; go in peace" (Luke 7:44-50).

Somehow, the woman's love was unblocked. Her warmth made it clear that forgiveness, the healing of her spirit, had taken place. To Jesus, the flow of her love was the sign that she was receiving the forgiving, healing love of His Father.

The Charismatic Dimension of Repentance

I made an important new discovery when I found that repentance sometimes cannot take place without prayer for healing. Nowhere have I ever found this stated in books on healing although Paul's long laments in Romans 7, where he describes how he does the very things he hates, should give us a clue that we need a lot more than the Law provides.

And yet I find that much Christian preaching is a preaching of law—of an ideal that some Christians fail to achieve. Preaching, even of the truth, just makes some sinners feel guilty without giving them the power to overcome their sin.

Some Christians are able, through discipline and will-power—and with the help of God's grace—to repent and overcome their sins. Others simply fail, over and over again; they are the ones who need the additional help of healing prayer.

To give you an example: some friends of mine once brought one of their friends to Merton House (then my residence in St. Louis). This lady was about fifty years old and was from a fairly well-to-do family, but she was dying of alcoholism. She had been a patient at one of the very best alcoholism treatment centers, and yet she continued to drink herself to death. So, as a last resort, her friends brought her to me for prayer. She even had to stiffen her resolve to see me by taking a couple of good, stiff drinks. After talking with her for about five minutes, I, with her friends, prayed, asking Jesus to free her from her need to drink.

From that point on (and for at least the next fifteen years) she never took another drink. Not only that but the shakes disappeared (they had tormented her every time she tried to quit drinking). Still more marvelous, she never had the struggle that most recovering alcoholics have—of being tempted every time she passed the liquor section in a drug store; it was as if she had never had a drinking problem.

Admittedly this healing was remarkable; with most alcoholics the struggle remains and we always encourage people who have a drinking problem to connect with Alcoholics Anonymous.

Similarly I have prayed with people who had tried to stop smoking or taking drugs or overeating and who had not succeeded in conquering their destructive habits through willpower and discipline alone. And the Lord has healed them.

Was their healing on the level of the will or of the body (an alcoholic's body truly craves another drink) or of an emotional craving (or even an addictive demonic spirit)? I'm not sure.

All I know is that many sins that preachers rail against can only be changed by a combination of *repentance and healing prayer*. Preachers who do not understand this are really back in the Old Testament in this regard and do not understand Paul's laments about the failure of Law to free God's people from sin and guilt.

Our greatest need for healing prayer as well as conversion lies in our inability to fulfill Christ's great commandment to love one another as He has loved us. And the hardest part of it all is to love our enemies (Matt. 5:44). I really don't believe most of us are able to love our enemies without God's special help. It's impossible. (And that's why the most that was commanded in the time before Jesus was to "love your neighbor as yourself.")

Over the years I have learned to pray for a person who is not able to forgive. In this prayer I ask Jesus to help the angry person see the enemy as Jesus sees him and to love the person with Jesus' own forgiving love. Over and over I have seen Jesus help the bitter person see his enemy in a new way, in a new light in which he had never seen him before. In seeing him in a new way the person is able to understand the other's motives in a more compassionate way and then to forgive him with God's own love—which is poured out into our hearts by the Holy Spirit (Rom. 5:5).

Repentance, in the New Testament, takes on a newness and a possibility that it never had before the time of Jesus. Truly we can become a new creation and share in the very uprightness of God Himself (2 Cor. 5:18-21)!

13 | The Inner Healing of Emotional Problems

The Spirit of the Sovereign Lord is on me,
because the Lord has anointed me
to preach good news to the poor.
He has sent me *to bind up the brokenhearted*,
to proclaim freedom for the captives
and release for the prisoners (Is. 61:1, italics added).

Somewhere between our sins and our physical ailments lies that part of our lives where we find many of our real failings as human beings—our emotional weaknesses and problems. After making our yearly New Year's resolution we find that, in spite of our good intentions, we often keep on repeating many of the same sins. Evidently, the cure of some of our failings does not depend altogether upon our willpower. Over and over we have tried; again and again we have failed.

Paul reflects this tragic human situation when he cries out:

I do not understand what I do. For what I want to do I do not do, but what I hate I do. And if I do what I do not want to do, I agree that the law is good. As it is, it is no longer I myself who do it, but it is sin living in me. I know that nothing good lives in me, that is, in my sinful nature. For I have the

181

desire to do what is good, but I cannot carry it out.
For what I do is not the good I want to do; no, the
evil I do not want to do—this I keep on doing (Rom.
7:15-19).

The tragic fall of certain TV evangelists, who have been
discovered falling prey to the very sins they have preached
against, is present-day evidence of the accuracy of Paul's
description.

Years ago I tried to counsel those persons who came for
advice to the visiting parlor of the seminary where I taught.
Yet I came to realize that my suggestions, even though they
were based on the Bible, seemed to have very little effect
on the lives of the people who were hurting the most. To
those persons who were well balanced I could offer some
helpful suggestions. But if they had deep emotional wounds,
then they usually could not merely use their willpower to
solve their problems.

Unfortunately, the only help I was trained to give was to
encourage them to use willpower with the help of God's
grace, and then to recommend some practical advice. What
troubled me was that this advice usually was not sufficient.
For example, the mentally depressed woman, who had been
enduring rather than enjoying life for as long as she could
remember, remained depressed. The best I could do was to
encourage her to keep going. I could also recommend that
she see a psychiatrist.

I found, of course, that my concern and caring were in
themselves a healing force. But I didn't have time to listen
to all the disturbed people asking for appointments. The psychiatrists, too, were overbooked. Unless a person had done
something desperate, he or she had to wait a month for a
first appointment.

What could I tell the mentally depressed woman who could

not believe that God loved her and whose whole experience of life simply demonstrated to her that no one really cared about her—especially if her husband had deserted her? The only one who would listen to her was a psychiatrist at $100 an hour. What could I say to the homosexual who simply was not attracted to women and whose tendency went all the way back as far as he could remember? What hope did he have for a change—what did my church offer him as a genuine help?

In the sixties, as the priests and ministers I knew studied the findings of psychology they gradually came to realize that *repentance* was insufficient advice for many of these problems that went deep into the person's subconscious— and hence, were largely untouched by willpower. They finally learned the wisdom of recommending that such suffering persons see a psychiatrist. In time, it seemed that I, like many other priests and ministers, was serving mainly as a referral service for other, more professional services, which could better handle the needs of suffering humanity.

At the same time, however, psychiatrists were referring their patients to me for spiritual direction. Through this experience I could see both the help that some patients were given by the psychiatrist's direction as well as observe the number of patients who progressed only minimally. I once talked, for example, to a mother and father who spent $70,000 on psychiatric help for their daughter. This professional help kept her alive and gave her a vocabulary to describe her problem but did not cure her. She has since been healed by prayer.

Years later I was to find that my wife, Judith (I had not then met her), had gone through her own vocational crisis as a psychotherapist, working in a Boston psychiatric unit. Why, she wondered, didn't her clients get healed? Through her own desperation she learned how to pray with her clients and, to her joy, found them healed.[1]

This caused me to reflect seriously. Why, if Christ came to bring salvation and freedom, wasn't there any realistic hope for some people who were badly wounded psychologically? Especially it didn't seem fair to persons who had given their lives to Christ as best they could—ministers, for instance. They would tell me, "I don't think God loves me." Physical sickness I could see as potentially redemptive. But if persons are mentally depressed they are prevented from experiencing many basic aspects of the Christian life:

1) The Christian is supposed to experience inner *peace and joy*, but the depressed person cannot.

2) We are to believe that *God loves us*, but the depressed person cannot.

3) We are supposed to relate to others in *community*, but the depressed person is often so saddened that he or she withdraws from community. Nor does such a person have the energy to *work* as others do.

4) Jesus had said that we should not be anxious, yet the depressed person is often in a continual *state of anxiety*.

Such people are, objectively speaking, living in a sinful state of depression, of lack of hope; but they are not subjectively guilty for it. Even so, guilty or not, there seems no way out for the suffering person. What does the message of the freedom and salvation brought by Christ mean to such a person?

Medicine and psychiatry do not always help, nor does the traditional remedy of repentance. Something clearly is missing. It is not right that such sufferers should be overcome by evil, when their willpower cannot touch it.

When we come to this area of emotional sickness, I find it hard to see how the person's suffering can be spiritually helpful. The mental depressive finds it almost impossible to trust his or her fellow human being. The scrupulous person feels that God is the enemy, not a friend. Consequently I was never able to accept the idea that psychological sickness was God's will for a suffering individual; it was destructive, not redemptive.

So, then, when I first heard through Agnes Sanford about inner healing, her message filled me with hope. Healing of the memories, as she termed it, made so much sense. It was as if the whole wall of an unfinished building suddenly went into place.

Inner healing made sense not only because Christ came to free us from the evil that burdens us, but also because it was in accord with what psychologists have discovered about human nature: We are deeply affected not only by what we do, but by what happens to us through the sins of others and the evil in the world. Our deepest need is for love, and if we are denied love as infants or as children, or anywhere else along the line, it may affect our lives at a later date and rob us of our peace, of our ability to love and of our ability to trust people—or God.

The basic idea of inner healing is simply this: Jesus, who is the same yesterday, today and forever, can take the memories of our past and

1) *heal* them from the wounds that still remain and affect our present lives;

2) *fill with His love* all those places in us that have so long been empty, once they have been healed and drained of the poison of past hurts and resentment.

I have found by experience that this kind of prayer is usually perceptibly answered. At times the healing is progressive and takes several sessions, but I believe that it is always God's desire to heal us of those psychological hurts that are unredemptive and that prevent us from living with the inner freedom that belongs to children of God.[2] When this kind of prayer is seemingly not answered I assume that we simply have not gotten to the bottom of the matter, either because

1) there is a need for *repentance*, usually a need for the person to forgive someone who has hurt him or her; or

2) there is a deeper, *more basic hurt* we have not yet discovered or reached; or

3) there is also a need for *deliverance* (see chapter 15).

When to Pray for Inner Healing

Inner healing is indicated whenever we become aware that we are held down in any way by the hurts of the past. We all suffer from this kind of bondage to one degree or another, some severely, some minimally. Any unreasonable fear, anxiety or compulsion caused by patterns built up in the past can be broken by prayer, provided we are also doing our best to discipline our life in a Christian way.

So many Christians are hindered in their lives by such things as a haunting sense of worthlessness, erratic fits of anger or depression, anxiety and unreasoning fears, and compulsive sexual drives. These or other problems they would like to change, but find they cannot cope with them on the basis of repentance and a decision to change. More and more books have been written, such as *The Secret Life of the Unborn Child*,[3] which show the influence of the past upon our present and the need for breaking free of the patterns of immaturity. Some of these patterns we change through adult decisions, but often we find that the powerful memories of the past rise to fill us with fear and anxiety, whether we wish these fears or not. We cannot wish them away by an act of the will.

What Is Inner Healing?

The idea behind inner healing is simply that we can ask

Jesus Christ to walk back to the time we were hurt and to free us from the effects of that wound in the present. This involves two things, then:

1) *Bringing to light* the things that have hurt us. Usually this is best done with another person; even the talking out of the problem is in itself a healing process.

2) *Praying* to the Lord to heal the binding effects of the hurtful incidents of the past.

Some of these hurts go far back into the past. Others are quite recent. Our experience coincides with the findings of psychologists: Many of the deepest hurts go far back to the time when we were most vulnerable and least able to defend ourselves.

A good deal of evidence even suggests that some hurts go back before birth while the child was still being carried in the mother's womb.[4] Just as John the Baptist leapt in Elizabeth's womb when she heard Mary's greeting, so every child seems sensitive to its mother's moods. If the mother does not really want the child or is suffering from anxiety or fear, the infant seems somehow to pick up the feelings of the mother and to respond to them.

In praying for inner healing I have actually seen an adult woman reexperience in an amazing way the time before birth, and verbalize it during the prayer. "I'm not going to come out!" she said. "I'm not going to be born!" Such early memories up to the time we are two or three years old seem to be crucial in setting the patterns for our future behavior— long before we are free to make our own personal decisions.

If a person has always felt unlovable or has always been restless or fearful, the need for inner healing probably goes all the way back to the very earliest years of life. In general, we find it hard to be loving (and to fulfill Jesus' great commandment of loving one another) unless we have first *been loved* into existence ourselves.

The Setting for Prayer

Since the need to talk about these deepest, earliest memories is painful—often involving feelings of guilt or shame—the prayer for inner healing is ordinarily something to be done privately with only one or two persons present. There should always be freedom for a person to ask for prayer without being forced to pray in a large group or to have to pray with a particular person for whom he or she feels no special affinity. This kind of prayer is so sensitive, so delicate, that the person asking for prayer should have the freedom to select the person or persons he or she would like to confide in and pray with. Often, too, these traumatic childhood experiences have to do with sexual matters that the person finds most painful to talk about.

The ideal, then, is that people qualified by a gift of the Spirit coupled with a knowledge of psychology or with great sensitivity be available for persons who wish to pray for inner healing. Those who do the praying should never force themselves upon others.

A sign that you may be called to pray for inner healing is when the person has first come to you and unburdened him or herself of the things that are hurting within and that are beyond conscious control. This can happen, of course, in such a natural setting as morning coffee when a neighbor comes over to share confidences. You can ask the person then if he or she would like you to pray for inner healing. If the person has never heard of inner healing you can explain very simply what it is.

If the person is suffering deeply, chances are he or she will not feel able to have much faith. This is especially true for mental depressives. So do not ask the person to claim any more faith than he or she has.

The depressed person will usually tell you that no one has

been able to help—that even God does not care. In fact, you can expect to hear, "I've prayed about this many times before, and nothing's ever happened." In praying for physical healing we do well to ask the sufferer to make an act of faith, but in praying for psychological healing sometimes we only add to the sufferer's feeling of hopelessness if we ask for more faith than he or she can elicit. Assume that any faith required must come from you.

The atmosphere should be of great peace and gentleness. The time you give to the person should be generous and unhurried. In fact, if I don't have at least twenty minutes I usually don't feel I can pray adequately for inner healing. An hour is a good amount of time: forty-five minutes to talk and fifteen to pray. Sometimes it takes longer still, and there should be provision for a follow-up.

Getting to the Root

In preparing to pray you can ask some questions that will usually reveal the basic wounds to pray for:

1) *When* did this all begin? Agnes Sanford got at this by asking if the person had a happy childhood; if not, the person would say no and then naturally tell about what happened. If the person said, "Yes, I had a wonderful childhood," she then asked when things first began to go wrong. I find that most deep emotional problems go back into our distant childhood, although many people have later been badly hurt in school, through unhappy sexual experiences, or still later through broken marriage relationships.

2) Do you have any idea *why*—what caused it? Often the answer to the first question reveals the reasons for the ancient wounds—most of which go back to rejection and to broken relationships. Our relationships with our parents are especially important; whether or not we truly experienced the felt love

of our parents is crucial.

If there is a lack of love between the child and one or the other parent, chances are the person will carry the hurt on into adult life. If the mother did not hold the child enough, if the father came home from work tired and seldom talked to the child or punished it harshly, if there were too many children for a sickly mother and she had no time to show them affection, or if one of the parents died while the child was little—all these painful events leave their wounds and deeply affect the person's basic feelings about him or herself, about others and about life.

Sometimes the person does not really know what happened; then we ask for God's revelation or wait until such a time as the deep need comes to the surface. If the person can remember how it all began and why, we then ask Jesus to walk back with us into the past while we ask Him, in as vivid a way as possible, to heal each of the principal emotional hurts the person sustained. Since it is our inner child of the past who is being healed we need to pray in as childlike, imaginative a way as we can.

Jesus, as Lord of time, is able to do what we cannot: He can heal those wounds of the past that still cause us suffering. The most I was ever able to do as a counselor was to help the person bring to the foreground of consciousness the things that were buried in the past, so that he or she could consciously cope with them in the present. Now I am discovering that the Lord can heal these wounds—sometimes immediately—and can bring the counseling process to its completion in a deep healing.

At times, these hurts may seem slight to an adult mind, but we must be sensitive to see things as a child would. I remember once praying for a woman whose complaint was that her inner life was always bleak and boring, even though her professional life was in itself full and exciting. When we finally found what had caused her to shut off the flow of life it was an incident that happened when she was ten years old.

"Our Hearts Are Restless Until..."

After the prayer for the healing of the hurt (the negative part, as it were), we can pray for Jesus to fill up in a positive way whatever was missing in the person's life. Since we have such a basic need for love, the conclusion of a prayer for inner healing usually involves a filling with God's love of all the empty places in our heart.

If the person does not feel loved by God, I ask Jesus to speak to the person within his or her own heart and spirit— at a depth where no human voice can reach—to call the person by name and to say that He loves the person, even in the midst of weakness and failure. If the person lacked a father's love I ask God the Father to fill the person with His own love in fulfillment of Jesus' prayer to His Father: "That the love you have for me may be in them" (John 17:26b). Then I ask the Father to make it as if the person had a father who sat the child on his lap in the evenings to talk over the day and to tell stories; who took the child by the hand and went walking down the street, sharing his vision of life and his ideals; who carried the child on his shoulders and threw the child up in the air and caught the child again.

Such a prayer may sound very simple, very childish—and it is. On paper it may even seem sentimental. But when we actually say such prayers they are very moving. Through them God heals the brokenhearted.

When we pray we need to follow the guidance of the Spirit. No formula of prayer guarantees results; only God can heal. The Spirit may lead you to say a prayer that you would never have thought up on your own; if you follow that inspiration you may find that your spoken prayer perfectly matches the interior, unspoken needs of the person you are praying for. One unstructured way of ministering to a broken person, which leaves the prayer open to whatever Jesus might wish to do—and leaves us out of any possible manipulation of the prayer—goes this way:

First, you talk to the person you are going to pray with and, if you have any counsel to give, you give it. Then pray to enter into the presence of Jesus. Some do this best with songs or prayers of praise; others find they enter God's presence more easily when they keep silent and listen for anything God might choose to say or reveal: "When he opened the seventh seal, there was silence in heaven for about half an hour" (Rev. 8:1).

After coming into an awareness of God's presence as best you can, then ask Jesus to come to the person and take him or her back in memory to the wounding time in his or her life (for example, of sexual abuse) or to the broken relationship that has left the person with a broken heart. Then leave it up to Jesus to minister to the person (while you remain silent) as He sees fit. More often than not, in my experience, I have found that Jesus ministers to heal the person in extraordinary and sometimes unexpected ways that I myself would never think of or be able to invent.

Here is one testimony, among many, of how the Lord heals when we turn the prayer over to Him:

> My dad died of leukemia when I was just thirteen. After Judith's talk I was so filled with the love of God the Father, Abba, I wept for joy. Then I knew He was asking me to go back to before Daddy's death in the hospital room. I said, "Only if You will go with me, Jesus." Then it was as if I was in the hospital room, by the bed, and my daddy was in the bed. I

looked at him and, for the first time since a few months after his death, I was really able to see his face. (I forgot what he looked like so quickly because I didn't have any pictures of him.) I saw every detail of it—the smile lines, the receding hairline, the shadow of reddish whiskers. Everything *exactly* the way he looked. I looked at him for a while, taking it all in; then I said, "I love you, Daddy." At that point I broke down and *wept* and it was so painful I could hardly stand it, and I said irritably, "Jesus, You *said* You would be here."

Then, of course, there in the right hand corner of the room, sitting in one of those orange vinyl, modern-style chairs that only hospitals have, was Jesus. He got up and stood at the foot of the bed with His hands on Daddy's feet. I was still crying, but not so much in pain. I took Daddy's hand (it felt so familiar!) and held it for a while; then I leaned over and kissed him on the cheek. I could even feel the softness of his skin beneath his whiskers. It was so good to kiss that cheek! Finally, Jesus walked to the other side of the bed and lifted Daddy in His arms and walked out of the door. On the other side of the doorway He stopped and put Daddy down and Daddy walked away. I wasn't crying now, just feeling expectant and peaceful. Then, best of all, Jesus turned back toward me with the biggest, most beautiful smile you could ever imagine. It was so full of joy and light—a smile as big as the room. I had been standing over the empty bed, but then I sat down in that same orange vinyl chair, and Jesus got a towel and began to wash my feet. Not just splash a little water on and lightly pat them dry, but really to clean them and rub them. It felt so good and clean. Then He left. I was somehow clean and free and *ready*. It is difficult to describe and explain, but it was the most *complete* healing time.

Of course, such an extraordinary vision does not happen every time people pray; we cannot manufacture or manipulate such beautiful times of healing. But they do take place a significant number of times when we pray and leave it all in the Lord's hands.

Much more could be said about this beautiful ministry. Inner healing brings so much peace and joy to people it is a pity so few understand and pray this kind of prayer.[5] Nor is everybody equipped with the gifts needed to pray for inner healing. Moreover, it takes time to pray; it is exhausting. But it is worth all the time and effort to see the transformation from sorrow into peace or joy that almost always follows.

Typical of God's transforming love is the following testimony of a young woman who had prayed to be released from a long-standing inner problem:

Peace and all good things to you. It's 10:15, "the morning after." I thought I should share with you somehow some of what has happened since we prayed together yesterday.

You may recall that during our visit I kept asking, "Where is the fire? I thought I would be on fire," etc. Then we prayed and I felt—not a burning—but a quiet cooling of my whole spirit.

We parted then and as soon as I was able to be alone I became conscious of a strange sensation. I was being washed and/or cleansed. Closing my eyes I could "see" waterfalls and rushing rivers. I *was* that river, that running water!

Throughout those first few hours, each time I was quiet and reflective and not distracted, I would become conscious of it again. Coming home, I sat for a while in the quiet darkness and just rested in the Spirit—in the whole experience. I thought that after a few hours it would go away, but it is still with me.

I opened the Bible once today, to John 4. The first words on the page were an introduction to the text: "This passage introduces us to the symbolism of living water....Just as Moses made water spring from the rock, Jesus will give living waters springing up to life everlasting. Christ, when glorified, will give the Holy Spirit, living in abundance for all who believe."

The passage itself is about Jesus and the Samaritan woman. The verse that touched my depths, naturally, was: "Whoever drinks the water I give him will never thirst. Indeed, the water I give him will become in him a spring of water welling up to eternal life." Praise Jesus! (If I go on I will begin to "babble like a brook"—or is that what the Spirit is already effecting?)

One thing more: I was alone here this morning except for one other friend who I thought was a bit tired of testimonies. So I began to write this letter; then she came in and I said, "Look, I've got to share this with someone," and then we read the passage together. At verse 14 ("but whoever drinks the water I give him will never thirst"), I broke down and cried like a baby. That probably is not important except that I almost *never* cry, and perhaps this is part of the whole healing process, the healing of the emotions.

Praise Jesus—my heart is very full.

At times some people question whether inner healing is "scriptural." We reply that it is simply the application of Christ's healing power to what we now know of the emotional nature of human beings. In no way does it deny the gospel, but rather it relies upon the healing message of Jesus and applies it to our wounded humanity.

Inner healing simply carries out the mission of Jesus that He proclaimed when He unrolled the scroll of Isaiah (Luke 4:16-22):

> The Lord has anointed me
> to preach good news to the poor.
> He has sent me to bind up the brokenhearted,
> to proclaim freedom for the captives (Is. 61:1b).

A remarkable incident that seemed to confirm the confluence of revelation with science occurred not long ago. I was praying together with a husband for his wife who was suffering from a feeling of inferiority and anticipated rejection. She was always afraid of making a wrong decision for fear of what others—and especially God—might think of her. Those fears went back to the deep hurt of her own mother abandoning her at birth.

After a beautiful, moving prayer, we left her to pray alone while her husband drove me back home. In the silence of prayer the thought came to her, "Read the Song of Songs chapter 3, verses 1-4." She didn't know the Bible so she had no idea of what was contained there, but she opened up her Bible and to her profound consolation read:

> All night long on my bed
> I looked for the one my heart loves;
> I looked for him but did not find him.
> I will get up now and go about the city,
> through its streets and squares;

I will search for the one my heart loves.
So I looked for him but did not find him.
The watchmen found me
  as they made their rounds in the city.
  "Have you seen the one my heart loves?"
Scarcely had I passed them
  when I found the one my heart loves.
I held him and would not let him go
  till I had brought him to my mother's house,
  to the room of the one who conceived me.

This was a beautiful confirmation of exactly the healing for which she had prayed—an application of Scripture as it related to her situation.

Our most basic need is to know that we are loved—not for anything we can achieve or do, but simply because we are. If we do not know God's love in this way, Jesus eagerly desires to show us how much He cares for us by healing us of those ancient hurts that have withered or broken our hearts and spirits.

A bruised reed he will not break,
  and a smoldering wick he will not snuff out,
till he leads justice to victory.
In his name the nations will put
  their hope (Matt. 12:20,21).

14 | Praying for Physical Healing

Of all the kinds of healing, physical healing is perhaps the hardest for us to believe in; it is far easier to believe that prayer can lead to repentance or can change a person psychologically. Yet real physical healings take place regularly in the prayer groups I know. Often a dozen or more occur on retreats when we take the time to pray for the sick.

So if you have the faith that the Lord still heals people as He did 2,000 years ago, launch out and learn to pray for the sick. Although physical healing may stretch your faith (have you ever prayed for a blind person?), it is also the simplest kind of prayer. It is often simpler and shorter, say, than a prayer for inner healing.

The Confidence to Launch Out

To pray for the first time requires courage. I used to feel foolish, as if I were pretending to be someone special when I knew I was just an ordinary person. Who was I to pretend to be the great healer, to act like Christ? This was, of course, merely false humility; Christ Himself instructed His followers to pray for the sick. In some ways praying for healing requires more *courage* than faith.

What a joy when we find that God really answers our prayers and heals the people we love! The praise of God spontaneously rises from our hearts. The following excerpts from three letters show the kind of healing that often takes place as we learn to share in the healing of God:

> March 16, 1973
>
> I am the diabetic over whom you prayed at the retreat March 2 and it is with great joy I want to tell you that the Lord has healed me. Praise the Lord with me, for since March 4 I have taken no medicine, and I feel great. Never in a million years did I think that this would happen to me.

On October 22, 1973, she wrote:

> I have the doctor's verification, for I went to see him last week and he can't find anything wrong with me. I shared with him last April when I returned from the conference, and he was amazed, but this last week he was convinced that strange things do happen. I thank the Lord every day for healing, as now I am able to do my housework, which last year I could not do. My heart has been healed, too; I do not feel the pressure I felt before, when it was enlarged and was beating irregularly. I could not walk up the stairs, and now stairs do not bother me at all. I feel ten years younger, praise the Lord.

In answer to my letter she wrote again on February 5, 1974:

> As you know, I had been a diabetic for ten years; my eyesight was failing, my heart was very bad, I could not walk up the stairs without resting every few steps, my feet were swollen all the time, I had to be on a special diet, I lost a lot of weight, and had to take seven pills a day just to live. It is almost a year now since my miraculous healing, and I feel

as strong and healthy as in my youth. I can walk up the stairs, and run if I want to. My eyesight is improving, and my heart is peaceful and strong. Praise be to God, and thanks to you, for you did intercede for me.

As to the doctor's confirmation, I was taken care of by a Jewish doctor who has since retired....I went to another doctor on my return to Florida, and then again two months later to see what he would say. He could not find anything wrong with me, but as to putting it in writing, he was not sure he knew my case well enough.

Well, I am sure, for I know how I feel. A year ago my husband had to do all the housework for me; now I can do it all, and be on my feet ten hours without any trouble.[1]

If you have confidence that Jesus might use your prayers to heal the sick, then you need learn only a few simple steps. They are easy enough to remember; we do not need a graduate degree to learn to pray for physical healing. Many of my missionary friends, especially in Bolivia, and Ralph Rogawski and Helen Raycraft, who work with the migrants in Texas, are teaching poor and illiterate people to pray for the sick in their neighborhoods. They report that about eighty percent of these unlettered people are healed or notably improved as they pray for one another.

There is no one method or technique that always produces results. God wants us to depend on Him—not upon a technique. Even so, some simple steps flow out of the very nature of prayer for healing, and these I want to share with you.[2]

Listening

The first step is always to listen in order to find out what to pray for. Just as the first step for a doctor when he meets a patient is to find out what to treat, so we need to find out what we are meant to pray for.

A doctor is looking for the right diagnosis. In prayer for healing we are looking for the right discernment—which is the same thing as right diagnosis in the realm of prayer.

We are actually listening in *two* ways:

1) to the person who asks for healing and tells us what seems to be wrong; and

2) to God, who from time to time shares with us (through the gift of knowledge) the true diagnosis whenever the person is not sure what is wrong.

My friend Tommy Tyson, who is one of the best listeners I know, says that he gives only one ear to the sick person. The other ear he gives to God. In this way the Spirit comes to enlighten us when we seem to be in the dark about what to pray for.

To some people this knowing seems to come in a special way in the form of definite mental images or verbal impressions. To many of us, however, the knowledge of what to pray for comes in a natural way, like a simple intuition. We may not be sure whether we are inspired by God or not; we learn by experience to sift out our intuitions and to find out what works out in practice. "By their fruits you will know them."

Often, after I have followed what seemed to me a simple intuition about how to pray, the person I was praying for has told me that I touched on those very things he or she had not directly mentioned but had hoped that I would pray for. When these intuitions work out time after time, you learn to trust that God is working through them.

Among those things we learn to listen for are the following:

1) *Whether or not to pray.* There are multitudes of sick people. Some of them are not ready to be healed, even when

they ask for prayer. In the case of others, who will be healed, I am simply not the right person to pray for them. I cannot presuppose that I am supposed to pray for every sick person I meet.

My friend Rudy Evenson, who runs a prayer home for alcoholics, tells the story of how he was set on fire with enthusiasm when he first heard about healing. This former prizefighter attacks every problem directly with courage and zest. Armed with his newfound faith, Rudy decided to try it out in the local hospital.

Upon entering the first ward, he proceeded to go from bed to bed, laying on hands and praying for healing. When the hospital authorities found out about what was happening they threw Rudy out. This didn't bother Rudy too much. After all, he thought, we must expect persecution. What did bother him was that none of the patients got out of bed; none was healed.

In his room that night, Rudy prayed in anguish: "Lord, I believed in You. Why did You let me down? What went wrong?"

Then it seemed to Rudy that he heard a voice saying: "Rudy, who told you to pray for the people in the hospital? Did you ask Me?"

"No, Lord," replied Rudy. And he got the point.

The first discernment we need is whether or not we are meant to pray *for this person at this time*. Some people know this very clearly; they are the ones with the special gift of faith. Others know that they are supposed to pray for someone by reason of a sensation of warmth, or something like a gentle flow of electricity that courses through their hands, as a sign to them that God's healing power is present.

For others the knowing is almost natural: a feeling of peace or joy when they should pray; a feeling of darkness or heaviness when they are not meant to pray. This feeling, of course, has to be carefully sorted out from the feeling of heaviness that may oppress us when a deliverance commences. As Agnes Sanford has written:

> It is not the duty of every Christian to pray for everyone. Our prayers will help some and will not help others, for reasons beyond our understanding or control. Only the Holy Spirit can safely direct our healing power. And if we will listen to the voice of God within, we will be shown for whom to pray. God directs us most joyfully through our own desires. The impulse of love that leads us to the doorway of a friend is the voice of God within and we need not be afraid to follow it.[3]

When I first began the healing ministry I met a man who was introduced as a true worker of miracles. At the time, however, he was suffering from mental depression and exhaustion: People had found out about the wonderful way God used him, so they would call him at all hours of the day or night to visit the sick.

If someone had been in a car wreck, friends would call him to the hospital in the middle of the night. Because he was compassionate he would get out of bed, dress and drive over to the hospital where he would stay all night in prayer with the mangled accident victim. After several years of this, he himself had a breakdown and needed rest and prayer.

God wants us to pray about whether or not we are to pray for someone—even when their needs are crying out to our own humanity. One of the hardest things I have had to learn to say is no when someone in obvious need asks for prayer.[4]

God often uses our natural intuitions and desires as a channel to lead us, if we will give Him the chance. Those experienced in following these intimations sometimes receive a strong impression that they are *not* to pray for healing for a given person. (You can still pray for the person and give him a blessing.) After talking to many people experienced in the healing ministry, I have been impressed by the variety of ways in which God guides people as to how and when they are to pray.[5] In all this, our main desire must be to sort out genuine spiritual guidance from the inclinations rising from our own nature which may be colored by our own human limitations and prejudices.

Even those of us who seem to receive no clear guidance one way or another can still pray for healing. In the absence of other guidance we are safe, provided we make no presumptuous demands on people (to claim their healing, for example), if:

a) we pray for persons who come forward and ask for prayer. I assume, barring any counterindication, that God has inspired them to ask for help. Christ is especially present in suffering people who are humble enough to ask for help.

b) we pray when our compassion inclines us to want to visit or pray for someone who is sick.

Extraordinary manifestations of knowledge and of sensations of healing are all helpful, but they are not necessary. Many of the extraordinary healings I have seen have taken place without any unusual manifestations at all. All that happened was that a person came forward and asked for a prayer for healing; the group prayed for what the person asked; and the person was healed.

2) *What to pray for.* The person asking for prayer, of course, is the one who usually tells us what we need to know about what to pray for. As we listen, we are trying to pick out the basic things, the root system of the problem that we need to emphasize in our prayers for healing. As we listen we must decide which of the four kinds of healing the person needs. Even when the person has a physical ailment, we should be alert to the possibility that some deeper healing may be needed.

If we are just dealing with physical healing, we don't need to spend a long time discussing symptoms. On the other hand, inner healing usually requires a fair amount of time for counsel (twenty minutes to an hour) with the possibility of follow-up. If there is a need for repentance as well, the person will also need to ask for God's forgiveness. If the person further needs deliverance, we will ordinarily seek the assistance of several experienced people with plenty of time to follow through and help the delivered person afterward. Since these types of prayer are so different, we need to listen well and make a wise decision about what to pray for.

In addition to listening to the person, we should also be alert to the promptings of the Spirit who may enlighten us, especially when we don't know what to pray for. It is not healthy to be unduly problem-oriented and symptom-centered. If we are truly united to Jesus Christ and His Spirit, the source of healing, we can rely upon His positive inspirations about what to pray for. In the abundance of His health and life, sickness will be overcome; in the brilliance of His light, darkness and ignorance will be dispersed. (Examples of the kind of inspiration often given by the Spirit are given in Chapter 13 on "Inner Healing" and Chapter 18 on the "Eleven Reasons People Are Not Healed.")

Laying on of Hands

In actual praying for the sick, the laying on of hands is a traditional Christian practice: "They will place their hands on sick people, and they will get well" (Mark 16:18). Certainly this act is not essential; if you feel the person you are praying for would be embarrassed or would feel more comfortable if you stay at a distance, then by all means be sensitive to his or her feelings. But if it seems right, the New Testament practice of the laying on of hands has several advantages.

In the first place, a current of healing power often seems to flow from the minister of healing to the sick person. Precisely what this is we are not sure, but it seems like a transfer of life-giving power. Jesus Himself seems to have experienced this flow of power in such a way that He could sense it:

> And a woman was there who had been subject to bleeding for twelve years, but no one could heal her. She came up behind him and touched the edge of his cloak, and immediately her bleeding stopped.
> "Who touched me?" Jesus asked.
> When they all denied it, Peter said, "Master, the people are crowding and pressing against you."
> But Jesus said, "Someone touched me; I know that power has gone out from me" (Luke 8:43-46).

Some people experience this same transfer of power, sometimes like a gentle electric current, sometimes like a flow of warmth. Whatever it is, it is often connected with healing. It almost seems like a transfer of life.

Because of this sense of power flow, I have a theory that some persons with long-standing ailments could be prayed for effectively maybe fifteen minutes a day with the laying on of hands, almost like a cobalt-radiation treatment. Tommy Tyson in fact talks about "soaking prayer" in which you just soak a person in prayer and in God's love for an extended period of time.[6]

This brings us to the other benefit of the laying on of hands, and this is the human one: Concern and love are communicated far more by touch than by words alone. After a group has gathered round and prayed for a person, that person is usually sorry to see the prayer end. A sense of community and love is experienced in a deep way.

I remember once praying with a sixty-year-old woman who

was to have an operation for cancer the next day. We gathered all her friends around and they prayed with the laying on of hands. When it was over tears were streaming down her cheeks and she said, "I have never felt the love of my friends as deeply as I have tonight."

The Actual Prayer

In praying for the sick person—with or without the laying on of hands—we can be spontaneous in making up the prayer for healing. Some people call this the "prayer of faith," because it summons up our faith to believe that God will truly heal the sick person. We can assume any posture that is most comfortable for us—sitting, kneeling or standing—where we can best forget ourselves and relax and concentrate on the presence of God.

Ordinarily the prayer for healing involves:

1) *The presence of God.* We turn our hearts and minds to the Father, or to Jesus; we know that it is only through Their love that anything will happen. The traditional form of Christian prayer is to pray *to* the Father, *through* the Son, *in* the Spirit. But some people feel more comfortable simply addressing the prayer to Jesus. After welcoming Their presence and praising God, we then turn to

2) *The actual petition.* Most ministers of healing suggest that we be *specific* in our prayer.[7] For instance, if we are praying for the healing of a bone we can ask the Father (or Jesus) to take away every infection, to stimulate the growth of the cells needed to restore the bone and to fill in any breaks. Such a specific request seems to enliven our own faith, as we see in our spirit what we are praying for. It also stimulates the faith of the sick themselves as they listen and picture in their own mind what we are asking God to accomplish in reality. This helps the sick persons become more actively

involved in the prayer, even if they say nothing. If they are up to saying a prayer themselves, so much the better.

Such a specific prayer should be *positive*, emphasizing not the present state of sickness but the hope of the body as we would like to see it—whole. Agnes Sanford for a long time had no success in praying for the sick at a distance when she was asked to do so. Contrasting this with the positive results achieved through a prayer group she knew, she wondered why she failed and they succeeded until she realized that, while praying, she imagined the persons sick in bed. The prayer group, on the other hand, thought of the distant patients they prayed for as whole and well. After changing to a more positive way of praying she, too, found that the persons she prayed for at a distance became well.

In this kind of prayer mental suggestion can, of course, have some influence. But the difference in results I am describing is much more than that. We are not playing psychological games, rather trying to share in the way God sees this person in His perfect understanding of how the person should be—whole and alive and well. Certainly such positive prayer helps our faith.

Imagine, for instance, someone coming to you asking you to pray for the filling of a tooth. If you should decide to pray for such a request, being specific about asking God to fill the tooth would be a genuine test of faith—much harder than just praying for the subsiding of the pain or for healing in general for the person. Many things we don't understand; but we know by experience that they seem to help.

For that reason some recommend that we form our prayers in a positive, concrete way to focus on the desired effect of the prayer.

Every time that we meditate upon God's life and light instead of meditating upon a headache, we are building into our inner consciousness a new thought-habit of health. Someday that new thought-habit will be stronger than the old one, and headaches will be no more.

If the thought, "Oh, dear, I'm afraid I'm getting the flu," crosses our minds, let us correct that idea right away.

My nose and throat and chest are filling with God's light and if there are any germs there, they are being destroyed immediately. I rejoice and give thanks, O Lord, for thy life within me, recreating all my inner passages in perfect health.[8]

With Confidence

"Have faith in God," Jesus answered. "I tell you the truth, if anyone says to this mountain, 'Go, throw yourself into the sea,' and does not doubt in his heart but believes that what he says will happen, it will be done for him" (Mark 11:22,23).

As mentioned in Chapter 8 this kind of faith is a gift—to know that *this person* we pray for *will be healed at this time*. But we can all have the faith that God in some way will hear and answer our prayer—always.

For a long time a kind of tradition has led most of us to end all our prayers with the phrase "if it be Your will." The idea behind the practice, of course, is that we don't always know God's will, so we don't have the confidence that everything we ask for will be given us. Instead, only those things that are truly good for us will be given.

This insight is true. Yet it seems to weaken our confidence in prayer. It amounts to "I don't really believe anything is going to happen."

Such an attitude is a far cry from the words of Jesus:

"Therefore I tell you, whatever you ask for in prayer, believe that you have received it, and it will be yours" (Mark 11:24). The answer is that we should pray for the discernment to enter into God's mind when we pray; having discovered God's will we can then pray with confidence for what we know He already desires for us. When we pray, we do not pray to change God's mind, but rather we are entering into His mind to restore wholeness that He has long desired for us.

By experience we find that the phrase "if it be Your will" seems to weaken the effect of prayer because our inclusion of that phrase usually indicates that we don't believe that *ordinarily it is God's will to heal persons who ask*. For most people that phrase puts an element of doubt where doubt does not belong: We attach the "if" to God's basic will to heal us of our disease. "If it be Your will" is a convenient escape hatch, so that if a person is not healed through our prayers, we can say, "Well, it doesn't seem that God wants to heal you."

With such doubt centered on God no wonder these prayers are seldom answered. "But if you can do anything, take pity on us and help us," said the father of the epileptic demoniac. In response to this "if," Jesus retorted, " 'If you can'?... Everything is possible for him who believes" (Mark 9:22,23).

Even so, there is such a thing as healthy doubt: a doubt as to whether I know all the factors in the case—whether I know the root cause of the disease in order to pray for causes and not just symptoms, or whether there may not be some hidden purpose in the sickness, or whether I am the person whose prayer God will use to bring about the healing.[9] All these are open questions unless God should reveal to me that He intends to heal this person at this time through my prayer. If He does reveal this, I can pray with utter certainty—even a prayer of command: "Stand up and walk."

But if I am praying without such a revelation it seems best

to say, "Let this be done *according to Your will*." This may seem only slightly different from "if it be Your will," but there is considerable difference in that the doubt in this case does not center upon God's basic will to heal. Instead, it places the doubt upon whether we *know* all the factors needed to bring about a healing. Yet we still believe God is answering prayer "according to His will," as He sees best.

I do know, however, of at least one prayer group that prays, "if it be Your will," and through their prayers healings have taken place, because they do believe in God's basic will to heal. Their understanding of "if it be Your will" does not place the "if" upon God's will to heal, and they do pray with confidence, with no hesitation in their hearts.

For most of us, though, it helps to leave out "if it be Your will" because of the phrase's ambiguity. If we feel inclined to add anything, let it be "according to Your will."

With Thanksgiving

John writes:

> This is the assurance we have in approaching God: that if we ask anything according to his will, he hears us. And if we know that he hears us—whatever we ask—we know that we have what we have asked of him (1 John 5:14,15).

If we believe that God answers our prayers always (not always as we think He will, but always, nevertheless) we naturally have a heartfelt desire to thank Him. We can thank Him even during the prayer: "I thank You, Lord, that even now You are sending Your healing love and power into Bill and are answering our prayer." Our attitude should be that of Paul: "Do not be anxious about anything, but in everything, by prayer and petition, with thanksgiving, present your requests to God'' (Phil. 4:6).

Pray in the Spirit

Those who pray in tongues, when they are not sure precisely what to pray for, turn the prayer over to the Spirit, believing that

> in the same way, the Spirit helps us in our weakness. We do not know what we ought to pray, but the Spirit himself intercedes for us with groans that words cannot express. And he who searches our hearts knows the mind of the Spirit, because the Spirit intercedes for the saints in accordance with God's will (Rom. 8:26,27).

Often when I have been pressed for time, with a crowd waiting for prayer and no chance to speak to each one, I have simply gone from one person to another, laying my hands on their heads or shoulders, praying in tongues about thirty seconds for each person. I do the same thing in foreign countries when I do not know the language. In this way many have been healed; several remarkable outpourings of God's grace have occurred at such times as this, when I simply turned the prayer over to God's Spirit, not even knowing what the needs were of each Peruvian, Colombian or Bolivian who came forward.

And occasionally we have experienced the Pentecost phenomenon where the persons being prayed for heard the prayer in their own language, just as the Parthians, Medes and Elamites heard Peter's message in their own language on the day of Pentecost.

15 | Deliverance And Exorcism

Some might wonder what a chapter on praying for deliverance from evil spirits is doing in a study on healing. To tell the truth, I did think of leaving it out—especially since it is such a controversial subject. Nevertheless, it is a part of healing in the broader sense of freeing us from all the evil that burdens us and prevents us from being fully alive and free. Anyone who exercises a ministry of healing must at least understand the four basic kinds of healing, including the last among them—deliverance.

Here I would like to make a distinction between

1) *exorcism*, which I understand to be a *formal* ecclesiastical prayer to free a person *possessed* by evil spirits, and

2) *deliverance*, which I understand to be a process, mainly through prayer, of freeing a person who is *oppressed* by evil spirits.

For example, formal exorcism in the Roman Catholic Church requires the permission of the bishop and is rarely exercised. Deliverance, on the other hand, is a relatively common occurrence—at least in some Christian communities.

I tried to avoid the ministry of deliverance as long as possible, since I was already worn out praying with all the people who desired prayer for inner and physical healing. Why get involved, I thought, in the unpleasant business of praying for deliverance?[1] Healing is such a beautiful and positive kind of prayer that I had no desire to get involved in something I felt was ugly.

The little I had seen of this ministry in prayer groups seemed to me unbalanced and exhibitionistic. As a psychiatrist friend had observed, "Who will exorcise the exorcists?" I still have enough intellectual pride not to want to be associated with the stigma of fanaticism. Richard Woods, in writing about diabolism, reflects the common disdain of the intellectual world for the image of the exorcist when he writes, "Catholic priests and Protestant pastors (so far, no rabbis) have told me contentedly of the informal exorcisms they regularly perform, clucking their tongues at the sad number of young people still, however, in the grip of Satan."[2]

Nevertheless, in spite of my fear of losing a somewhat respectable image, experience has forced me to realize that there are some people I simply cannot help merely by praying for healing. Prayer for deliverance sometimes is clearly called for. Some people who come to me know this and are quite calm and rational in describing truly extraordinary manifestations of apparently demonic attacks. For instance, I received a letter from a woman who asks about a pastoral problem common to anyone who has experience in the healing ministry:

> Do you know where I can get some information on deliverance and healing? What's the difference between praying for deliverance and exorcism? How does one know when a person needs either? There's a twelve-year-old boy on our block who exhibits strange "symptoms." I visited the parents the other day and without saying what I think (and I don't have any background on these things) the child might be suffering from, I talked and prayed with them.

The boy, they say, has an unidentifiable disease; he keeps twitching, except for a few intervals, gets real bad at night, sometimes says words they don't understand or vulgar words and doesn't communicate. His eyes are like far away and his mother says that at night he moves his head, with his eyes open, back and forth. His hands look paralyzed and he just keeps twitching.

One night I asked him to say, "Jesus Christ, help me." He could say, "Help me," but he couldn't—or wouldn't—say "Jesus Christ." We prayed for a while and he fell asleep before I left. He stopped twitching, his hands went limp and were no longer stiff and twisted. I feel there is much more to do.

Meeting such strange cases myself, as well as having these questions addressed to me, I realized I would either have to learn something about deliverance or not help such tormented persons beyond referring them to the psychiatrist. I would willingly have referred these cases to someone with a proven expertise in deliverance, but there simply weren't that many experts in deliverance that I knew about. Some of the people I had heard about who were performing exorcisms didn't seem to have balance or to use common sense. Some were claiming every sickness was demonic and were thereby splitting prayer groups apart.

People who needed deliverance were phoning in from the East and West Coasts to ask for appointments; I wanted to refer them to someone in their own cities for help. But I didn't know of anyone to refer them to. One person called a local bishop's office to ask for prayer for exorcism and was told to see a psychiatrist. In view of all this, I realized that I would have to learn something about deliverance in order to complement what we had already learned about repentance, inner healing and physical healing.

Is There Such a Thing as
Demonic Possession or Oppression?

As I have said, my initial avoidance of the deliverance ministry came from a fear of moving into an area that savors of superstition and primitive religion. Some of my closest friends find it easy to accept healing as a beautiful ministry of God's love, but to them any emphasis on the demonic seems like a retreat from reason into the realm of superstition. The evil that is in our human nature, they say, is enough to explain what is wrong with the world; when Jesus is reported to have driven out demons, He was just speaking according to the mentality of His age which attributed mental illness to evil spirits. Talk of demons seems like a throwback to the Middle Ages or to the witch-hunts of Salem.

Consequently, I assume that some intelligent readers will question the very existence of demons and wonder if the resurgence of exorcism isn't more of an unhealthy regression than a move toward health. To propose adequately the need for such a ministry is clearly beyond the scope of this chapter, but I would simply like to indicate that, in addition to the evidence of the gospels, I personally have been convinced by:

1) The constant teaching of the Christian church, going back to the times of the apostles. This teaching can be found in the present day in the Roman Catholic Church, the Pentecostal churches and in many of the growing nondenominational churches. For example, Pope Paul VI wrote the following statement (which was, incidentally, much criticized):

What are the greatest needs of the church today?
Do not let our answer surprise you as being over-simple or even superstitious and unreal: one of the

greatest needs is defense from that evil which is called the devil....

Evil is not merely a lack of something, but an effective agent, a living, spiritual being, perverted and perverting. A terrible reality....

It is contrary to the teaching of the Bible and the church to refuse to recognize the existence of such a reality...or to explain it as a pseudoreality, a conceptual and fanciful personification of the unknown causes of our misfortunes....

That it is not a question of one devil, but of many, is indicated by various passages in the gospel (Luke 11:21; Mark 5:9). But the principal one is Satan, which means the adversary, the enemy; and with him many, all creatures of God, but fallen, because of their rebellion and damnation; a whole mysterious world, upset by an unhappy drama, of which we know very little.[3]

2) In addition to this long tradition of the church, my own *experience* has convinced me more than anything else. *Before* prayer for deliverance many of the phenomena, such as the behavior of the boy described in the letter, impress me as most easily explained as demonic in origin. Admittedly, this kind of criterion needs to be used cautiously, but the gift of discerning spirits finds its purpose in helping us know whether we are simply dealing with a human problem or whether the problem is caused or aggravated by evil spirits.[4] To call a person a schizophrenic or a mental case still does not explain how and why those particular symptoms were caused.

If the cause is demonic, then the proper cure would be exorcism. At one time I thought that if a person was psychotic the only remedy was to refer the person to a psychiatrist or mental hospital. I now have come to believe that many of these same patients can be helped through prayer for deliverance *if* the cause of the psychosis is demonic. This kind of prayer should be done ideally working in conjunction with the patient's psychiatrist.

I have, for instance, before me two letters from a woman who was in a mental hospital for twelve years being treated for schizophrenia. In February 1973, I prayed for her deliverance and an immediate change took place. On June 9 she was released from the hospital and on October 5 she wrote:

> I went to see my psychiatrist today. He said I was
> well. I told him I wanted to visit the hospital because
> I miss the dances there. He said that he didn't agree;
> the hospital is for people who are sick and I am well.

In short we have tended to diagnose various personality problems as neurotic or psychotic; but such labels do not necessarily get at the root cause of the problems. We believe that a view which holds that some of these problems could be demonic in origin is primitive and superstitious. Yet to call a person "schizophrenic" only describes symptoms and may not help the person recover at all.

In dealing with someone who is psychotic it would be unwise to jump to the conclusion that such a person needs deliverance. On the other hand, those who are not open to the possibility that such problems as schizophrenia can be caused by demonic intervention are blocking the cure of that patient, *if* the cause of sickness of that particular patient is demonic in whole or in part.

During prayer for deliverance I have also seen unusual phenomena take place which I think can best be explained by demonic activity. Such phenomena would include being thrown to the ground, and what purport to be demons speaking through the person (saying, for example, "You will never drive us out; we are too many and too strong for you"). I know that these phenomena can be explained in other ways, but to me now the best explanation is the more direct one: that these voices can be demonic in origin. I know some of the people who have prayed for deliverance from one or another problem, and they are as rational and sophisticated in their understanding of these matters as anyone. Yet during the exorcism they were surprised by what they found taking place.

After prayer for deliverance a transforming change often takes place in persons who have not been helped by any other means. This change is sensed immediately by the person ("I just felt something leave; I feel a tremendous weight lifted off me") and is recognized by others in the new freedom and joy the person experiences.

As one person wrote after praying for deliverance:

> I feel so privileged and special to God that He led me to this weekend, so that I might be healed and transformed into a new person.
>
> You might have some idea how very, very important this is to me—a matter of life and death. My gratitude will take the form of total surrender to God. At last I have the ability to be open to Him completely without the old obstacles keeping me from Him.

These past few years' experience has convinced me of a vital need to understand the deliverance ministry.

Problems With Terms

When people talked about exorcism I used to think about people being "possessed." Clearly this was a rare phenomenon; there were a few famous incidents like the celebrated case that inspired Peter Blatty to write the novel

The Exorcist (with the subsequent movie). But these rare, dramatic instances were hardly worth reading about unless we were influenced by morbid curiosity.

The problem is in the term "possession." Real possession, when an individual's personality is submerged by an alien, evil force, is certainly rare. It is nothing most of us need to be concerned about. But the word in the New Testament which is often translated as "possessed" actually means, in the original Greek, "demonized" or "to have a demon"— which is a much broader term. I find that possession is rare, but people who are "demonized," who are attacked or *oppressed* by demonic forces, are a relatively common occurrence.

If a person is oppressed by evil spirits, then an informal exorcism, a prayer for deliverance, is in order. Derek Prince has compared this kind of oppression to the invasion of a city in which the person has control over the main part of the city, but where *certain areas* of the city are under enemy control. When a person has a problem of compulsive behavior in a particular part of his or her life—drug addiction, for instance—it *may* be an indication that prayer for deliverance will free the person.

Indications That Deliverance Is Needed

The following are signs that may indicate a need for prayer for deliverance:

1) The element of *compulsion* just mentioned. When a person tries over a period of time to change but is unable to, even after doing everything possible to achieve self-discipline, then either prayer for inner healing or prayer for deliverance (or both) may be the answer. Common problems that often involve inner compulsion include drug addiction, alcoholism, self-destruction, compulsive masturbation. Discernment is

always needed to decide the proper approach to each of these problems: a) repentance and self-discipline, or b) inner healing for the wounds of the past, or c) deliverance. But compulsion is one indication that demonic forces may be an influence.

2) The *person asking for prayer often knows* that the problem is demonic and will tell you. Of course, the person may simply have too lively an imagination, and after reading vivid accounts of demonic activity may have decided that his or her problems must be demonic. This is similar to the problem of suggestible people who read medical books and imagine that they have contracted the diseases they have read about.

Consequently, when people come asking for exorcism, we are right to question them closely. Most of us, however, have been trained to be suspicious of any such tale of demonic horrors and to ascribe it to hallucination or other psychic aberrations. Some of the people who describe these wild stories are psychotic, too—which does not help in the sorting out.

My own impression is that ministers who have an adequate intellectual background tend to disbelieve any story of diabolic activity, while unofficial exorcists with little or no training tend to believe everything is exactly as told and create all kinds of havoc by seeing demons where there are none. In this way those who should be performing the needed exorcism or deliverance abandon the field to those least qualified—and then criticize the results.

My own experience leads me to believe that many people have had experiences of evil they would like to talk about and be freed from. But the skeptical response they have so often met from their priest or minister has led them to keep quiet about their deepest suspicion that the real source of their problems is demonic.

3) If prayer for inner healing seems to accomplish nothing,

then it may be an indication that deliverance is needed. I have come to expect that prayer for inner healing will ordinarily have a perceptible effect. If, after prayer, a person says, "I still have a feeling of being tied up inside," it may indicate a need for further counseling or support in community or more prayer for inner healing—or, possibly, for deliverance.

From what I have seen of the activity of demons they ordinarily try to convince the afflicted persons that they are unworthy, unlovable, doomed to failure, headed toward death and disaster, hated by God and filled with irredeemable guilt. Yet all these problems of a "loser's script" can also be caused by the psychological wounds of an unhappy past. Clearly, then, any deep personal problem can have a number of possible causes:

• One person who is mentally depressed needs to repent of a secret sin that weighs him down;

• Another has a problem of hormonal imbalance and needs medical attention, or prayer for healing (for example, postpartum depression);

• Still another never experienced the love of a mother and father and needs psychiatric help and/or inner healing;

• Yet another, oppressed by demonic powers leading to thoughts of depression and despair, needs prayer for deliverance.

In all this we clearly need the gift of *discernment* to be sure of the presence of evil spirits. If we ourselves don't have this particular gift, we can find someone we know and trust who does have it, and then join that person to our team. Lacking that, we have to go by observing the activity of the persons we are praying with (or listening to their story) and making the best cautious, human judgment we possibly can. Then we must proceed from there.

Because of the delicate nature of this ministry, the one who prays with someone for deliverance, more than any other minister, needs this gift of discernment. When you pray for healing and it does not take place, providing the ministry has been in an atmosphere of love, the patient is still blessed. But if you pray for deliverance and nothing happens, then the person may fall under a pall of condemnation, believing that you have seen demonic activity in him which has not been driven out and which still remains. Deliverance should be ministered, then, with great caution, and only if in prayer you judge that demonic activity is truly present and that the Lord wants you to pray *for this person at this time*.

Prayer for deliverance is radically different from prayer for healing in two ways:

1) Whereas prayer for healing is addressed to God, a prayer of deliverance or exorcism is not really a prayer but a command directed to the oppressing *demons*.

2) Whereas prayer for healing is ordinarily a petition, prayer for deliverance is a *command*. For a person who has the gift of faith, prayer for healing can be a command—"In the name of Jesus Christ of Nazareth, walk" (Acts 3:6b). But prayer for deliverance is always a command to the demonic forces, ordering them to depart in the name of Jesus Christ, as Paul did to the spirit influencing the soothsaying slave girl: "In the name of Jesus Christ I command you to come out of her!" (Acts 16:18b).

The exorcist, then, is one who, invested with the authority of Jesus Christ, commands the evil forces to leave. This commanding need not be done with shouting, as I have seen it done in some prayer groups, but it does need to be done with firmness and authority.

For a variety of reasons this ministry should be reserved to those who have been called to it. First of all, because it is a prayer of authority, those who feel strained in situations of authority—who are timid or insecure—are not suited to this ministry. They will either be so frightened that nothing will happen through their prayer, or they will mask their insecurity by false posturing that will only make their ministry look ridiculous.

On the other hand, just because it is a prayer of command, involving confrontation, persons with aggressive tendencies may feel called to this work, when in reality they are working out their own aggressions. Since their motivation is mixed, the results of their ministry are likely to be mixed. The sensitivities of the person being prayed for may be deeply hurt by what one observer once described as "spiritual rape."

Furthermore, because of the need for sorting out the complexities of good and evil and knowing when to pray, what to pray for and how, the exorcist must be experienced, wise and discerning. Simplistic people who tend to see everything in terms of black or white often seem drawn to a deliverance ministry where they help some people while they harm many others. This, in turn, gives deliverance a bad image, frightening away the very persons who might be best able to exercise a discerning ministry of deliverance.

Our concentration on driving out demonic forces must never overwhelm our priority of ministering Christ's healing and mercy to a wounded human being. We are not primarily ministering anger to demons, but we are *ministering love to wounded people*. The persons we minister to must be able to sense that we love them. A balanced deliverance ministry has to be seen in the context of a much larger healing ministry.

Just Before the Prayer for Deliverance

The following points represent the consensus of those persons I know who have the most experience and wisdom in the deliverance ministry:

1) Prayer for deliverance should not be entered into without

prayer and discernment beforehand. Like major surgery, it should not be lightly suggested. Many people have a need for prayer of deliverance, I believe, but the time cannot be hurried and there is a great need for follow-up. If follow-up cannot be provided, if there is no Christian community to help the person grow, we should hesitate before embarking on a prayer that cannot be finished; the last state of the person may end up worse than the first.

Bob Cavnar of Dallas at one time was engaged in praying for a number of people for deliverance. They were all in great need, calling upon him at all hours of the day and night. But when he stopped to pray about the situation, his guidance was that he should pray for only one man who was in the most severe need. This Bob did, and over a period of months the man was freed from the oppression that had held him paralyzed in his bed. During those months of prayer Bob learned a great deal by this experience, almost as if he were being given a course on deliverance.

2) Ideally, the prayer should be in private, so as not to appeal to the curious (the crowds packing in to see the movie *The Exorcist* show how deep this curiosity is). Only mature persons should be allowed to participate.

3) Ideally, prayer for deliverance should be done with a *team*, rather than alone. At times, I have had to pray for deliverance alone, but a team is preferable for a variety of reasons.

The most evident reason for a team approach is that the diversity of gifts belonging to the Christian community can be brought to bear. One person, for instance, may be more suited to say the actual prayer of deliverance (ideally the minister) because of his or her spiritual authority. Another may have a gift of discernment to know what to pray for at any given moment, while still others can offer prayer support to the person prayed for, as well as the one praying the prayer of deliverance. Sometimes the prayer is short, but at other times the prayer can go on for several hours—in which case simple fatigue and the need to concentrate make a team approach the most suitable.

The Actual Prayer for Deliverance

1) As the prayer begins it is wise to pray for *protection*. I pray that the power of the blood of Christ surround and protect every person in the room. Some also ask for angelic protection and support. I pray that no evil force be able to harm anyone in the room—or anywhere else—as a result of demons being cast out through our prayer for deliverance.

The way each person prays will of course be different, but it is wise always to pray that no harm befall anyone as a result of the fallout from our prayer. Often we find that spirits, once cast out or stirred up, redouble their attacks upon the afflicted person—or upon others:

> The evil spirit answered them, "Jesus I know and I know about Paul, but who are you?" Then the man who had the evil spirit jumped on them and over-powered them all. He gave them such a beating that they ran out of the house naked and bleeding (Acts 19:15,16).

In this instance the exorcists (the sons of Sceva) apparently were not Christian and did not have the spiritual authority needed to perform the exorcism. Similarly, problems can arise for us if we do not pray for God's help or are not called to this ministry which deals with such powerful spiritual forces.

2) I always pray, then, that the force and power of any demons *be bound* and lose their force to resist. I do this by a command in the name of Jesus Christ. This command seems

to help the deliverance take place more quickly and more effortlessly.

For example (and for those who have not witnessed these things I simply ask you to suspend judgment until you have had a chance to investigate them for yourselves), during prayer for deliverance some persons feel as if they are being choked by some invisible hand, or they may be thrown to the ground, or they suddenly go blank. All these manifestations temporarily interfere with the prayer until they are dealt with. Consequently, I pray that the powers of evil be bound, and in this way avoid as many unpleasant side effects as possible.

Richard McAlear of Newburgh, New York, states that *most* evil spirits oppress people because of wounding that has happened in their past (for example, a spirit of rejection). He and his colleague, Betty Brennan, find that these spirits leave quietly if the spirits are bound by the blood of Jesus and forbidden to affect the person's mind and emotions. They then pray for inner healing, and once the healing is accomplished the spirit no longer has a hold on the person and leaves without further ado.

3) Often we need to find out the identity of the demon we are driving out. Usually these demons are identified by their predominant activity: for example, a spirit of self-destruction or a spirit of fear.

Again, I know this must sound strange to someone who has not been involved in this type of prayer, as it once did to me. Nevertheless, the demons do seem to have identities and names[5] which they reveal to us in several ways:

a) *The person asking for prayer knows* who the demon is or what its characteristic activity is. For instance, *if* sexual sins in a given instance should happen to be demonic in causation, then the prayer can be directed against a spirit of lust. This is not to say that all sexual problems are demonic; only that *if* this is the case, then the spirit can be addressed.

b) Through the *gift of discernment* the persons doing the praying know what should be prayed for. This is the most direct way, the quickest, of knowing what to pray for. But the genuine gift—which is not guesswork—is relatively rare in my experience. There are only half a dozen people that I know and trust whom God inspires with discernment in the kind of situation we are describing.

c) Through *commanding the demons to identify themselves*. They answer this command, either by speaking through the oppressed person (often to his or her great surprise) or through suggesting very strong mental pictures or ideas to the person's mind. These thoughts are ambiguous signs in that they can simply emerge from the subconscious of the person, so here again genuine prudence and discernment are needed on the part of those praying to be able to sort out precisely what is happening.

4) If an area of demonic interference is recognized, then the person should *renounce any sin* connected with it. If, for instance, a spirit of hatred identifies itself, then the person should forgive any persons who have ever wronged him or her, and thus cut away the sin or wound that has given the demonic force a hold upon the person.

In addition, the person himself can *renounce the spirit* of hatred, or whatever else it is. If the evil spirits do not have a deep hold upon a person, self-deliverance is a possibility. (Chapter 17 in Don Basham's *Deliver Us From Evil* describes how this can be done.) Furthermore, if the person has been involved in spiritualism or other forms of occult activity, he or she should renounce by name each one of these activities.

5) Next I ask the tormented *person to command* the demon to leave. Sometimes this is enough to cause the demonic force to depart. Some persons, especially those involved with the occult, are not able to do this. Some find themselves unable

even to say the name of Jesus; the demons block them.

6) If the demon (or demons) has not yet departed, then I myself pray for deliverance. This deliverance prayer has several definite components:

"In the name of Jesus Christ..."

It is not by our authority that we cast these demons out, but we name the power to which these demons must bow. "Lord, even the demons submit to us in your name" (Luke 10:17).

"...I command you..."

This is a prayer of authority, not of entreaty. This kind of prayer is like a parent telling a child to do something; if there is doubt or hesitation, the child picks it up immediately and will not obey. The person commanding can speak quietly but must truly believe that the authority of Christ will rout the forces of evil. In praying for deliverance I find it helps to look directly into the eyes of the person being prayed for.

"...the spirit of..."

Identify the spirit, if possible, by name: "spirit of hate," "spirit of despair" or whatever else it is.

"...to depart..."

"...without harming _____ (the person being freed) or anyone in this house, and without creating any noise or disturbance..."

There have been instances where other people have been attacked by the demons leaving or the person being prayed for has been needlessly tormented. These problems can all be precluded by praying for God's protection. Since deliverance tends to be a spectacular or ugly performance, if the demons are unchecked, it is advisable to command the demons to be quiet and not to create any disturbance.

"...and I send you straight to Jesus Christ that He might dispose of you as He will."

Some persons prefer to command demons to "return to the abyss" or to hell, but personally I prefer to leave their immediate destiny to the wisdom of Christ. Jesus Himself allowed the legion to depart into a herd of pigs (Mark 5:13). As David DuPlessis once told me, there is an occupational hazard of exorcists becoming infected by what they combat; they may become harsh and judgmental over the years. As Jude remarked: "But even the archangel Michael, when he was disputing with the devil about the body of Moses, did not dare to bring a slanderous accusation against him, but said, 'The Lord rebuke you!' " (Jude 9).

7) The person being delivered seems to know when a given demon has departed. Sometimes there is no discernible change to an onlooker; the person just looks up and says, "It's gone! I feel so much better now."

If there are many demons, the person, too, seems to know when they have all gone. There is a sense of freedom, of joy; at times, it's like the lifting of a weight or some other very physical relief such as the removal of some gripping pain.

Often, too, the demons come out with a struggle: Sometimes they cry out or throw the person to the floor (phenomena mentioned in the Gospels) or they come out in a fit of coughing or retching. All these symptoms, of course, are unpleasant and make the work of deliverance an unsavory task. If these phenomena become too exhibitionistic I command the demons to keep quiet or to stop tormenting the person or to cease whatever else they are doing. The coughing or retching (why it happens is a mystery) does seem to have a part in expelling the demon; when it is over the person usually has a definite impression that a particular demon has departed.

All these phenomena are bizarre and distressing. Much as we may dislike them, we must be prepared to face them if we are going to help those persons who need deliverance.

Other Considerations

In dealing with demons we ordinarily seem to find a principal one, something like the taproot of a tree around which the rest of the root system clusters. Getting rid of them is something like digging out a tree stump. Sometimes it is best to drive out lesser spirits that have less of a hold upon the person; it's like chopping off feeder roots, so you can get more easily at the main root.

Other times, the lesser ones won't move until you identify them and drive out the principal spirit. I say "lesser" because some of these demons seem stronger than others. These demons, like vices, seem to go in clusters. When you find "anger," for instance, you may also find "resentment," "jealousy," "depression," "sadism" or such specialized forms of anger as "hatred of women."[6]

Demons usually identify themselves by the title of a particular vice:

"In the name of Jesus Christ, I command you, evil spirit, to identify yourself. Who are you?"

"Lust."

"In the name of Jesus Christ, I command you, spirit of lust, to depart...."

Several of the spirits that tend to surface early and block the prayer for deliverance are these:

1) *Mockery.* The person may start to laugh derisively and may say something like "You can't drive us out. You don't have enough experience."

2) *Dumbness.* The person can't move his mouth or talk.

3) *Confusion.* The person becomes confused and can no longer think.

Here again the persons praying must have the discernment,

knowledge and experience to know the difference between demons and the very natural human distress that the person may be experiencing so as not to misidentify the problem.

After praying the prayer of deliverance, the leader and others will find it helpful to praise God or to sing. Those who pray in tongues should do so. This kind of prayer goes on until the demon releases whatever hold it has upon the person and leaves. If there is no change, then the person leading the prayer needs the discernment to know how to proceed from there.

If the person being freed has had any dealing with spiritualism or with the occult (such as the Ouija board), the person should ask God's forgiveness for this. If there are demons (such as a demon of divination) that entered through this kind of influence, they should be the first to be driven out; otherwise they will block anything else from happening. Those spirits involved with the occult are usually the hardest to drive out, especially if the person has been involved in witchcraft.

Following the Deliverance

You should consider three important factors in following up on any deliverance. If there is no follow-up, chances are the condition of oppression will return.

1) You should *pray immediately after* the deliverance to *fill* the person with God's love and grace. Anything left empty by the departure of the demons should be filled by the presence of Jesus. Above all, the persons ministering deliverance should show genuine *love* toward the person who has just been freed and remove any sense of condemnation that so easily attaches to the recipients of deliverance ministry.

2) The person should be taught *to break the habitual behavior patterns* that originally led to the demonic infestation. If the problem was in the area of despair, for instance,

some kind of spiritual discipline, mutually agreed upon, is needed to combat the area of human weakness that caused the problem in the first place.

In addition, the person should be taught how to rebuke any forces of evil and keep them away, once they have been driven out. "Submit yourselves, then, to God. Resist the devil, and he will flee from you" (James 4:7). I once spent two hours praying for a person to be delivered from a number of evil spirits, a principal one being resentment. The person was delivered, but within an hour an incident occurred which aroused resentment in her. Unresisted it led immediately to a return to her previous state (although the last prayer for deliverance was much easier and only took about forty minutes).

3) The person should also adopt a regular schedule of prayer, of reading Scripture and (if he or she belongs to a sacramental church) of receiving the sacraments.

4) Ideally, the person should then become part of a Christian *community*. Just as alcoholics have found that they cannot, for the most part, remain dry without the help of people who understand and care (such as members of Alcoholics Anonymous), so people who have been delivered need the prayer and loving support of community. Tragically, today's churches have few such communities. I often don't know where to send people who can't make it without the help of community. The few strong communities we know about that take in people who need support are already overburdened with more people than they can handle.

Final Considerations

I might mention here that whenever I have prayed for deliverance I have almost always found that prayer for repentance or for inner healing was also necessary. Usually a very human weakness, such as an experience of rejection in early life, opened the way for the demonic. Unless this deep weakness is shut off, more problems may arise later. The person is something like a tree with a deep gash in the bark: If this is not covered over, the tree is always in danger of succumbing to the attack of insects or fungus which will then get in and rot it out.

On the other hand, most emotional problems, such as depression, are caused by very natural, human factors. Thus the appropriate response is not deliverance but prayer for inner healing or psychological counseling or spiritual discipline and growth.

Of all the areas of healing, deliverance is the most susceptible of abuse and creates the most problems. Yet I see how it is absolutely necessary that more of it be done by the right people. Nowhere are discernment and prudence more necessary than in this ministry. But nowhere is there more ignorance—especially on the part of the clergy, who are the natural candidates to perform this ministry.

For those who have had no experience in any kind of deliverance ministry, some of what I have written in this chapter may seem problematic if not downright medieval. I would only ask that you put it all on the back burner, as it were, until such time as you have a chance to see for yourself. In this area you will find books and articles voicing very strong opinions pro and con. Here I would simply like to share the beautiful aftereffects of deliverance from a minister who personally experienced it:

> So many wonderful things have happened since the Lord delivered me that I feel I must write and let you know.
>
> First and above all, my faith in the powerful love of Jesus has grown tremendously. The positive

assurance I have that He is with me in prayer astounds me. When I pray with people for healing or deliverance, I couldn't be more sure of His presence and desire to serve this person with me. Indeed, I feel that my already growing ministry of deliverance is just what I've needed to build my faith. Somehow, with each one (there have been eight in the last two weeks) my faith and the love of Jesus grow immeasurably.

My own ministry of deliverance has somewhat surprised me. And yet something seems to tell me that I've known all along that I was ordained for this....

I have not delivered anyone whose reaction was as violent as mine, although some have approached it. And I have already helped a young man in a two-hour session that included all four types of healing....

The most striking effect in my personal life has been the permanency of the cure. As I look over a list of demons cast out I am grateful that none of them has a hold on me anymore. My outlook on life is different now: I no longer feel like an outcast because of my problems. I am no longer beleaguered by doubts, fears, inadequacies or lust.

Of course, I am tempted in all the areas in which I was delivered. But it is so wonderful to have human and not demonic temptations! They are infinitely easier to resist....I never realized that a free Christian could give his life to the Lord so completely.... My life is filled with joy such as I have never felt before.

16 | A Case History: Flor's Story

In November 1972 and February 1973 our team gave retreats in Bogota and Cali, Colombia. On these retreats Senora Flor de Maria Ospina de Molina received a remarkable series of healings that illustrate the four types I have just described. Her story also illustrates the complexity of these different healings and how they intertwine.

Notice as you read, for example, how Flor's daughter was not healed until her mother was inwardly healed, some months after we had prayed for the daughter. Moreover, Flor apparently received a deliverance when she received an inner healing; whatever grip any evil spirits (such as resentment) had upon her was loosened and broken when she forgave (repentance) and received an inner healing. Furthermore, this case history illustrates how healing often takes time and happens in a series of steps as one log after another in the logjam that impedes the flow of life is taken out of the stream, until finally the key log is removed which sets a person free. Finally, note as well her faith (her chutzpah) as she traveled several hundred miles from Bogota to Cali in search of total healing.

This beautiful story of how God sets one of His people free is a translation from the Spanish (by Dorothy Curran) of the testimony given by Flor on February 18, 1973, in Cali, Colombia.

In October 1972, I was invited to take part in a study of the charismatic renewal by Padre Guillermo[1]; I attended every one of the conferences and this produced good results. Afterwards we went to Bogota to attend a retreat given by Francis MacNutt, Jeanne Hill and Ruth Stapleton. While there, we experienced a great and tremendous thing which initiated us into the movement of the Spirit. It was there for the first time that I spoke in tongues. On the second day of the retreat following the prayer for inner healing by Mrs. Stapleton, I found Francis in the hall and I asked him to pray for me and my children. This day I first learned to pray in tongues.[2] I felt happiness and I began to cry. A young man was standing there when this happened; having witnessed this experience, he kissed and hugged me and said, ''The Lord was with you.''

Four months later I heard that Francis was coming to Cali, Colombia. I remembered my experience in Bogota and all that I learned from him. I asked God not to let me miss one conference at my parish church and at the Presbyterian church. So I attended every morning conference, Monday through Friday. I brought my sick daughter, Maria Fernanda, with me the first day and I asked Francis to pray for her sickness. (There seemed to be no change in her after that first prayer.) I was also accompanied by my two half-sisters.

On Thursday, the day before the conferences finished, Francis prayed for inner healing. In the prayer he included all those persons who might not have been wanted by their parents or who never received the love they needed. At this time he asked us to reflect back on our lives—to think back to our infancy and childhood. It was then, too, that he asked us to pray for our parents if, by chance, they had not brought us into this world through love. At this moment, I felt a tremendous convulsion and a great desire to cry, because I was one of these unwanted children. I asked God to give me outward calm which I needed at this moment because I was in the presence of my two half-sisters, children of my mother's second marriage, who would not understand what was happening to me.

The only thing I felt at that moment was a desire to scream out and say that I was one of those unwanted children! I had been full of hate and revenge since my infancy and childhood; it seemed that I could hear my mother's first words when I had reached the age of reason, when I was able to comprehend and understand.

She said to me: "You and your brother are children of my first marriage. I don't know why destiny brought me to that marriage. You are the shadows of that cross; you always make me remember that part of my life."

Since I was a small child I didn't understand what she was talking about. My brother never lived with me or our mother; he always lived with my father's mother. I felt ashamed of my brother who suffered from asthma from the time he was a year and a half old.

I remembered how my mother married my father when she was very young. My mother had told me about my father in a great rage. She told me that my father had many bad habits and that he was irresponsible. They married very young, perhaps without love. My mother was an orphan, and perhaps she married as a last hope, thinking that through this marriage, she could change her life.

The first child, my oldest brother, died in forty days. Afterward my brother was born, but he was never reared with me. When I was born, my parents were already separated. I asked my mother if my father saw me after I was born. She said yes. He came because she called him and he loved me a lot. After that my mother never permitted him to visit and see me, because she did not want to live with him anymore.

Then, when I was one year old, my father was murdered—a terrible and horrible death during the time of the Violence (a civil war in Colombia). He died at twenty-eight years (almost the age I am now) from bullet wounds in the stomach, causing all his intestines to pour out on the sidewalk of the small town of La Cumbre. My mother told me that the death of my father gave her great happiness; she said it was better for a husband of this kind to be dead. From this moment, a legal battle started to decide where his children belonged. The law decided to leave my brother with my paternal grandmother while my mother claimed me.

Thursday morning, I was reliving my infancy and childhood: I grew up without a father. The only thing I knew of him was the worst. I had a distorted and horrible image of him—an image of sin and irresponsibility; even his death was horrible. I remembered, too, that my mother had said that when I was about thirteen years old I had a terrible argument with her and told her that she should at least respect him now that he was dead. I reminded her that I never ordered her to marry him—she had freely chosen to do that. My mother replied that the marriage was a disgrace and was something she never desired. Whenever I asked my mother for anything, she would say, "Your father never left you an inheritance so why should you be asking for things?"

At this time, too, my troubles began with my stepfather. I was still a child when he told me he desired me (my mother was out of the house), and that if I did not accept him, I would have to leave the house, or he would leave it. I had always been close to God and God was close to me. When my mother returned home that day, I told her what my stepfather had said. From that time on, hate was poured on me from both my mother and stepfather; I was face to face with humiliation as my stepfather continued to insist on his love for me.

When I was sixteen years old, I escaped from home. I realized that I could no longer find security there. My mother couldn't help me since she had five small children from her second marriage. I told her that I could no longer live in her house filled with hatred and malice. So I went to work for another family as a servant. After two months, I met my future husband and in four months we were married, another marriage of circumstances! Although I never really desired this marriage with a man ten years older than I, since I was like a child compared to him, I promised myself I would be a good wife and a good homemaker. I have kept this promise. I have been married ten years and I have three children. With God's help, I am giving a good example.

On Thursday morning, I reviewed all these memories. I recalled the past sufferings of my childhood and young adult life, which was never a happy one. I felt a desire to cry. I felt torment, a tremendous interior congestion within me. I asked God to help me because I was sitting between my two half-sisters who probably never knew the terrible suffering that their father had caused me.

I stayed on in church while my half-sisters went to get a cup of coffee. I felt a great need to talk to someone. Fortunately, Padre Guillermo, my pastor, was there praying. I told him all that I was experiencing and suffering that morning. I felt I was also suffering for my brother. I reflected that what I felt inside of me, my brother probably felt too. Just recently, my brother came to visit me and he asked about "that woman" whom he hates so much. I told Padre Guillermo that my brother hates our mother. I felt that perhaps the largest wound I have is that my brother hates our mother, because he does not know God.

Then I asked Padre Guillermo to pray for my brother.

But I also felt a great need for an interior healing. I felt I needed to be cleansed. I wanted it because I felt tremendous torment and confusion. The main thing I felt was remorse because I had never prayed for my own father, whom I never knew, nor for my mother. For the first time in my life, I knelt down and prayed for my father and my mother. I asked God to erase the horrible image within me that I saw! I was not clean inside of me. I also realized that I was not free. Something inside me prevented me from being completely free; something prevented me from gaining the complete freedom to live for God. I came to realize, from the talks Francis had given, that I needed still more; so I began to analyze my life further.

On Friday morning, Francis divided the group. I went to the basement of the church to pray for interior healing. There we formed a circle where others outside the circle would pray with us. At that moment I truly felt God's presence within me when Francis put his hands on my head and prayed for my interior healing.

Perhaps others can give a better testimony than I of what happened to me at that moment, for it was said that *something went out of me*. From that moment, I felt completely electrified. I began to tremble. The person next to me began to tremble also.

It seemed as if an electric current went through me—as if it were the grace of God, as if it were a cleansing.

We felt that our Lord Himself had descended upon us. God acted forcefully; I rested interiorly. I felt peace for the first time, because I forgave while I, in turn, was forgiven for what I had done, for what I had kept hidden within me for such a long time. When I returned to myself (I suppose I can say this) I felt wonderful!

There before me was Pastor Jose Fajardo of the Presbyterian church and Francis. Pastor Fajardo was crying really hard. He said: "Flor, it could be that you have been chosen for something great. Let's give thanks to God for you. You will with your testimony help many more people."

After this, we sat down to rest and I recalled my three children, especially Maria Fernanda who has been suffering with eczema for five of her six years. I remembered that I had tried everything—doctors, specialists, pilgrimages—although I never tried spiritualists or any other form of witchcraft.

Thinking of my sick child, I asked Francis how to pray for my child. "I brought her to you Monday and you prayed for her," and I repeated my request: "Teach me how to pray for my child! She does not get better."

Francis replied: "Flor, many times the sicknesses of children are not the child's fault, but are connected with their parents. You were suffering with something that has now been healed by God. I believe that now that you have forgiven your mother and father and have been healed by God, your child too will be healed."

This was on Friday. On Saturday, the child was a little better. On Sunday, the day I give this testimony at the Church of San Juan Battista, Maria Fernanda's hands are dry. They no longer have pus or any other infection.

Praise the Lord!

PART IV

Special Considerations

Therefore, strengthen your feeble arms and weak knees. "Make level paths for your feet," so that the lame may not be disabled, but rather healed.

Hebrews 12:12,13

17 | Discernment of the Root of Sickness

In talking about healing we have seen clearly how discernment is needed. Our spiritual and physical sicknesses are so interrelated that we need God's light often to untangle the complexity of human existence so that we will know how best to pray.

God is a mystery—and so is the human person.

Tommy Tyson shared the following incident[1] which illustrates a combination of several things we have talked about: discernment through listening to God, the need for repentance—especially in relation to forgiveness—and the need for healing of the human spirit before certain physical healings can take place:

> As I understand it the gift of discerning spirits is essentially this: As spiritual beings it is utterly impossible for us to live alone. We are always identified with other spiritual realities—bad or good or neutral. That is my premise, my understanding which governs my own approach.
>
> Now the gift of discernment of spirits is the gift whereby you are able to see that spiritual reality to which another person is most closely identified.
>
> Sometimes this comes as a visual representation—sometimes it is given as a word of knowledge. That

sort of thing began to happen to me one evening when I was holding a preaching mission down South. The pastor drove me out in the country until we had come upon a beautiful little mountain ridge overlooking a farm. The pastor said, "Tommy, I guess this is the reason we came on this drive, not just to see the view, but there is a home down there; I had forgotten about those people, but we should visit them."

We went down to this lovely farm home. There on the porch sat a man and his wife in their mid-sixties. Mae and Nelson were their names. Mae was sitting in a wheelchair with her right arm folded against her paralyzed right side. Nelson was sitting in the porch swing. The pastor and I pulled up a chair in front of them. I began to turn inwardly, being bathed in God's love. (I never give a person both ears anymore. I just give you one ear, but not my best one. While I'm listening to you from one ear, I'm really seeking to get heaven's interpretation from the other ear.)

The Lord began just to bathe my heart with love. People are aware of the power of love, aren't they? So I said to Mae, "Mae, something is happening— the Lord is giving me great love for you and I know He wants to minister to you." She said something through clenched teeth—she was paralyzed, you know. As I sat there some pictures began to come to my mind. I said, "Mae, if this is of the Lord you'll know it, and if it isn't, I need to know it."

I have discovered in this kind of discernment you can afford to be very cautious; you don't have to tell the people that the Lord is showing you something. That might frighten them. A lot of people might be afraid if you say that God is showing you something.

But you can say, "This idea has come to me," or "This idea seems to be of the Lord," or "May I share this with you?" I have found this to be much more helpful than just telling people everything you know. Just because you know something is not in itself a license to tell it, is it?

But as I say—this picture was coming to me: I saw a lovely home in a little village—I even saw a weeping willow tree in the yard. When I described the home Mae said, "That was the home I was raised in." I saw her as a young girl riding off in a horse and buggy with a young man, and I could tell they were running—it was just a mental picture. Then the whole thing dawned on me. I said, "Mae, I take it that Nelson came to town, and your folks didn't want you to have anything to do with him, so you ran off and eloped with him."

She said, "Yes, that's right." Then, as the picture developed, I saw her sitting at an organ—just losing herself as she played. Then, from that picture this interpretation came. I said, "Mae, you were disappointed in your marriage, weren't you? You discovered that your folks were right and rather than leave him, you lost yourself in your music. You have compensated for a disappointing marriage through music."

She was crying now as she replied, "Yes, that's right." Then I only could see a big block, so I said, "Maybe the Lord wants you to tell me what this is, or maybe we should just sit and wait for a while." Then she nodded at Nelson and said, "You tell him." Nelson said, "I suppose what you see now in this block is what happened down at the church....Everything you have said has been true. What happened

251

at the church was that a woman there who has a large family had a falling-out with Mae; they had a big argument. This woman said, 'Mae, either you or I with my whole family will have to leave this church!' Since there were only the two of us, we thought it best for Mae and me to leave.''

I said, ''Mae, how soon after that did you become paralyzed?'' She guessed it was about three months. So I said, ''Mae, where is your hand of fellowship? Where is your forgiveness?''

There it was; that was the problem.

In this case I don't mean to imply that all paralysis comes from lack of forgiveness. I think it is dangerous to imply that certain diseases have a definite spiritual cause, unless you are sure about it. Unless you are cautious you can bring people under grave indictment and guilt. I don't believe in doing that, but in this case her body was the sacrament of her soul: what her soul went through her body also underwent, and this had been going on for three or four years. I told her what I thought.

Nelson looked at me and said, ''There is one thing God hasn't shown you that maybe you ought to know. In the three years Mae has been paralyzed I've tried to make up with her and we've become sweethearts again.'' (God uses suffering, doesn't He?) Then I said to Mae, ''Will you accept forgiveness and cleansing from all this?'' She said, ''Of course I will.''

She had confessed her sin and I had heard that confession, so I laid hands on her and said, ''Mae, in the light of God's Word, you are cleansed from your sin and you are washed clean in the blood of Jesus.'' When I pronounced her forgiveness she became radiant, and we had a great time rejoicing. As I started to walk off the porch, I turned impulsively and said, "Mae, in your new life, let me be the first one to offer you the right hand of fellowship."

I reached out my hand, and hers—that had been paralyzed—came out to meet mine. For the next hour we helped her to learn to walk all over again.

18 | Eleven Reasons Why People Are Not Healed

For the most part we need encouragement to believe that God *does* heal people. But after we summon up the courage to launch out and start praying we may get discouraged when we realize that people are not always healed through our prayers. This is especially puzzling to those who have been exposed to a very simplistic approach to healing: "All you have to do is to have faith and claim your healing."

I remember in the early days of our prayer meetings in St. Louis one priest who had an agonizing interior struggle moving from his position of "suffering *sent by God*" to one of "suffering as part of the *evil* Christ freed us from." This man would often get up in the prayer meeting and give a short teaching on the redemptive value of suffering. Finally, he read a book "on the authority of the believer" which persuaded him that he ought to start praying for healing instead of for the acceptance of sickness.

The person he chose to pray for was a most difficult beginning: a patient dying of cancer. He gathered a group of friends, and with his newfound expectancy that she would be healed, he took his group to the hospital and prayed the prayer of faith. A short time later she died.

Crushed by this experience, he didn't pray again for

anyone for another year.

We need to understand, then, why people are not healed, so that we can understand the kind of faith we need to pray for healing. The best point of view, I think, is to see that *God's normative will is that people will be healed, unless there is some countervailing reason.* He gives some individuals the "gift of faith" to know that particular persons they pray for will be healed. The rest of us need to believe in God's healing power and pray for healing, while at the same time realizing that there is a mystery involved and that the person may not be healed.

To avoid simplistic approaches to healing we should be aware of the reasons people are not healed. In my ministry I have discovered at least eleven of these reasons and I imagine that we will discover several more:

1) *Lack of faith.* When the disciples could not cure the epileptic demoniac, Jesus upbraided them for their lack of faith (Matt. 17:14-20). I believe that this is still the reason we do not have more healings taking place in our churches today; a general skepticism about healing sees its occurrence as nothing more than a natural psychological process.

But even for those of us who do believe, we need to grow in faith. I find I have more faith than I did a few years ago. This was true even of someone with the fame of Kathryn Kuhlman. Many more were healed in her later services than there were in the early days of her ministry. We need to grow in faith—even those of us who have seen miracles of healing—in order that God may use us still more.

2) *Redemptive suffering.* Physical healing is not in itself the highest value in the world. At times God uses sickness for a higher purpose. There has been a long history of saints whom God called to suffer redemptively in union with the suffering of Jesus on the cross. If a person is called to suffer for the sake of the kingdom, or to learn a lesson, or as a

punishment, or for some other reason, then clearly he or she should not pray for healing.

I remember in 1969 when Agnes Sanford was visiting a monastery in Dubuque, Iowa, to give some lectures on healing to the Trappist monks. It was just then that an epidemic of Hong Kong flu struck the monks down. On the second day of the seminar Agnes herself, the renowned expert on healing, came down with flu and had to be taken to the Franciscan Sisters' hospital.

Nevertheless, a higher purpose seemed to be served by this as it gave Agnes a chance to talk to many sisters and nurses. As a result she was asked to give a workshop to them, and in this way she was able to influence an entire hospital staff. Paul recognizes the higher purpose that sickness sometimes serves when he says, "*It was because of an illness that I first preached the gospel to you. Even though my illness was a trial to you, you did not treat me with contempt or scorn*" (Gal. 4:13,14, italics added).

3) *A false value attached to suffering.* Having said that some suffering is redemptive and is for a higher purpose, we must balance that statement by saying that most sickness does not appear to be redemptive (cf. Chapter 5). I have been asked to pray for persons who didn't really want to be free of their suffering. It seemed to me that their sickness was destructive and was not a blessing sent by God, but they had been so conditioned by their training that they felt guilty about asking God to take away their suffering.

When you see a person depressed and unhappy under the weight of disease you can be fairly sure that it is not a blessing sent by God. But if the person believes God has sent the sickness, then he or she often feels guilty about asking for healing. Nor should we pray for a person contrary to his or her own wishes. Even if someone talks the person into praying, there will be a strong subconscious resistance that will block the healing.

4) *Sin.* If there is sin connected with the physical ailment (as was mentioned in Chapter 12)—especially resentment—no healing is likely to take place unless the sin is dealt with first. Once on retreat we prayed for the healing of a woman suffering a truly destructive illness, but nothing happened. The whole group remained in prayer filled with an expectancy that something should happen.

Then someone sensed that the disease was hooked up with a resentment of authority and a number of angry relationships. When this was brought up, the woman concurred that she felt this was truly the case; she asked forgiveness for her rancor. Immediately the healing began to take effect.

5) *Not praying specifically.* Especially in praying for inner healing, I think it is important to get to the root cause of emotional suffering, the initial harmful memory. Several times I have prayed for inner healing, knowing that we were praying about the right problem, and yet nothing happened. It was only when we went back and found the root incident, which had been forgotten, and prayed for Jesus to enter into that moment and heal it, that the healing finally took place.

Why can't God answer our general prayer and heal the person without our having to discover all these specific roots? I know He can and that He does. But experience has also indicated to me (not only my experience but that of several other people I know who pray extensively for inner healing) that there are a few people who do not seem to be healed until you touch specifically on the root incident that initiated the problem.

I remember, in particular, praying for one woman in Peru who had a rather common problem: Her life was altogether gray and dull. This boredom had nothing to do with her work; she was a missionary and liked her work. She knew that some kind of inner healing was necessary, for Christians should be filled with an abiding joy and zest for life. But you can't fake it either. So she spoke at length about all the things in her life that had caused her sadness. Nothing, however, was dramatic. All the events of her life seemed ordinary; there were no great crises.

Usually when you listen to a person something turns on when you get the key to the healing. You feel in your heart, "That's it; I know that's it." But there was nothing like that. We prayed, then, as best we could, for all the wounding incidents of the past that she could think of. Yet when the prayer was over, nothing changed. She experienced none of the peace, the joy, the lifting of the spirit that we have come to associate with a genuine inner healing.

The next day she came back and honestly admitted that nothing had happened. So again we (Barbara Shlemon and I) asked if she had thought of anything more we should pray for (often a person, out of shame, will omit the one incident that is the key to the inner healing). But she could think of nothing further.

So we turned in prayer to the Lord for the light that would help us. While praying, Barbara received a mental picture of a young girl, about ten years old, holding a dog in her arms. Barbara said, "This doesn't make sense, but let me tell you what I see."

The woman said that the picture brought something to mind she had forgotten: As a young girl of ten her best friend was her dog. But the dog was old and her parents took the dog away from her to "put it out of its misery."

As an adult she had put this out of her mind; that's what you do to old dogs. But to a young girl it was as if her parents, the people she trusted most in life, had taken away her best friend and killed it. If you get hurt that painfully when you love a friend and trust people, maybe it's better not ever to trust or love that much again. So as a little girl she turned off, as it were, the flow of life, so that she would never again be hurt so deeply. The result was that she could never again experience the joys or sorrows of life.

So we prayed for what had happened to a ten-year-old girl. The next day I received this beautiful note: "Life pours in. Rejoice! I feel so happy that I want to cry. This is the first time I have ever wanted to cry for being happy. Parts of my being are pulling back together."

It's a mystery why God wants some of these prayers to bring to light the precise incident that needs healing. I believe that it is because God respects the natural process of healing, which requires that incidents which have been covered up and hidden in our subconscious be *brought to conscious light* to be healed by Him. He brings His supernatural light to shine in the darkness so that these incidents may be brought out of the subconscious into the light; the supernatural reinforces and accelerates the natural process of healing.

How mistaken we would have been to tell that woman, after the first prayer, that she should accept the fact that we had prayed in faith and that she was healed. She was not in fact healed after the first prayer; only after the Spirit had revealed to us the specific wound that needed our prayer was she healed.

Not getting to the specific root of sickness is also one of the reasons people do not "keep their healing." Most evangelists teach that the reason why people who have been healed and later regress is that they lack the faith to hold on to their healing. True, that is one possible reason. But another reason for the failure is not in the sick person. Rather it's in the minister of healing who has only prayed for the healing of symptoms. These symptoms improved as a result of prayer, but because the underlying cause remained, the symptoms later reasserted themselves. Let us not be too hasty in accusing people of lacking faith.

6) *Faulty diagnosis.* In medicine doctors often fail in diagnosing diseases. Consequently, they fail to prescribe the right medicine and treatment. In the same way, the minister of healing, if he or she lacks discernment, is bound to fail from time to time.

To be specific, the most common failures I have found are these:

a) praying for *physical* healing, when *inner* healing was the basic need;

b) praying for *deliverance* from evil spirits, when *inner* healing was the basic need;

c) praying for *inner healing* when *deliverance* was the basic need.

For example, our team prayed for a young woman in Peru for inner healing for depression. She had known no father and had a series of traumatic sexual episodes in her childhood, so it seemed that inner healing was needed. But after prayer she remained as depressed as ever.

Upon further inquiry we discovered that her mother had called in a witch doctor to cure her of an abdominal infection. This doctor had prayed over her and given her a potion; immediately afterward, she fell to the floor in a trance and woke up cured. We knew then that deliverance was needed, and that we had missed it.

When our team prayed for her deliverance she was freed. The inner healing was free to take place and the depression lifted. In this instance, praying for inner healing was actually needed, but initially we missed the fact that deliverance was also necessary. We had failed to make the complete diagnosis, the full discernment.

At another time a leader of a prayer group decided to quit smoking. He wasn't able to do this by willpower (the first type of healing: repentance). So friends prayed for him for healing of his habit (the third type of healing) and others prayed for his deliverance (the fourth type of healing). None of these prayers seemed to help; he just kept on lighting up cigarettes.

The response of the prayer group leaders was to tell him that he was failing to "claim his healing." So his next step was to claim his healing. This he did—and still he went on smoking.

Some months later, hearing a talk on inner healing, he realized that his smoking habit was related to his teen years when smoking represented to him freedom and adulthood. In particular, it symbolized the freedom he needed from the overcontrolling authority of his father. Consequently, the key to his being freed of his smoking habit was connected with his need for inner healing and not to any of the other kinds of healing that his friends had prayed for.

When his friends told him that he had been healed, they were simply wrong. His relation with his father needed to be healed, and God was not about to heal the surface problem (smoking) until the more basic need was taken care of. God's withholding the healing was not a punishment, but rather a mercy—the painful embarrassment of smoking in front of people who had prayed for his deliverance gave him the motivation to search deeper until he found the deepest healing that God had in store for him.

Like good doctors we need to discern what is the cause behind those symptoms we can see. Otherwise, we simply don't know how best to pray. Often we are just guessing about the correct diagnosis. No wonder people are not always healed.

7) *Refusal to see medicine as a way God heals.* As I will make clear in the next chapter, I firmly believe that physicians and medicines are the instruments God ordinarily uses to bring about healing. This is what most people believe, and nothing should have to be said in defense of medicine.

In spite of God's revelation, coupled with common sense, we still keep hearing about ministers of healing who persist in setting up prayer (the "supernatural") in opposition to medicine (the "natural"). In recent years, for example, several persons are reported to have died of diabetes because parents or ministers encouraged them to stop taking their insulin as a sign of faith. Then the patients died. "By their fruits you will know them": Such actions are simply false doctrine unless a given person is genuinely inspired by God to rely solely on prayer and not to see a doctor.

As we rediscover the charisms of the Spirit in our day, some enthusiasts tend to misunderstand and oversimplify their operation. Healing is no exception—witness the history of the Pentecostal movement:

> In the early years of the movement, Pentecostals felt that it was a sin to take medicine or to visit the doctor. One Pentecostal preacher, F.M. Britton, once refused medical aid for one of his sons, and reported later that he "died without drugs." Some years later his wife also died after "refusing medicine." Although threatened with jail for refusing medical attention for his family, Britton never wavered in his views....Rather than an exception, these cases were the rule for many early Pentecostals.[1]
>
> One of the first schisms caused by personality clashes occurred in the Georgia Conferences of the Pentecostal Holiness Church in 1920, resulting in the organization of the "Congregational Holiness Church." The controversy producing this schism began over the doctrine of divine healing. Two ministers, Watson Sorrow and High Bowling, held a view that varied from the generally accepted ideas of the church at the time. The faction led by Sorrow

and Bowling held that it was not sinful to use remedies and medicines to aid in the healing of sickness. Another faction led by F.M. Britton and G.F. Taylor held that "the provision in the Atonement for the healing of the body was all-sufficient, and that it was unnecessary to supplement any human means to assist God in effecting a cure...."

In 1920, events came to a head in a trial which resulted in the expulsion of Sorrow and Bowling from the church.[2]

Time after time enthusiasts set into opposition the world that God has created with the "supernatural." This false opposition further damages suffering human beings and sets up a needless controversy with scientists that results in mutual suspicion between religion and science.

8) *Not using the natural means of preserving health.* Although most of us have a high estimation of the medical profession, many of us neglect the ordinary means of keeping balance in our lives. If we neglect these we should not be surprised if we fall sick and prayer does not cure us. I find in my own life that, if a cold or some other ailment begins when I am needed to give a conference, prayer always seems to cure the ailment. But if I have been working too hard and an open time in my schedule is available, the cold may run its ordinary course, rather than being immediately cured by prayer.

It's as if the body needs a rest, and God is saying through these circumstances, "Put more balance into your life. Unless you take ordinary care of yourself, do not expect to be cured of your sickness through extraordinary means. I want you to learn to keep your life in balance."

Similarly, in more serious illnesses, if some natural factor underlies the illness and should be attended to, patients cannot expect prayer to bring about a cure. They should be doing something about putting their life in order. If I have headaches because I worry too much, or if I suffer from hypertension because I work up to my breaking point, I need to change my life before healing will take place.

9) *Now is not the time.* For whatever reason there often seems to be the right time for a healing to take place. Christ urges us, like the importunate widow, to continue on in prayer if at first nothing happens. Four basic time sequences seem to take place in praying for healing:

a) Some healings are *instantaneous*.

b) Some healings occur after *a delay*. I have prayed for a person on Saturday, for example, and his healing occurred on the following Monday.

c) Some healings occur in a process, *gradually*.

d) Others *do not seem to occur*, at least on the physical level, at all.

We need not be disappointed, then, if there appears to be no immediate answer to prayer for healing. Perhaps now is not the time.

10) *A different person is to be the instrument of healing.* Perhaps I am not the one who has the discernment or the healing gift to pray for this particular person. Maybe I don't relate humanly to the person; maybe I don't have enough faith; maybe I don't have a ministry in this area of healing. These are some of the reasons why I am not the minister of healing for everyone who is sick. At times, I must be ready to let someone else take over and do the praying.

This willingness to let God choose the right instrument of healing was most clearly pointed out to me several years ago when I was giving a conference. At that conference I had spent several hours praying for a woman's deliverance and wasn't able to get very far with it, in spite of a great expenditure of time and effort. So I phoned long distance to my friend, Bob Cavnar, who I felt would have a ministry to the woman I had been praying for. He was able to give the needed help.

In turn, he and his group were praying for a man, and one of the group seemed to receive a vision of the man stuck full of nails with a spike through his heart. These nails and the spike were being loosened by their prayer, but they were not coming out. Their discernment in prayer was that, in four days' time, the nails and spikes would be removed, as it were, by a prayer for inner healing.

At the time they did not know that I would be passing through that city in four days' time. In four days' time their prophecy was fulfilled when I prayed for the man's healing. In the one instance, then, I was not the right minister to finish the healing, but Bob Cavnar was; in the other instance, I was to finish the healing that his prayer had begun.

Only when God calls us to be His instruments of healing will our prayer be successful. Jesus is the one who heals, and He uses different people at different times. In short, I need to be humble enough to know that sometimes I am not the one; I need to pray for discernment to know where to send the sick person for help, rather than to feel guilty if I am not always able to help.

11) *The social environment prevents healing from taking place.* Since we are meant to live in a community of love, some of the healing we need will not take place until our relationships and our society are healed. Earlier in the book (Chapter 16) you read Flor's testimony about how her daughter, Maria, was not healed, even after several prayers, until Flor herself was healed. Hatred and bad relationships cause all kinds of sickness, and that sickness usually remains until the root cause is removed.

When a married person suffering from depression or anxiety asks for healing and it is clear that part of the problem is caused by a tense relationship in the home, prayer can only deal with part of the problem. If a disturbed child is brought by its mother for healing, you know that you are only dealing with part of the problem until the entire family is brought into a more harmonious relationship. Much sickness in our society is caused by wounded relationships and will only be healed when the larger relationships are healed and when we have Christian communities where people can be loved into wholeness.

In 1 Corinthians 11, Paul specifically states that many in the Corinthian community are weak and sick and some have even died (v. 30) because they haven't discerned the body of the Lord. By this he seems to mean that the community itself is sick because the poor go hungry while the well-to-do eat their fill (vv. 19-22).

> So then, my brothers, when you come together to eat, wait for each other. If anyone is hungry, he should eat at home, so that when you meet together it may not result in judgment (vv. 33,34).

Perhaps the reason, then, that we have so much sickness in our society has to do with a need for more Christian love, especially in relation to the poor in our midst.

> When we are judged by the Lord, we are *being disciplined* so that we will not be condemned with the world (v. 32, italics mine).

I do not expect that most readers will want to remember all these reasons why people are not healed. The key thing is for us to know, deep down, that there is *more than one reason why people are not healed*: Lack of faith is not the only reason, and ministers of healing who imply that it is are simply leading innocent people into all kinds of false guilt. They also cause intelligent, honest people to question the whole concept of healing when they honestly observe that many people are not healed—including people who seem to have the utmost faith in prayer.

The healing ministry is perhaps the most dramatic and one of the most beautiful demonstrations of God's love for us. We have no need to overstate the case or to lead the scientific community to disparage it. If we think we have all the answers we are shut off from God's light. Healing is a mystery of God's love.

Whom does He want to heal? When? Through whom?

You should be open to being used for healing or for not being used. Wait upon God's wisdom in all simplicity, like a child. We are face to face with the mystery of God's providence.

19 | Medicine And Healing

Sometimes it happens that persons asking for healing receive an inspiration to stop taking their medicine or to act as though their sickness were cured even though the symptoms and pain still remain. That was the case of the woman (cf. Chapter 9) who asked her seminar group to pray for the cure of her endometriosis, whose only medical cure is surgery. I have kept in touch with her, so I know that this healing has lasted for many years since that conference took place. Her inspiration to stop taking her medication has proven out in its effect.

Such faith experiences that pass beyond ordinary medical remedies do happen often enough. They have, unfortunately, led some persons to generalize and to separate medical healing from prayer for healing, as though a patient should always abandon the ordinary human means of consulting doctors or taking medicine. Do you have faith in this prayer or not? is the question that some ministers of healing pose to the sick person who comes to them for prayer.

The sequel, after praying for healing, is this: Now that we have prayed, believe that your prayer has been answered, that you are now healed. You can disregard any symptoms you may still have. And, as a sign of faith, stop taking your medicine. We have spoken about this in Chapter 8, "The

Faith to Be Healed,'' but we must point out here that an artificial opposition between medicine and prayer has been set up in this way by a few faith healers who have over-generalized from their genuine experiences.

We cannot assume that, just because some people receive real inspirations from God to stop taking their medication and to disregard their symptoms, this is the way God works in all cases. God not only works directly and miraculously through prayer, but He is also at work in all of His creation and in all human intelligence, provided it is subject (even unconsciously) to Him.

To say that God inspires some people to stop taking their medicine, and even to disregard their symptoms, is, according to my experience, true. But to say that this is the way He always works leads some people into a serious problem of faith: They are torn between believing in their doctors or in someone who claims to represent the mind of God. They are forced to make a false choice between faith (not taking the medicine, and not accepting the appearance of disease symptoms) and science (the doctor's judgment according to what he sees before him).

Such theories of healing—which, in effect, oppose faith and medicine—also lead to discrediting the entire ministry of healing in the view of those doctors and psychiatrists with patients who have gotten worse after being told at healing sessions to disregard their physicians' orders. If a physician's first introduction to prayer for healing comes through patients like these who refuse his suggestions, the chances are he will write off all healing prayer as quackery, and dangerous quackery, at that.

In consequence, we see almost contradictory attitudes among Christians: Some have little faith in prayer for healing, coupled with a healthy respect for the medical profession; other Christians have a newly discovered faith in God's ability to heal. But in ruling the medical profession out of God's healing plan, they in effect drive away those very people who have devoted their lives to healing as a profession, the doctors and nurses who could most profit by discovering the power of praying for the sick.

There we have it all: a belief in prayer for healing as well as a recognition that God also cures through the skill of the doctor and through medicine. Medicine and prayer are not opposed; the doctor, the nurse and the person with the gift of healing prayer all together form God's healing team.

In our prayer group in St. Louis we were privileged to have several doctors who pray for their patients before, during and after operations. The beautiful thing is that they, too, have seen cures wrought through prayer when they came to the limits of their medical art.

At other times, doctors, relatives or friends have asked us to visit the hospital and pray for patients. Some then underwent successful operations; others were not even operated on, for the growth disappeared or the condition was cleared up beforehand. The very first person we prayed for in our St. Louis prayer group was a young woman who was scheduled for an operation for nodules on her vocal chords. When the doctors examined her larynx before beginning the operation, they found that the nodules had disappeared.

The following story is typical of what we have come to see as the ordinary working together of medicine and prayer in God's providence:

> I underwent surgery on March 13, 1972. A week later, on the 20th, I was told that barium sulfate was leaking at the juncture of the parts of the colon that had been sewn together. If mother nature did not heal it within two or three days, a temporary colostomy would be required which, in effect, meant two more

271

surgical operations. The next evening, Francis stopped to see me. After a quiet visit of about twenty minutes we prayed together for about ten minutes. Later, shortly after 1 a.m., I felt that Francis's request that "all channels be open" had been heard and I was certain that I would be all right. About 7 a.m. the surgeon told me that I was doing wonderfully well and that he was going to change my diet from liquid to a regular diet. (He skipped a few in-between kinds of diet.)

There was no further talk of surgery. Before being dismissed, I asked one of the surgical residents how they knew I was all right. He said, "Your temperature suddenly dropped to normal. Your white count also suddenly dropped to normal. You remember we also took another X-ray which showed that the barium had been cleaned out of your system." How that barium, seen in an earlier X-ray, got back into the colon and out of my system is still a mystery to me. I praise and thank the Lord for this healing.

To set up any opposition between prayer for healing and medicine is contrary to common sense. Sometimes God cures directly through prayer; at other times through nature, assisted by doctors who have learned how the body can be assisted to throw off the sickness that oppresses it. As Paul Tournier put it:

Sometimes what happens is that a patient's relatives refuse, for religious reasons, to entrust him to technical medical care, claiming that if he is converted he will be healed without such treatment. It can only harm a patient to realize that instead of being properly treated, his sufferings are being made use of as a means of bringing him forcibly to accept the doctrines that someone wishes to impose upon him. Nothing is more surely calculated to turn him away from the faith....

We have something better to do than to enter into controversies between partisans of religion and those of science. To do so is to perpetuate the awful habit of thinking of faith as being opposed to technology.

People are suffering. Medicine is a very difficult art. There are not too many of us persons of good will to work together to heal the sick.[1]

To some readers this may all seem obvious. Yet it does need to be said, because a few Christians pray for patients and then, as a general rule, tell them to stop taking their medicine and to disregard their symptoms. If an individual person has a genuine inspiration from God to do this, fine, but if this disregard for ordinary channels of healing is set up as a general faith principle I cannot imagine its doing more than sowing confusion and self-condemnation in the patients not cured, and opposition to healing prayer on the part of the medical profession.

Since the Lord often teaches us through experience, one incident stands out especially as teaching me about the interrelation of prayer and medical care. It happened in Houston where I was visiting the home of my good friends, Harry and Ruth. At dinner I shared with their family what I had been learning about the healing ministry. At the end of the evening, as I was about to leave they asked me if I would pray for their son, Randy, who was suffering a great deal from attacks of asthma. So before I left we gathered the whole family around Randy and prayed for him that the Lord would cure him of his asthma.

The next day I left Houston; it was a whole year before I was again in Houston and had a chance to visit Harry and

Ruth. I had forgotten all about Randy, but while we were at dinner Harry asked if he had ever written to tell me what had happened. Then the entire family began laughing—which I didn't understand.

They explained what happened: When I had left, after praying, Randy went through the worst asthma attack of his entire life. In fact, the attack was so severe that they had to make an emergency phone call to a doctor who lived down the street from them. This doctor, who was not Randy's regular doctor, came right over and gave him some medication to quiet the attack until morning. Then they took Randy over to their neighbor's office in the morning, where they ran him through some tests and came up with a new diagnosis. This diagnosis, in turn, resulted in different treatment which effectively took care of his asthma.

The prayer, then, had been answered in a way helpful to my humility: Randy got worse. But the prayer was answered nonetheless: His getting worse resulted in his getting another doctor, whom they wouldn't otherwise have consulted, who in turn discovered the correct diagnosis which eventually worked the cure. It was as if the effect of our prayer was to find the right doctor through whom God wanted to cure Randy.

Prayer and Psychiatry

A similar relationship should exist between prayer for inner healing and counseling, psychology and psychiatry. I think it is probably true to say that psychiatry is stronger in its analysis of problems than it is in cures. But what we know through the study of psychology can be a great help in knowing precisely *what to pray for*.

Of course, God can move beyond human knowledge and help people know what to pray for through the gift of discernment. Nevertheless, I have ordinarily found that the knowledge born of study and experience—knowing what the danger signs are—can be a great help in prayer. Just as we cannot give up ordinary study in other areas of life, so we cannot expect to be used for a ministry of inner healing if we do not cooperate by learning what we can of the workings of the human mind.

Yet here again I find that some persons who pray for healing display a fear of psychology; they often treat it as unnecessary, if not actually dangerous. Perhaps the fear of Freud and other psychological innovators who have, on occasion, attacked traditional Christian morality, has made Christians fear their genuine discoveries. At any rate, I have frequently found an antipathy toward the study of psychology among Christians who practice a ministry of healing or deliverance (exorcism).

This attitude, which would scrap psychology as useless if not harmful, is typified by such statements as these:

> To put the issue simply: the scriptures plainly speak of both organically based problems as well as those problems that stem from sinful attitudes and behavior; but where in all of God's Word is there so much as a trace of any third source of problems which might approximate the modern concept of "mental illness"? Clearly the burden of proof lies with those who loudly affirm the existence of mental illness or disease but fail to demonstrate biblically that it exists.[2]
>
> Rogerianism, therefore, must be rejected *in toto*. Every remnant of this humanistic system exalting man as autonomous must be eradicated.[3]
>
> Depressed persons whose symptoms fail to show any sign of a biochemical root should be counseled on the assumption that they are depressed by guilt.[4]

Such a completely condemnatory attitude toward the knowledge discovered by psychology is based upon a biblicism that holds that there is nothing worthwhile discovered about the human personality which is not already in the Bible. The answer is again, I suggest, that we must learn to distinguish, as do Karl Stern (*The Third Revolution*) and Paul Tournier (*The Person Reborn*) between the true discoveries of psychology and those which are contrary to Christianity.

The basic discoveries of psychology help us to understand people's problems and often suggest how to cope with them. The gospel indicates how we can bring God's healing power to bear upon these problems. Psychology helps to bring problems to light for what they are; then once they are brought to light, we can use God's healing power to cure them.

Those of us who pray for inner healing should know something about the intricacies of the human mind if we are going to help the people we pray for. If we don't know, for instance, how crucial the time of our childhood is—especially the time between eight and eighteen months—we are not likely to consider the time of childhood seriously when we counsel with a person who wants to pray about some chronic emotional problem.

Paul Tournier was a wonderful example of a practicing psychiatrist who believed in the primacy of grace and prayer. For those interested in investigating the relationship between psychology and healing I highly recommend Dr. Tournier's book, *The Person Reborn*, in which he gives examples of the need for science and faith to work together:

> A young student comes to see me in the throes of a psychological crisis. He has lost interest in everything, is becoming unsociable and finds it impossible to concentrate on his work. We use technical

methods in order to throw light on the situation. They reveal a crisis of retarded adolescence in a young man who has remained morally dependent upon his parents.

But he is soon telling me that he is conscious that in reality he is going through a religious crisis behind the screen of his psychological crisis. The reason why he has been unable to detach himself from his parents is that he had no strength of personality, and he feels the emptiness of an impersonal religious attitude, which he had inherited from his family tradition....A case such as this seems to me to illustrate clearly the necessary relationship between the technique of psychology and the cure of souls. Everybody has complexes, and comes to some sort of terms with them.

When they begin to cause real suffering, this is because they are standing in the way of the realization of a person's profoundest aspirations. Such aspirations are always religious in kind—taking the word in a nonformal sense. Technical means must then be used to break up these complexes....

Technology of itself is negative. "Psychoanalysis," says a letter from a patient who herself has undergone it, "reveals evil, with its hundred faces and its thousand tricks. But where is good?"...I do not think that analysts will contradict me if I maintain that, strictly speaking, no problem is ever resolved. We bring them out into the daylight in order to be honest about them....A repressed tendency poisons the mind and disturbs its functioning. On the other hand, the always humbling process of bringing it out into the light opens the door to a real experience of God's grace, even if no word of religion has been uttered by doctor or patient.

People come to me for my help in "solving" their problems. No one knows better than I do that all human effort is powerless to solve any problem. In fact, when I try to understand their difficulties, I discover nothing but insoluble vicious circles. Faith is needed to experience God's grace, and God's grace is needed in order to find faith....

Our patients often tell us how unjustly hurt they feel when they are plied with exhortations and advice: "You only have to believe. All you need is willpower. Just love others and forget yourself. It's only a matter of confidence." Psychology cures us of this oversimplified view of personal problems. It shows us that they are tenacious and terribly complicated.[5]

And these same people who, from the security of their faith and health, are so free with their "all you need is..." (which always means: "all you need is to do as I do") would soon discover, if they themselves were assailed by doubt and depression, that things are not so simple....

I believe that problems can be dissolved by grace, like a mist is dissipated by the sunshine....In the climate of faith, a life that has seemed to be nothing but a tangle of problems looks quite different. The problems disappear without anyone actually solving them. This process of dissolution is all the more definite if one does not try to find human solutions, but relies rather upon God's grace....

This is the way that, in my experience, technology and faith work together. Psychoanalysis explores the problems in order to bring them out into the daylight. Grace dissolves them without our ever knowing exactly how.[6]

In an earlier chapter we have shown how, through prayer for inner healing, God's love can be brought to bear upon our problems to heal them. The arts of medicine, counseling and psychiatry are ordinary ways in which God can work to create wholeness in broken human beings through freeing the forces of nature (which God also has created) to move toward health. Unless there is some obstacle, nature (our body, mind, emotions) always moves toward health; the doctor or counselor works to uncover these obstacles whether they be a virus or a painful past, in order that the patient might grow toward that same health for which we pray.

The ideal situation is when doctors, counselors and psychiatrists pray for their patients asking God to do what they cannot do, as well as to guide their diagnosis, their counsel and their skills in areas where they do have human competence. But even where they do have competence God can perform healings that medical science might be able to provide; He may do them more speedily, with no expense, and without the tearing and destruction to the human body that medication or a surgical operation often wreaks.

Sometimes God works through nature and the skill of doctors; sometimes He works directly through prayer, and sometimes through both. But always there should be cooperation, mutual respect and an admiration for the variety of ways in which God manifests His glory.

20 | Anointing Of the Sick

They went out and preached that people should repent. They drove out many demons and *anointed* many sick people *with oil* and healed them" (Mark 6:12,13, italics added).

This passage, along with James 5:14-16, shows the connection that early Christians saw between healing and anointing. Consequently, we too need to understand how anointing can be helpful in our healing ministry today.

One helpful fact I would like to pass along to you is my discovery that anointing with oil was a basic medical treatment for wounds in the time of Jesus. Medicine, as we know, was then in a very primitive state; so anointing with oil was, as it were, the first-century combination of prayer and medicine.

The Good Samaritan, for instance, is a good example of medical treatment in the time of Jesus.

> But a Samaritan, as he traveled, came where the man was; and when he saw him, he took pity on him. He went to him and bandaged his wounds, pouring on oil and wine (Luke 10:33,34a).

Realizing this first-century understanding of anointing, which we in the twentieth century might not realize at all if someone didn't tell us, I started reflecting on how the root meaning of anointing might influence our healing ministry in today's world.

I think this understanding means first of all that we should pray over any medications that we ourselves use or administer to others. I know one Christian nurse, for instance, who prays every morning over the medicines she is to dispense in her hospital ward. She asks the Lord to use these medicines as channels for His healing power; in addition, she asks Him to prevent any harmful side effects and to guard the patient from any effect other than the beneficial effect intended by the doctor.

As we know, most medicines have some harmful side effects, some of them serious. Yet through prayer we have seen patients on chemotherapy who have experienced none of the expected side effects: Their hair didn't fall out; their appetite didn't disappear; their energy level didn't dwindle. This kind of prayer, I believe, is today's extended meaning of the first-century custom of anointing with oil.

But anointing with oil—especially if it has been blessed— seems also to have its own effect and to be very helpful in ministering healing. Something like the handkerchiefs and aprons that touched Paul (Acts 19:12), oil fits into the category of objects that have somehow been touched by God through His servants in such a way that they emanate the healing presence of God. For me, one sign of this has been that when I have, upon occasion, anointed with oil people who needed deliverance, they have recoiled as if they had been touched with a red-hot poker. The demonic forces in them could not stand the presence of God brought so close to them: "What do you want with us, Jesus of Nazareth? Have you come to destroy us?" (Mark 1:24a).

History of Anointing

The history of anointing and of praying for healing is fascinating.[1] For the first three centuries of Christianity Christians had a lively belief in prayer for healing. Then in the third and fourth centuries this belief diminished.

This decline was hastened when Jerome translated the Bible into Latin (c. 400 A.D.) and somewhat obscured the celebrated passage about anointing in the epistle of James. The New International Version (and other contemporary versions) translate this passage with the following emphasis on healing:

> Is anyone of you sick? He should call the elders of the church to pray over him and anoint him with oil in the name of the Lord. And the prayer offered in faith will make the sick person well; the Lord will raise him up. If he has sinned, he will be forgiven. Therefore confess your sins to each other and pray for each other so that you may be healed. The prayer of a righteous man is powerful and effective (James 5:14-16).

Unfortunately, Jerome used the Latin word for "save" where we have the translation of "heal" or "raise up." The emphasis then came down upon saving your soul rather than healing your body. Since Jerome's translation (the Vulgate) was the only official translation allowed in the Catholic Church, the focus on anointing the sick was on the spiritual benefits, while bodily healing came increasingly to be regarded as of secondary importance.

Yet anointing with oil, even by lay people, continued to be seen as a help in healing of the body as well as the soul. For instance, in the fifth century, the oil for anointing was blessed by the bishop. Then the oil was taken home by the people and kept in their equivalent of our medicine cabinet, to be taken out and used whenever anyone in the house fell sick. In those days there were two kinds of anointing: one performed by the sick person, or by relatives or friends; the other performed by the bishop or a priest.

The prayer used in blessing the oil asks God to give it a curative power so that it becomes a means of removing every sickness and disease for the soundness of soul, body and spirit, and for perfect well-being (*The Euchologian* of Serapion, d. after 362 A.D.). In those days it was still clear that anointing with oil was intended for healing and could be administered by ordinary people.

Then, in the Carolingian reform (c. 815 A.D.) in the Frankish Kingdom, anointing by lay people was suppressed, as part of a movement aimed at renewing and bolstering up the ministry of priests. More regulations (whose purpose was to stamp out abuses) resulted in connecting anointing with deathbed penance. Gradually, anointing came to mean the "last rites" (extreme unction) and its purpose was seen primarily as a preparation for the soul to meet God. By the end of the thirteenth century the most influential theologians had come to teach that a sick person could only be anointed when death was imminent and recovery was despaired of.[2] In the Catholic Church anointing of the sick came to be regarded as one of the seven sacraments.

The Protestant Reformation did little to renew the practice of praying for healing or anointing the sick (although some individuals like Martin Luther came to experience the value of praying for healing upon occasion). In the Catholic Church anointing of the sick continued to be seen as having a spiritual effect and, upon occasion, it could lead to physical healing.

Then, with the Pentecostal awakening at the beginning of the twentieth century and the charismatic renewal beginning in the fifties and sixties—along with the rediscovery of the full dimensions of the gifts of the Spirit—came a dramatic rediscovery of the healing ministry and the value of anointing with oil. In this same century the Roman Catholic Church began to return to its roots in the Bible and, as a result, there were many reforms, especially promoted in the Second Vatican Council. One of these reforms was the renewal of anointing of the sick (which went into effect on January 1, 1974) in which *healing* is once again emphasized as its purpose—healing on all levels, bodily as well as spiritual.[3]

In the mainline Protestant churches came also a rediscovery of the healing ministry and the value of anointing the sick, through such groups as the Order of St. Luke. Consequently, we are seeing a remarkable renewal of the healing ministry in most of the main Christian groups. Anointing of the sick with oil is part of this extraordinary explosion in which ordinary people are finding a renewed ministry, centered on the baptism of the Spirit and an understanding of the priesthood of all believers.

A danger always exists that people will take a kind of magical view of something like anointing. For example, I have met some people who don't seem to feel comfortable praying for the sick unless they have oil. I think we always need to realize that, while anointing with oil is helpful, it is not necessary in order that healing take place. Personally, I try to listen to the inspiration of the Spirit as to whether or not I use oil.

21 | Questions Most Often Asked

People at workshops frequently ask a number of questions that don't exactly fit under any of the topics covered so far. In the practical order some of them are important, so I will do my best to answer them.

How do I tell if I have the gift of healing?

This is a delicate question, one that I don't feel comfortable in answering—just as I experience a mixed reaction when someone says, "I have heard you are a healer."

In the first place, it centers too much on the person. It sounds as if I can say I *have* something that I can control, that I can turn on and off at will.

What I can do is to pray—that I can decide to do. But whether or not the person is healed depends on God, not on my own powers. This is not magic or superstition. I don't change God's mind by prayer, but cooperate with God's plan for us (which includes my prayer); His plan is always basically directed toward life and health.

In a given instance, because of some obstacle or because of some higher positive purpose, healing may not take place. Healing, then, is more like my having a potential to be used by God than it is a gift[1] which is under my power. The gift is not for the minister of healing, but for the sick person—

the one who actually receives the gift of health.

I believe that every Christian has the potential for being used in healing. Christ is the one who does the healing and since He, the Father and the Spirit reside within each Christian They will, upon occasion, work through the prayers of any Christian: "Everything is possible for him who believes," said Jesus (Mark 9:23b). We are all encouraged to pray for healing. In particular, we have a special responsibility to pray for those who are close to us in any way: Parents are used by God to pray for their children, husbands and wives for each other. Friends, too, have a special bond of love God uses for healing when they pray for one another. Ministers, because of their position as leaders and counselors of the Christian community, have a special gift of healing connected with their ministry.

Nevertheless, some persons seem specially gifted in the area of healing and develop a *ministry* of healing when others in the community recognize this gift. Paul says that *some* are given the gifts of healing (1 Cor. 12:9), so it is clear that others are not given this gift—at least to this extent. In context Paul is speaking about special ministry gifts given for the sake of the community. Clearly, that kind of remarkable gift is only given to some persons, but I believe every church and prayer group should have some persons who are recognized by the group as having more healing ministry than others.

When people ask how to tell if they have the gift of healing, this special ministry gift is what I presume they are asking about. The only real test that I know is *if people are healed* when they pray. The ones who will be the first to know are the other members of the local community, so it is not the kind of thing a person needs to worry about.

The gift of healing—like love—admits of more and less. It's not so much a question of having it or not having it. It's not that simple. Any gift of healing allows for growth; most of us have it to some extent, and so it is hoped we can grow in that gift. There need be no hurry to prove that we have the gift.

My experience leads me to believe that anyone who has an extraordinary gift in this area is spotted very quickly by other persons. Very soon he or she will have to try to hide—as our Lord did—rather than to wonder whether or not he or she has the gift. If you have a real gift of healing as a ministry there will soon be no doubt about it. Those who are not sure had best wait and just continue to grow.

Some persons seem overanxious to find out if they have the gift of healing. Perhaps their motivation is not altogether pure; along with a laudable desire to help others, they may also have an excessive need to be needed. Such persons somehow manage to make their appearance at most prayer groups and there announce, in one way or another, that they have a ministry of healing. They may attend one of our workshops on healing and then feel they have been certified in some way. If anyone at the meeting seems to be ailing, this person proceeds to take over and lead the prayers or takes the person aside in order to minister privately. They are persons who think they have a ministry, and they are anxiously looking for someone to minister to.

No one feels comfortable in such a situation. Things are turned around. Maybe the person is helpful to some people and so you hate to discourage him. I find that people with problems know intuitively to whom they should go, with whom they should pray. Ordinarily the sick should be free to seek out the minister of healing—just as in the natural order they phone the physician of their choice. The reverse, a doctor looking for patients, is a sign that something is wrong. If a doctor is successful, he or she doesn't have to go around looking for work

Sometimes the pressure to be recognized is subtle; the person wants a special ministry of healing to be set up by the prayer community so that people can only come through certain channels to him. At times, of course, a prayer group needs to recognize and establish a team for ministry—to protect persons in the group from poor teaching and from people who think they have a ministry but who do more harm than good. In general, though, people will eventually surface in a prayer group or community who have a genuine ministry. Most of the community will recognize who they are; they won't have to push themselves forward. If time is made available for those people who wish to consult and pray with them, freedom will be preserved. The harm is caused by people who need to feel important, who need to minister more for their own sake than for that of the sick.

For all these reasons, I feel somewhat uncomfortable when people ask how they can tell if they have the gift of healing. If people are healed through their ministry, the community—the sick in particular—would be the first to recognize that gift.

Most of us can just pray for the sick when the natural opportunities present themselves. In this way that gift of healing we all have as Christians will have the chance to grow and increase as we gradually grow in faith, love and wisdom, the deep foundation of healing power.

Are there physical phenomena that accompany the healing gift?

Yes, there are. And sometimes these can be a help, but they are only indications and effects and not the gift of healing itself. The gift is only clearly manifested when someone is actually healed.

Agnes Sanford used to experience various sensations when praying for healing while her husband did not. Yet persons were healed through his ministry as well as through hers.

Some of these phenomena include:

1) *Heat*. This is the most common of all physical phenomena connected with healing. Often it centers upon the affected organ and sometimes remains as an indication that the body is being healed long after the prayer is over.

2) A gentle *trembling of power*. Some people feel their hands shake as a kind of current of power moves through them. This trembling lasts as long as the healing prayer continues.

3) Something like an electric current or a filling of power, but *without the trembling*.

These sensations can be helpful. Some persons, for instance, who experience the trembling have learned to pray as long as the power seems to be there and to stop praying when the sensation stops. This time varies, sometimes lingering for awhile, as if it were a cobalt radiation treatment. At other times, it is brief.

Other persons who have learned to associate healing with heat or a sensation of some kind of current in the hands believe that this helps them know when to pray and when not to pray. If they feel this sensation, for instance, during a prayer meeting they know through experience that someone in the group needs healing and can receive it.

Those with a ministry of healing need not seek after such phenomena. Yet I find that these various sensations are frequently experienced without their being sought. When persons receive such manifestations they need not be surprised or take pride in them but should simply regard them in a matter-of-fact way. They should see if they can find any factors that give these manifestations some kind of practical meaning.

Do they, for example, help us to know when to pray? Do they help to build up our confidence that God can use our prayers for healing? The emphasis should not be upon these phenomena in themselves but upon any significance they may have. They should neither be feared nor scorned—nor should they be overprized. They can be a great help in assisting us to understand our own healing ministry.

On the other hand, I know some friends who experience a slight trembling when they pray for healing and who believe that this is simply a weakness of the human body which is not yet accustomed to the power of God. They incline to the opinion that for those who are more accustomed to the presence of God these physical phenomena are almost nonperceptible.

Is it best to pray for healing in community?

At times there are advantages to praying in community; at other times it is best to seek individual prayer. No one answer will suit every individual or every occasion.

Individuals with a ministry of healing include some who have special gifts of discernment that help in difficult cases. But there is a power in group prayer: "For where two or three come together" (Matt. 18:20). In general I think we can say:

1) In praying for *physical healing* it helps to pray in community.

2) In praying for *inner healing* and for *deliverance*, it is usually best to provide for prayer with a small team or, occasionally, one-on-one. Christian counselors, for instance, will often be in situations where they will pray one-on-one in their office. The kind of confidence that is often shared, the revelation of deep hurts, requires the greatest respect for privacy.

A small *team* is useful: 1) to make use of the special gifts, such as discernment, that are given to different individuals; 2) to have a man and woman praying together for a healing of past hurts; and 3) to avoid any kind of compromising situation that might develop in a one-on-one situation.

In praying for physical healing, why not combine the advantages of both group and individual prayer, by having persons *with the gift of healing lead the entire group in praying* for the sick?

What about praying at a distance?

Distance seems to be little of a problem when praying for *physical* sickness. I have heard of many instances when, at the very time a group prayed for someone in a distant hospital, the sick person experienced the presence of Christ and was healed.

In praying for *conversion* and *inner healing* of any sort (or *a fortiori*, *deliverance*), where the person's own active part in the healing is important, it is usually helpful for the person to be present. Prayer is not magic and God does not bypass the person's own part in the healing if it is needed— as it is in inner healing. Ordinarily, if a person comes up and asks for prayer (for instance, for a relative suffering from emotional problems), I usually suggest that it would be better to have the sick person, if he or she really wants help, to come and ask for prayer. Yet there are exceptions.

I know of conversion and inner healing being occasioned through distant prayer (with the suffering person's subsequent inner cooperation). In the Gospels we read about the Canaanite woman who came pleading for her daughter to be freed from the torment of evil spirits—and the daughter was freed from the moment that Jesus prayed (Matt. 15:21-28). In November 1972, I prayed with Pastor Jose Fajardo and his wife at a retreat in Bogota, Colombia, for the conversion of his son, who at the time was at home in the city of Cali. At that precise time, about 1:00 a.m., his son was awakened from sleep and underwent a tremendous conversion experience in which he committed his life to Christ and came off drugs—without any apparent external influence (but still with the cooperation of his own will).

Are other gifts involved with healing?

Among those gifts mentioned by Paul in 1 Corinthians 12,

the following have a clear connection with healing: the discerning of spirits, the gift of faith, the word of knowledge and the working of miracles. Although the purpose of each of these gifts is not altogether clear, there seems to be a common consensus among ministers of healing that the gifts have these uses:

1) The *discerning of spirits* enables us to ascertain whether healing is needed, or a deliverance—and what kind of deliverance.

2) The *gift of faith*, as was said earlier, enables us to know whether or not the sick person is to experience healing at this particular time. It also imparts the confidence needed to act upon that knowledge and to pray the prayer of faith.

3) The *word of knowledge* enables us to discern the roots, the causes of sickness for which we should pray, even when sometimes the person himself doesn't understand fully what is wrong. This gift is especially helpful with inner healing or when physical sickness is somehow hooked up with a deeper wound.

4) The *gift of miracles*[2] differs, I believe, from the gift of healing in that it actually creates something that is missing, while healing hastens or changes what would ordinarily be accomplished by the healing process of nature.

All these gifts clearly are a great help working toward the full and perfect working of the gift of healing. The gifts of healing and miracles have to do with God's *love and power* in curing sickness, while the gifts of discernment, knowledge and faith enable us *to know* when and how to minister God's healing love.

Can you pray more than once for healing?

For some reason many people who believe in healing also believe that they can only pray once; to pray again indicates to them that they lack faith in their first prayer. Some evangelists apparently give this kind of advice, too. So far as I can judge this kind of absolutism goes contrary to the clear teaching of our Lord in the parables of the importunate friend (Luke 11:5-8) and the importunate widow (Luke 18:1-8). "I tell you, though he will not get up and give him the bread because he is his friend, yet because of the man's persistence he will get up and give him as much as he needs. So I say to you: Ask and it will be given to you" (Luke 11:8,9a).

Nevertheless, there are those times when a person prays once and then seems called upon to accept the fact that he or she has been healed. But to raise any one factor here to the status of an absolute—"We can only pray once and then we must claim healing"—is to create a new legalism and to make an idol out of a method. Each person should pray and then make a decision as to how best God wants him or her to pray: once or several times or many times.

Praying for chronic ailments of long standing, for example, is usually a matter of continuing prayer over a long period of time. Ordinarily (again, not always) ailments such as arthritis are gradually healed. When parents ask prayer for a mentally retarded child, I teach them how to pray every day, with the whole family, for the child. What usually seems to happen is that the child improves gradually—and much faster than the medical prognosis would call for. For long-term, deep-seated ailments a kind of "soaking prayer," repeated often, seems to bring the best results.[3]

What about leg-lengthening?

For those who have never seen this kind of prayer—and for some who have seen it—"leg-lengthening" may sound somewhat bizarre. It simply means that the patient, suffering from some such ailment as a lower back injury, sits in a chair and then holds his legs out in front of him, where their length can be compared by putting one heel against the other. Since most people have an imbalance in leg length, some difference usually shows up. The group gathers around and prays while one or more persons hold the feet, watching one leg move out until it is the same length as the other.

To many people the whole process seems ridiculous, something like a sideshow. Friends of mine, whom I respect highly and who have a genuine ministry of healing, want to have nothing to do with this practice, which they feel lends a circus atmosphere to prayer groups. They feel it leads people to seek after the spectacular, instead of keeping their mind on God.

Since I have tried to remain open to whatever is genuine, no matter how unpromising it seems at first, I have to admit that my own experience (as does that of so serious a minded person as Derek Prince) convinces me that it is a valid way of praying. I have seen extraordinary healings take place, especially of back problems, through praying in this way.

To put this peculiar ministry in focus several things need to be said:

Actually, "leg-lengthening" is a misnomer. If anything is wrong with the alignment of the spine or hips, it affects the alignment of the legs. What goes on is not really a lengthening of the legs; the change in length is more likely caused by changes going on in the spine or hips.

As any doctor will tell us, measuring leg length accurately requires more than the kind of rough measurement that goes on with this "leg-lengthening" prayer. To claim an accuracy that does not exist only holds this kind of prayer up to medical ridicule.

Nevertheless, rough measurements or not, misnomer or not, something seems to happen almost every time we pray for someone with a spinal or hip problem. This particular method helps, too, in that the people in the prayer group can actually *see* something happen as an effect of the healing that is going on. Remarkably, the persons prayed for usually report that they actually feel a shifting and a healing in the spine as if things were moving into place.

A dramatic instance of prayer of this sort that I experienced was in praying for a man who had been diagnosed at Mayo Clinic as suffering from a deterioration of the hip that would eventually require an operation to install an artificial hip socket. When we measured his legs there was a big difference—about three inches. As we prayed, in the course of five minutes, the shorter leg gradually extended until both legs seemed the same length. He then stood up and for the first time in two years was able to walk using his heel. The following morning he told us that he had been able to sleep on his back for the first time in six years and that he was now able to walk without a limp.

Exactly why this kind of prayer seems to work so well, I don't understand. All I know is that it serves as a powerful visual help for people who are skeptical about the healing ministry and that—at least in my estimate—about ninety percent of the people I have seen prayed for in this way for back ailments seem to be cured or notably improved.

How do you know this isn't just suggestion?

Some of it may be. God works in many ways through the various facets of His creation. But as far as I am concerned, the great mass of evidence points in the direction of a power far greater than unaided human powers.

What do you make of psychic healers?

I believe that, in general, three forces can be at work in healing:

First, there is the *divine power* of healing. "Ask for anything in my name and you will receive it" (see John 16:23,24).

Then there seems to be a *natural force* of healing, based on love, which is given to some people. Various experiments are presently being conducted regarding this phenomenon. Some evidence, shown through special photography, suggests that people with a strong life energy are able to transmit some of this to other people through the laying on of hands. If this is shown to be true, I see no reason to fear it any more than any other natural force that we discover, for it ultimately reflects glory to God, its creator.

For example, Dr. James Lynch in *The Broken Heart*[4] shows the effect that love and touch have in reducing the danger of heart disease. In one diagram[5] he shows the dramatic difference a nurse can have in stabilizing and decreasing a comatose patient's heart rate simply by holding the patient's hand. The whole point of Dr. Lynch's book is that loneliness can increase the risk of heart disease, while the effect of human love and companionship tends toward the healing of heart problems.

Last, I believe that there are *demonic forces* which can work toward healing anything they themselves have inflicted. Satanic covens and witch doctors work with this kind of healing force. To seek healing from anyone whose powers are connected with the demonic is ultimately to invite far greater evils, even if a cure should take place in some subsidiary area of a person's life. Discernment sometimes needs to be exercised as to the source of the healing power. If the power is not of God, directly or indirectly, we should stay away from it, no matter what the claims of the healer, nor how great the need for healing may be.

In regard to this matter, Agnes Sanford learned through experience not to pray for anyone who has been involved in spiritualism. At one time she had prayed for four people in a short period of time—each of whom had been involved in spiritualism. Not only were they not cured, but death struck each one's family a short time after the prayer.

Four times in a row! That was enough for me. Whatever the explanation of this phenomenon might be, I was evidently not a good person to pray with for anyone involved in spiritualism. This troubled me greatly, for there were times when with all my determination I could not help it. I might find myself involved with a group and find out later that there was a spiritualist among us. The results were not so drastic in a group, the mind of the group overshadowing and to some extent protecting the participants. But even when thus shielded, I have known undesirable aftereffects of praying in such a group, and as far as I know, no healings have resulted....

The reader may bring forth all kinds of reason as to why this ought not to be. But, praise God, this book is not a series of lectures but is merely an autobiography, and I do not have to argue about the reasons! I am merely stating facts.

However, I myself greatly desired to understand and, if possible, to be set free from this hampering restriction concerning those for whom I might pray.

Therefore, when a chance came to me, I consulted a woman whom I consider a final authority upon all matters of the occult; her innate wisdom and acquired knowledge are great and so is her real devotion to Jesus Christ.

"What can I do to prevent these things from happening?" I asked her.

She replied, "You can do nothing except to abstain.

"You may meet socially with these people interested in spiritualism, but you must not pray for them. This is for their own protection."

"Why?"

"Because they do actually conduct a current of supernatural power from the lower regions, and you happen to conduct a particularly pure current of supernatural power directly from heaven. Now these two currents are inimical. They cannot mix together, as direct-current electricity cannot mix with alternating current. One must choose one or the other. When you do mix the two, there comes an explosion of a destructive nature. You are surrounded with protection, and it cannot touch you, so it rebounds upon the other person...."

"But many good people are involved in spiritualism!" you may cry.

Yes, it horrifies me to go to Christian conferences and see books about Edgar Cayce, and other spiritualistic literature, for sale along with my books. They do not belong together. This confusion between the power of the Holy Spirit and the danger of spiritualism is the greatest menace to the Christian church today. It is our duty to combat it however we can.[6]

Regardless of whether you can accept her friend's theory about why the problem exists, there is a serious problem here and a Christian has no business confusing Christian healing with any healing coming from spiritualistic sources. On the other hand, I find some Christians too ready to condemn any form of healing that is not explicitly Christian but which might be a natural power—putting it on a par with witchcraft. I think the wisest course is for us to learn to experience the beauty and power of Christian healing, to *abstain* from, while not condemning, any forms of healing prayers that are not Christian, while clearly *warning* people to stay away from any healing connected with spiritualism or witchcraft.

Healing and the Incarnation

by Tommy Tyson

These words are taken from a talk given at a healing seminar in February 1973, in Mexico City, at San José del Altillo. Tommy Tyson is a Methodist evangelist from North Carolina who has traveled extensively giving retreats. The following is a rendition I transcribed and edited from a tape recording of his talk.

The ministry of healing means that we take the Incarnation seriously. The Incarnation means that God is here. Not only is God with humanity, but God has become human.

Jesus is God, as it were, coming down; it is not a humanitarian reach for heaven. A humanitarian understanding leaves you with a psychological approach to healing. Your ministry will be a diagnostician's approach; you will be problem- and symptom-centered. The Incarnation is not humanity reaching up, but God becoming human and perfecting within Himself that which concerns humanity. It is simply Jesus being Himself.

This is what I understand about healing! We are not ministering salve to sores; we are ministering love to suffering people. It is *Jesus Christ living within us*, who has perfected our humanity, who is ministering to suffering people. He is not simply a spiritual being, but He has become flesh. He is now spirit and body: this is the Incarnation. Jesus does not reveal a compartmentalized life. Rather, He reveals the marriage of opposites, with spirit and matter becoming one. God and humanity becoming one—heaven and earth becoming one. Heaven coming to earth, and earth being caught up into heaven. In this way we have the supernatural made manifest through the natural, and the natural lifted up to the level of the supernatural. That's what we are talking about when we talk about healing.

This means that all methods are ours. For instance, we use natural methods: We build hospitals, we train doctors and we train nurses—all in God's image. Yet we believe in the supernatural. So we pray, and the natural and the supernatural come together. It is not either/or; it is both/and. All things are ours, for God has married all these elements in Jesus. As one of the early church fathers put it, "Jesus became what we were that we might become what He is."

Our Father now shares with us what He has achieved in Jesus Christ, and this achievement includes the redeeming of humanity—a new kind of humanity. Jesus comes into the all of us, becomes mind of our mind, becomes spirit of our spirit, becomes bone of our bone and flesh of our flesh. God's purpose is to conform us to the image of Jesus Christ; God intends for us to be like Jesus—not in the abstract, but in the concrete here and now. He accomplishes this by the power of His Spirit working within us.

This is what we are talking about when we are talking about healing: We are talking about being conformed to the image of Jesus. That's wonderful, isn't it? Jesus ministers to us from the realm of the resurrection and shares with us His own achievements. There are limitless ways in which He accomplishes this.

Nevertheless, some specific issues are involved. For example, Jesus Christ reveals Himself, sharing our humanity, for our instruction, in several basic ways. Most important of all, He accepts Himself in terms of His union with the Father. He never tries to minister what He has not worked out within Himself. He does not heal in order to prove that He is the Christ; He heals *because He is* the Christ. His healing power comes from His very being.

That reverses the usual order. In the natural order we are judged by what we do: This man is a minister, this one an attorney and this one a banker. But in the kingdom of the Father our doing comes out of our being. Jesus Christ manifests Himself from within.

For instance, here comes the man with the withered arm. Jesus Christ does not begin by diagnosing the cause of the man's problem, but He goes within Himself to His Father. Through His union with the Father He sees the creative power of God: He sees this man *as whole* before God. And from that inner level of union with the Father He speaks, "Stretch forth thy hand."

The same thing with Peter. His name is Simon, which means "a reed"—a reed blown about by every wind. At Caesarea Philippi, Jesus asked His disciples, "Who do men say that I am?"

"Some say you are Elijah, some say you are John the Baptist, some say you are another great prophet." Then Jesus looks at His disciples and says, "Who do you say that I am?" And Simon says, "Thou art the Christ, the Son of the living God."

Jesus says (I'm going to paraphrase at this point), "You did not discover this by natural means, but you have been before my Father, and my Father revealed to you who I am. Now, Simon Peter, I've been before the Father about you. So while those around call you a reed, I see you before the Father's throne, and I see a rock. You're not a reed; you're a rock" (see Matt. 16:13-20).

Who told Jesus that? How did He know it? It was revelation

303

that came from His union with His Father; in that union He saw Peter as the rock on which the church was to be built. That is the way the healing ministry of Jesus works—yesterday, today and forever: He sees people before the Father. He manifests outwardly what He sees by the Spirit. That is glorious!

You really glimpse the glory of God when you see the heart of Jesus. He looks at people and He sees them not as trees, not as goats, but as sheep without a shepherd. That is glorious—isn't it?—that before the Father people are sheep. That is healing.

How do you see people? How do you see people in your heart? That is the very key to your healing ministry. How do you see *yourself* before the Father? Do you let Jesus Christ establish in your heart who you are in the light of His love?

This is what the Holy Spirit does. He shows us who we are separated from God, and then He shows us who we are in relationship to God. Then we simply make that exchange; that is what repentance is all about. We come to repentance because of a conviction of our sin.

We are saying, "Apart from God, this is what I am. I neglect my husband; I get mad at my children; I ignore my church. Apart from God I am all these things and more."

The minister says, "You are right: and the truth is you are a lot worse. But where sin did abound, grace does much more abound. And so, here is who you are before God. And here is how you go about appropriating that grace." These ways of appropriating grace are simply a bridge to where people ought to be in Jesus.

That is healing. That is what repentance is supposed to do for people: It gives them a bridge to move from where they are to where they ought to be in Jesus.

One basic element of healing is helping persons to accept themselves in relationship to God even while they still have the sickness. Now this is basic, and yet so often we don't do it. We give people the impression that they are sick because of their meanness: "If you do not get right you are going to get sicker. There is not much hope for you anyway; God makes you sick in order to make your spirit sweet." That is the impression we give.

But that isn't the gospel; that isn't our ministry. That doesn't bring anyone into union with Jesus. The gospel says that God loves us as we are; that while we were still sinners Christ died for us. When Christ was crucified there wasn't a single Christian—not a single Christian—in the world.

There wasn't even a Catholic.

Just one Baptist.

By the grace that is in Jesus we belong to God. By His healing power we belong to God. Don't you know that most sickness is rooted in the people's sense of not belonging? They are sheep without a shepherd. They don't know the shepherd; they don't know they belong. So we come in Jesus' stead and tell the precious people, "You belong to Jesus, and I've come to tell you this."

That is the real power of our healing ministry. If we don't know this much about people, our ministry of healing will be greatly limited. Our healing ministry should come out of a conviction that we have been sent by God to lay His claims on people, and God's claim is "You are mine!" Haven't you seen miracles happen through that kind of commitment, through people who know that they belong to Jesus?

You ministers know this. You are ministering to hungry, starving people. You know it, not just intellectually, but experientially. But they will come to know God's love as you manifest it in your relationship with them. For if you believe you belong to God, they will know that they belong to Him, too, because you are in God's healing ministry. This will really get you involved with people through the compassion of God. If you are afraid of getting your hands dirty, stay out of the healing ministry.

In that story about Peter and John at the Gate Beautiful, Peter reached out and touched the man. He had perhaps been lying there nearly forty years—no salve, no Band-Aid, no penicillin. He was a stinking mess, and yet Peter reached out and touched him.

Are you afraid of touching people? Stay away from the healing ministry if you think you are too good to get involved with people's mess. Stay out of the healing ministry because you will have to minister with the compassion of God—you belong to God and you have come to tell people, "I've come to love you! I've come to transmit to you what I've experienced of the love of God."

So we get people to accept themselves in relationship to God in the midst of the sickness, *but* we don't stop there. I think often the church has stopped there—that we have let people know they belong to God even if they are sick and we tell them that God can give them the grace to bear the sickness. So often we have left the impression that grace is the power to bear, the power to endure suffering.

Now grace *is* the power to endure, but more than that, grace is the power to overcome. As we help people to accept themselves in relation to God, we also have a teaching ministry to let them know what their inheritance is in God. You see, very few people have difficulty believing God *can* heal, but so often people do not know He *wants* to heal them.

This is where we are in the healing ministry: helping people to know that their inheritance is health and healing. Jesus called it the "children's bread" (Matt. 15:27). That's a wonderful descriptive phrase for healing—the children's bread. Every child deserves bread from its father. No father makes a child pay for its own meals. "Thank you, Father. Thank you, Mother." "You're welcome" is their response.

This is true of our ministry to people. We are ministering to them their inheritance: "God loves you; God wants to heal you." This is not only true of healing for the body but also for the mind and spirit. I used to hear people testify of the healing grace of God and I knew it was real—I knew it was real for them, but I felt my case was different—I didn't deserve it! I had no right to ask for it, so all I could say to God was, "God, have mercy!" and ask Him to help me endure the pain.

But on the contrary, the Word of God comes and says, "I love you. I've taken your sins into my body and by my stripes you are healed. This is your bread; it's your inheritance."

"Father, you mean I have a right to the saving grace of God, a right to the healing love of Jesus? You mean that Jesus loves me in this way?"

Yes, this is what people need to know: that Jesus loves them in this way, that they have a high priest who is touched by their infirmities. God forgive us if we try to have a ministry separated from the suffering of those whom we love. I rejoice with those who rejoice, mourn with those who mourn and suffer with those who suffer. I stand in the gap so that the grace of God may be transmitted through me. This is our ministry: letting people know what their inheritance is.

This means our healing ministry is committed to those to whom we minister. Otherwise, it is just so much academic procedure. We want involvement with life, which means coming into a real awareness of the love of Jesus as we begin to see what our inheritance is and to learn ways of appropriating the grace of God.

Are you just a minister in robes carrying on a beautiful liturgy, or are you ordained of God as a minister of life?

We are ministers of life! We must be!

God's grace is the life that is in Jesus Christ.

Epilogue

The Story of the Three Indians

In an earlier version of this book the first chapter was called "The Story of the Three Indians." I put the story there as a kind of test of our belief: Can we really believe that such a healing as the Indians told about in this account actually happened? After reading that story, the editors all agreed that the Indians' testimony might be too much for the average reader to believe—they were afraid that we might lose most of the readers before they got past the first chapter.

Agreeing to the wisdom of their observation, we relocate the story here. Test it out with your own reactions. Do you think that what these Indians relate could possibly have happened?

Appropriately enough, I heard the story of the Indians at Blue Cloud Abbey (Marvin, South Dakota). I had been invited there as one of six persons who composed a team which was conducting a nationwide series of workshops on prayer for priests. These workshops were held in seven areas of the country during the early seventies.

This particular workshop was attended by a bishop and forty-five other priests from the upper Midwest. My part in these workshops, as part of the team, was to give a talk on charismatic prayer.

On the way to the workshop our team met at the airport in Minneapolis, from where we were to catch a plane to Watertown, South Dakota. There, at the airport bookshop, we bought copies of *Bury My Heart at Wounded Knee*, which had just come out in paperback. It seemed especially appropriate to read this book as background for the land we were to visit, for the Battle of Wounded Knee had taken place in South Dakota, the heart of Sioux Indian territory.

We were met at the Watertown airport and driven to Marvin, South Dakota. On the way we were joking about the isolation of the spot where we were headed; all the previous workshops had been held in large cities where I could bring in local people to amplify my talks by giving their own testimony of how the Holy Spirit had touched their lives. In Houston, for instance, members of the Episcopal Church of the Redeemer were invited to share what the Spirit had done in helping them build up their remarkable community. Marvin, South Dakota, would be a real test—a challenge to discover a charismatic prayer group in the midst of that prairie land!

When we got there, sure enough, the prior, Father Odilo, told me that there was a prayer group of Indians that met right there at the abbey. But when I asked if members of the group could share their experiences Odilo said no; he was afraid of embarrassing these Indians who might be too shy to address a group of priests. So we gave up that idea.

After my talk Wednesday afternoon, April 26, I was asked to give another talk that evening, a free evening, since there was no place for anyone to go out there on the prairie. So I gave them an additional talk about the healing ministry as it pertains to the life of a priest. As I neared the finish of my talk, Odilo's call bell rang, so he got up and left.

A short time later, he returned, came up to the lectern and whispered that three Indians had just arrived at the abbey, looking for the key to the library to borrow a book on Sitting Bull. He said they had recently experienced healing and might be willing to talk about it in spite of their habitual reticence. Would I want them to speak, if they were willing? "Yes," I said, so out he went again.

Just as I finished speaking these three Sioux Indians suddenly appeared from behind the movie screen at my back. Odilo introduced the unexpected visitors: Simon Keeble, his wife, Lucy, and Nancy, a young woman about twenty years old.

In the following transcription from the tape recording I have not changed the style or the grammar. (The rhythm and the way of speaking are hauntingly reminiscent of the statements of the Indians which preface each chapter of *Bury My Heart at Wounded Knee*.) The first to speak was Lucy Keeble:

> I like to praise my Lord every day for what He has done for me. I used to be a wicked woman: I liked to gossip, and go around telling peoples, hate peoples, and talk about them and do things like that. But one time I needed prayer, and the people, they come and they prayed for me. And Jesus set me free from all the things, all the bad things I was going through, especially the Indian dances, all the witchcraft and everything I've done. He set me free when I opened my heart and dedicated my life to the Lord. He healed me from many things; He healed me from my sickness. Every time I get sick I pray and then He heals me.
>
> Last Sunday we was up to Minneapolis and we went to a healing service. And just when we got there—my boy was with me—he said, "Mom, I got a toothache. They are having a healing service over

311

there. Why don't we go over there?"

So we went over there. He went up and this man prayed for him. And right there Jesus filled seven of his tooth that had cavities. He filled them with silver. This is really so. That's how powerful Jesus is. He can set you free from all your troubles, all your miseries. I never read a Bible when I was out in the world. (I'm in the world, but, you know, when I was out there having a good time and things.) But when I'm closer to walking with Jesus, that's when He showed me many things—all the miracles He could do. Really have faith in Jesus!

And this is what He has done Sunday for my son. He healed my son, filled his cavities and he come home. There are some other things He has done; you can't believe it! How Jesus could work—how He was healing those persons.

I was setting there watching them—how the peoples are going in line, and they get healed. And how powerful Jesus is, because I have that touch from Him. When that man touch me like that, I just went out of myself.

So He can fill you if you have faith in Him and give yourself to Him and open your heart to Him. He'll come in. He'll fill you with the Holy Spirit.

Next to speak was Nancy, the young woman, dressed in the slacks in which she had been working all day. What was most convincing about her testimony was the fact that she was shy and didn't like to talk: She was just saying it because that's the way it was.

I didn't believe that Jesus can heal anybody. I didn't believe, because I have never seen anything happen like that, but these people from Minneapolis took me up there. We went to the prayer meeting, and we walked in the door and I sat down.

I was sitting there, and the man that was standing up there come up to me and told me to come up front. He said, "You don't believe: you never did really accept Jesus. I want to pray for you." I didn't say nothing. I just stood there. He said, "Do you have any fillings?" I said, "No," and he said, "Do you have any gold fillings?" I said, "No." He said, "Do you have any cavities?" I said, "Yes, but I am going to go to a dentist." He said, "Well, I'm going to pray for you. I want you to put your mind on Jesus. Forget everything else." I did what he said, and he started praying for me. I started feeling funny—you know, shaking inside and getting hot. Then he looked in my mouth and said, "You have never had any gold filling or silver filling?" I said, "No," so he called a lady up there and told her to look in my mouth. She say the top part of my mouth had gold in it and the bottom had silver fillings. I still didn't believe him. He knew that, so he told me to go home and look in the mirror.

I went back home that night, and I looked in the mirror. I could see the gold and silver.

I went to the dentist; the dentist said, "You sure have some unusual fillings."

That's when I started believing.

I know it takes a lot from a person to really try to follow the way of the Lord. And it takes a lot to stand up and tell you people about Him.

Father Odilo had just said a prayer for the Indians of the Dakotas and was about to conclude the meeting, when Simon Keeble asked to speak. He began:

You read Acts 1:1-9.
Jesus goes out forty days,
And nobody knows what He does—
How many prayers He uses,
How many faiths and loves He got.
You read that; you will see.
But you in your own heart
You really believe in Him.
He will show you right off,
God can heal you!

But it is the person—you—who will heal.
You have to forgive the sick man yourself,
    and to give him time:
You ask him, "Do you have faith?"
    "Do you love God?"
And he answers,"Yes, yes, sure!" You
    question him. You tell him he must
    leave all his sins at the bottom.
You ask him again, "Do you believe Him?"
He says, "Yes."
Then you go touch him and you heal him right
    now. Powerful how Jesus acts!

I found that out.
It comes through here (pointing to his heart).
I can feel it—just like you get hold of
    electricity.
Is all in your body—makes you sweat.
Then gets you warm and touch you.
And you can heal.

We heal quite a few people in Sisseton.
They sometimes backslide and that's bad.
Jesus don't like that.

But Jesus forgives;
He likes the sinner.
He don't want nobody die.
He wants to be good to everybody.

Now, who likes Jesus? Raise your hand!
(Here the priests didn't know what to expect.
They all raise their hands hesitantly.)
How many of you ever heal anybody? (Here only
   two hands go up.)
How come? How come you know Jesus and you
   no heal nobody? (Dead silence)

The question of whether this story can be true confronts us all, as it did forty-five priests that evening. With most cures we hear about we can imagine a natural process being speeded up; we often harbor a deep-down suspicion that perhaps a natural explanation can be found for what happens. But the filling of teeth? How can we imagine that?

The call for a faith decision—"How come you know Jesus and no heal nobody?"—was taken seriously by at least one man who began from that very night to pray for the sick, and now has seen for himself: "We no longer believe just because of what you said; now we have heard for ourselves, and we know that this man really is the Savior of the world" (John 4:42).

Endnotes

Preface

1. In 1977 we produced a film, "The Power of Healing Prayer," which we filmed at St. Vincent Hospital, Toledo, Ohio. This film documents our teams' praying for twenty-four patients in two days' time, under medical supervision. In the end the chief-of-staff, Dr. Stiff, summed up by saying that twenty of the patients reported that they felt a change in their condition. Of those twenty, the change was medically verifiable in fifteen patients. One of the patients was totally cured of lupus erythematosus (I was able to follow up on this for several years), and a woman was notably improved in her condition of ALS (Lou Gehrig's disease), although I was not able to stay in touch with her afterward.

Chapter One

1. New York: Harper and Row, 1960.
2. Old Tappan, N.J.: Fleming Revell Co., 1969.
3. Edited by Claude A. Frazier, M.M. (New York: Thomas Nelson Inc., 1973).
4. One of the least publicized aspects of the healing brought by the Pentecostal movement has been the healing of relationships among whites and blacks:

"This striking interracial phenomenon occurred in the very years of America's most racist period, those between 1890 to 1920. In an age of Social Darwinism, Jim Crowism, and general White Supremacy, the fact that Negroes and whites worshipped together in virtual equality among the Pentecostals was a significant exception to the prevailing attitudes. Even more significant is the fact that this interracial accord took place among the very groups that have traditionally been most at odds, the poor whites and the poor blacks." Vinson Synan, *The Holiness-Pentecostal Movement in the United States* (Grand Rapids: Eerdmans, 1971) p. 165.

5. *First Latin-American Charismatic Leadership Conference*, reported by Francis S. MacNutt. Private printing by Thomas Merton Foundation, 4453 McPherson, St. Louis, MO 63108 (now out of print).

6. In 1988 I talked to Ralph, and he reported that they have helped start some *400* neighborhood prayer communities in the neighborhood of Brownsville, Texas!

7. Kathryn Kuhlman's *I Believe in Miracles* (Englewood Cliffs, N.J.: Prentice-Hall, 1969) and Emily Gardiner Neal's *Where There's Smoke: The Mystery of Christian Healing* (New York: Morehouse-Barlow, 1967) are two such books. On the other hand, books attacking the healing ministry are also out, such as *The Faith Healers* (Buffalo, N.Y.: Prometheus Books, 1987) in which James Randi investigates the charlatanry of some healers and implies that all Christian healing is trickery.

8. New York: Signet, 1969, reprinted from the 1959 edition.

9. From *The Journal of Pastoral Counseling*, vol. VI, No. 2, pp. 38-41.

10. *Op. cit.*, Robert Miller, "The Effect of Thought Upon the Growth Rate of Remotely Located Plants," pp. 62, 63.

11. "But the average orthodox clergyman is not much

interested in practices that would convey healing. The 'orthodox' Christian, whether liberal or conservative, has little exposure to such sacramental acts and little or no interest in physical or mental healing through religious means. This fact has been brought home to me graphically on several occasions. One was the experience just a few years ago of a friend who is state commissioner of health for one of the large Eastern states. At this instance a group of doctors and clergy were called together to discuss the whole subject of spiritual healing. While the physicians as a whole were deeply involved in the discussion, the clergy who attended hardly treated the subject as a serious one.

"At about the same time a similar meeting was called by a large Western hospital which has a department of religion and health. A select group of clergy and medical men were invited to meet together and discuss the problems. All but one of the physicians responded and eighty percent of them came, while barely fifty percent of the clergy even answered the letter and less than thirty percent of them attended the meeting." Kelsey, Morton T., *Healing and Christianity* (New York: Harper & Row, 1973) pp. 5, 6.

12. *The Spiritual Renewal of the American Priesthood*, edited by Rev. Ernest Larkin and Rev. Gerald Broccolo, with seven other authors (including Francis MacNutt) (Washington, D.C.: U.S. Catholic Conference, 1973) p. 18.

Chapter Two

1. This particular conference (ECCLA in its Spanish abbreviation) has since grown to meetings of hundreds of leaders from all over Latin America.

2. An interesting illustration of this stereotyped image was the title of an article written on my early work in praying for the sick of St. Louis: "Pentecostalism Comes in From

the Tents'' (*St. Louis Review*, August 29, 1969).

3. Morton Kelsey in his fine work, *Healing and Christianity* (cited in Chapter 1), traces the dramatic shift in belief from early Christianity, when healing was considered as God's ordinary will, to the present, when sickness is presented as God's ordinary will for us. This great shift took place between the third and fifth centuries A.D.

4. Louis Evely, *The Gospels Without Myth* (New York: Doubleday, 1970) p. 25.

5. Matthew 13:24-29.

Chapter Three

1. "Salvation and Healing," *The Way*, October, 1970, pp. 302, 303.

2. *Cf.* Morton T. Kelsey, *op. cit.*, p. 185.

3. This ending is not in the earliest manuscripts; many scholars believe that Mark 16:9-20 was added by the early Christian community. If so, it shows that the faith of the early Christians continued to expect the power of healing as an ordinary activity of their community.

Chapter Four

1. The understanding of this passage of James was much affected by the only official translation of the New Testament sanctioned by the Catholic Church for nearly 1,500 years: the Vulgate. This translation from the original Greek to the Latin was done by Jerome around the year 400 A.D. In it the Greek words for (1) *save* and (2) *heal* are both translated by the Latin word *salvo*—save. It makes a real difference in the understanding of the passage whether it is translated "Therefore confess your sins to each other and pray for each other so that you may be *saved*" or "...you may be *healed*."

In this way, the very texts of the Bible that would encourage the faithful to pray for physical healing were translated to emphasize the spiritual aspect alone.

2. Morton T. Kelsey has a clear summary of this history in Chapter 8 ("Healing in the Victorious Church") of *Healing and Christianity*.

3. Henry Suso, *The Exemplar*, tr. by Ann Edward, O.P. (Dubuque: Priory Press, 1962), I:37-38.

4. John T. Noonan Jr., *Contraception* (New York: Mentor-Omega, 1967), pp. 187, 188.

5. *A New Catechism* (New York: Herder and Herder, 1967), pp. 468, 469.

6. First came baptism with its anointings on the forehead, chest and back; then confirmation (anointing on the forehead); then holy orders (anointing on the palms); and finally, the last anointing (with anointing of all the senses).

7. James Randi in *The Faith Healers* (Buffalo, N.Y.: Prometheus Books, 1987) attacks a number of Christian healers for "preying upon the sick" and taking their money in exchange for false hope.

8. Kelsey points out that in the most comprehensive survey of recent theology, John Macquarrie's *Twentieth Century Religious Thought*, not one of the 150 theologians surveyed discusses the effect of man's religious life on his mental or physical health. *Op. cit.*, p. 307.

Chapter Five

1. Quite the contrary, the earliest manuscripts of Mark say that when Jesus met the leper (Mark 1:41), He is described as "being angry," presumably because leprosy is an evil. In later manuscripts the verb is changed to "filled with compassion."

A similar attitude toward sickness in which Jesus treats

it rather like a demon to be exorcised is reflected in Luke's account of the healing of Simon's mother-in-law (4:38,39) in which Jesus "rebuked the fever, and it left her."

2. Except, of course, in His own hometown of Nazareth: "He could not do any miracles there, except lay his hands on a few sick people and heal them. And he was amazed at their lack of faith" (Mark 6:5,6).

3. It is significant, too, that the Gospels usually connect healing with the casting out of demons; healing and exorcism are parallel ministries. They are both connected with evil; sickness is no more God's will than is being tormented by demons. "They drove out many demons and anointed many sick people with oil and healed them" (Mark 6:13).

4. Some of the early manuscripts have "...by prayer and fasting." But the earliest merely have "...by prayer."

5. Agnes Sanford, *Sealed Orders* (Plainfield, N.J.: Logos International, 1972), p. 259.

6. Rufus Moseley. *Perfect Everything* (Macalester-Park, St. Paul: 1952). Revised edition, pp. 49-51.

Chapter Six

1. Happily there are many signs of change in isolated congregations of various denominations where the ministers hold regular healing services.

2. The account of his work with drug addicts can be read in *The Cross and the Switchblade* (New York: Spire Paperbacks, 1964).

3. "The young man was gaunt-blond, trembling slightly, his strained face and close-cropped hair saying pretty clearly that he had recently been to war and had picked up a communicable disease of that war—heroin addiction. Under his arm, he had a fatigue jacket and two Army blankets. He stood only in the back of Bethel Tabernacle—the squat, white

Pentecostal church in Redondo Beach, California, where miracles are supposed to happen....

"Then one young man slowly rose from where he had been kneeling and picked his way through the sprawled congregation to the ex-serviceman in the back of the church.

" 'Welcome, brother.' A hand was extended, and tentatively, briefly accepted. 'You're welcome here.'

" 'Jesus can help you.'...

"It was over in less than a minute. The young man's sobbing gently eased, almost as if mesmerized he began to join those surrounding and supporting him in the simple prayers of thanksgiving. 'Oh, man! Oh, Jesus, thank you.'...

"Bethel Tabernacle's famous 30-second heroin cure had worked again. The guarantee of no withdrawal agonies, no sweats, no pain if you accept Jesus Christ had been fulfilled. One more thoroughly surprised but completely convinced member had been added to Bethel's rapidly growing, spreading, dispersing congregation."

Brian Vachon, and Jack and Betty Cheetham, *A Time to Be Born* (Englewood Cliffs, N.J.: Prentice-Hall, 1972), pp. 1, 2.

Chapter Seven

1. Pamela Carswell, *Offbeat Spirituality* (New York: Sheed & Ward, 1961), pp. 219-223 *passim.*

2. C.S. Lewis, *A Grief Observed*, copyright 1961. (New York: Seabury Press), p. 9. Used by permission of publisher.

3. *Ibid.*, pp. 9, 10.

4. *Ibid.*, p. 11.

5. *Ibid.*, p. 26.

6. *Ibid.*, p. 27.

7. *Ibid.*, pp. 35, 36.

8. Fyodor Dostoyevsky, *The Brothers Karamazov* (New

York: Signet, 1957), p. 226.

9. This heart-rending kind of question is asked in a letter I recently received:

"My sister died last summer. She was a wonderful religious girl who went to church every day of her life until part of this year when her condition became worse. She was a very exceptional girl—never complained in her illness or pain. She had very severe treatments, lost her hair, could not eat or taste food at the end. But always a smile.

"But my great concern now is my mother. My mother as long as I can remember was always a very religious person. Church every day of her life, down on her knees every night praying. My mother was our life and strength.

"My sister's death has completely shattered her. My mother truly believed a miracle would take place.

"My feeling now is, why? We believed, prayed and hoped. She had so much to live for and was so good.

"But I know God's ways are not our ways. It is my mother whom I am greatly concerned about now. She has completely turned her back on God. No prayers, no more belief in God. It is almost two months now and she screams and blames God for everything. This is not my mother, but no one in the family can seem to help or console her in any way."

10. As Paul warns us, "They will turn their ears away from the truth and turn aside to myths" (2 Tim. 4:4).

Chapter Eight

1. Louis Evely, *The Gospel Without Myth* (New York: Doubleday & Co., Inc., 1971), p. 52.

2. *The Word of Faith*, January 1972 (published by Kenneth Hagin Evangelistic Association, P.O. Box 50126, Tulsa, OK 74150).

3. X Y stands for a noted evangelist who stresses a faith

that disregards symptoms of sickness as a precondition for healing.

4. *Under the Shelter of His Wings*, p. 2. A pamphlet published by Macalester-Park Publishing Co., St. Paul, MN.

5. This is only to say we do not need to be anxious about results. In one sense we can pray for a person, then walk away, leaving the results up to God. On the other hand, we do need follow-up: we need to encourage the person to thank God for hearing and answering our prayers. Moreover, there may be a need for further prayer, and for that we need to know the results—or lack of results—of our initial prayer. Most important of all, many healings are progressive and require the continued support of a Christian community.

Chapter Nine

1. Paul Tournier, *The Person Reborn*, pp. 20, 21. Copyright 1966 by Paul Tournier. Reprinted by permission of Harper & Row, Publishers, Inc.

2. The distance between the intellectual world and the experience of healing is pointed out by Morton T. Kelsey:

"Either there is a place for Christian healing in today's world or there is not, and this can only be decided on facts. But Christian theology does not seem to be looking at the facts—although, as we have seen, these are certainly not lacking. Instead one has the distinct impression of a foregone conclusion. The most comprehensive survey of recent theology, John Macquarrie's *Twentieth Century Religious Thought*, makes this quite clear. Healing is simply overlooked today. Of the 150 theologians discussed in that book, *not one* emphasizes the effect of man's religious life on his mental and physical health, as do the more perceptive psychiatrists and students of psychosomatic medicine. Few of these religious thinkers, in fact, even bother with the arguments against healing.

"Of course there are some who, on the side, poke fun at the theological vagaries of Mary Baker Eddy and others, or decry the extravagances of 'faith' healers. But the real reasons for ignoring the possibility of healing are much deeper than this. Our culture has no place for such experiences. Men feel helpless when confronting them, and theology has no answer. Indeed, Christian thinkers cannot consider experiences of healing today because of the tacit acceptance, philosophically and theologically, of a world view which allows no place for a breakthrough of 'divine' power into the space-time world" (Kelsey, *op. cit.*, p. 307).

3. In such instances it is possible that persons other than the sick person could know that he would be healed. Put the sick person himself would ideally have this leading confirmed by his own interior inspiration. Certainly his freedom, his own view of the situation, should not be coerced by outside pressure.

4. Paul Tournier, *The Person Reborn*, pp. 93, 98. Copyright 1966 by Paul Tournier. Reprinted by permission of Harper & Row, Publishers, Inc.

5. Oral Roberts Publications, Tulsa, OK 74102, 1970, pp. 14-16.

6. Allen Spraggett, *Kathryn Kuhlman, The Woman Who Believes in Miracles*. Copyright 1970 by Allen Spraggett. With permission of Thomas Y. Crowell Company, Inc.

Chapter Ten

1. Glenn Clark, Introduction to *The Healing Light*, by Agnes Sanford (St. Paul: Macalester-Park Publishing Co., 1947).

2. Paul Tournier, *op. cit.*, p. 58.

3. Allen Spraggett, *op. cit.*, p. 129.

Chapter Eleven

1. For Christians, of course, there are illegitimate channels of healing, such as spiritualists or psychic healers.

Chapter Twelve

1. Howard R. and Martha E. Lewis, *Psychosomatics: How Your Emotions Can Damage Your Health* (New York: The Viking Press, 1972), p. 7. This whole book, giving a popularized version of medical research that connects many diseases with an emotional and moral component, is worth reading.

An excellent best-selling book on the relation of emotions to sickness, especially cancer, is Bernie Siegel's *Love, Medicine and Miracles* (New York: Harper & Row, 1986). Dr. Siegel writes: "Acceptance, faith, forgiveness, peace and love are the traits that define spirituality for me. These characteristics *always* appear in those who achieve unexpected healing of serious illness" (p. 178).

2. *Ibid.*, p. 160.

3. Bernie Siegel, M.D., *Love, Medicine and Miracles* (New York: Harper & Row, 1986), p. 26.

4. Vinson Synan, *The Holiness-Pentecostal Movement in the United States* (Grand Rapids, Mich.: Eerdmans, 1971), pp. 195, 196.

5. "The Gospel According to Matthew," *The Jerome Biblical Commentary* (Englewood Cliffs, N.J.: Prentice-Hall, 1968), pp. 72, 73.

6. Jean Vinchon, "Diabolic Possession" in *Soundings in Satanism*, ed. Frank Sheed (New York: Sheed and Ward, 1972), p. 4.

Chapter Thirteen

1. Her testimony, on cassette, can be obtained from Christian Healing Ministry, 438 W. 67th St., Jacksonville, FL 32208.

2. There are many fine books on inner healing. Among them are *Healing the Hidden Self* by Barbara Shlemon (Notre Dame: Ave Maria Press, 1982); *Healing Life's Hurts* by Matthew Linn, S.J., and Dennis Linn, S.J. (New York: Paulist Press, 1978); *Healing for Damaged Emotions* by David Seamands (Wheaton, Ill.: Victor Books, 1981); *How to Pray for Inner Healing for Yourself and Others* by Rita Bennett (Old Tappan, N.J.: Power Books, 1984); *The Healing Gifts of the Spirit* by Agnes Sanford (San Francisco: Harper & Row, 1966); *Transformation of the Inner Man* by John and Paula Sandford (Tulsa, Okla.: Victory House, 1982).

3. By Thomas Verny, M.D. (New York: Summit Books, 1981).

4. With my wife, Judith, I have recently written a book on this important topic: *Praying for Your Unborn Child* (New York: Doubleday, 1988).

5. In fact, some Christians even feel impelled to attack inner healing. *The Seduction of Christianity* (Eugene, Ore.: Harvest House, 1985) by Dave Hunt and T.A. McMahon is one such book. In rebuttal for those who are interested, several books have been written: *The Church Divided* by Robert Wise (S. Plainfield, N.J.: Bridge Publications, 1986) and *Seduction?? A Biblical Response* (Buffalo, N.Y.: Buffalo School of the Bible, 1986).

Chapter Fourteen

1. Letters from Mrs. Sophie Zientarski, New Buffalo, Michigan.

2. The book I have found most helpful in describing how

to pray for the sick is Agnes Sanford's *The Healing Light* (Plainfield, N.J.: Logos, 1972—in paperback).

3. Agnes Sanford, *The Healing Light*, p. 86.

4. In Chapter 9, "Having to Say No," in my book *The Power to Heal* (Notre Dame, Ind.: Ave Maria Press, 1977), I discuss this vocational problem of the healing ministry at greater length.

5. For some, the first intimation they have they are called to a healing ministry is this current of energy vibrating in the hands (often during a prayer meeting) which seems to be God's way of alerting some people and encouraging them to pray for the sick.

6. Chapters 2 and 3 in *The Power to Heal* (*op. cit.*) share what I have learned about the benefits of "soaking prayer."

7. I do know one couple, though, who pray for healing and simply relax, empty their minds of all effort and let the love of God flow through them. And people are healed. It's just another reminder that we shouldn't absolutize any method.

8. Agnes Sanford, *The Healing Light*, (Plainfield, N.J.: Logos), pp. 28, 29.

9. *Cf.* Chapter 18 of this book, "Eleven Reasons People Are Not Healed."

Chapter Fifteen

1. Don Basham in his book *Deliver Us From Evil* (Washington Depot, Conn.: Chosen Books, 1973) describes a similar reluctance to get involved in the deliverance ministry. (Basham's book is eminently practical, and I certainly recommend it.)

2. *The Devil* (Chicago: Thomas More Press, 1973), p. 14.

3. "Deliver Us From Evil": General Audience of Pope Paul VI, Nov. 15, 1972. Reported in *L'Osservatore Romano*,

November 23, 1972.

4. Persons who have the gift of discerning spirits go beyond what we are able to observe in the person and are actually able to sense the presence of evil spirits. Some of my colleagues are not only able to "see" the spirits but are able to identify them by name.

5. In July 1972, I prayed for a woman who had been consecrated to Satan in Brazil at the age of eleven. The particular demon she had been consecrated to serve is mentioned in Job 18:14. In the Jerusalem Bible this demon is personified: "He is torn from the shelter of his tent, and dragged before the King of Terrors." In the New American Bible and the New International Version the capital letters are removed and it is changed into a non-personified "king of terrors." It is important to realize that these powers are not impersonal forces of evil; rather we are dealing with real entities that have a name.

6. In the teaching of the Rev. Richard McAlear what seem to be clusters of spirits are really one spirit with a number of different aspects (to the number of six or more). Through discernment he finds out the name of the principal demon (for example, fear) and its aspects (for example, shame, rejection and others). He then binds the aspects to the principal spirit and away from the person's will, mind and emotions. After that he casts out the spirit or if (as is usually the case) the spirit came in through the person's being wounded, rather than their sin or their involvement with the occult, he also binds up the spirit itself and proceeds directly to pray for the person's inner healing. Once this is accomplished the spirit leaves quietly, on its own.

An excellent series of fourteen tapes (audio and video) on deliverance can be obtained from Christian Healing Ministries, P.O. Box 9520, Jacksonville, FL 32208. These tapes include teachings by Richard McAlear, Betty Brennan, the

Rev. Tom White, with Francis and Judith MacNutt.

Chapter Sixteen

1. Padre Guillermo is now Bishop William Weigand of Salt Lake City, Utah.

2. This was not what I was praying for; I was praying for her children as she had asked—another instance of the mysterious and beautiful way in which God answers our prayers.

Chapter Seventeen

1. Tommy spoke about this in a talk he gave for the Christian Preaching Conference Convention in Toronto in 1968. This incident has been transcribed from the tape recording of his talk.

Chapter Eighteen

1. Vinson Synan, *The Holiness-Pentecostal Movement in the United States*, p. 189. Used by permission.

2. *Ibid.*, pp. 192, 193.

Chapter Nineteen

1. *The Person Reborn*, p. 10. Copyright 1966 by Paul Tournier. Reprinted by permission of Harper & Row, Publishers, Inc.

2. Jay Adams, *Competent to Counsel* (Grand Rapids: Baker Book House, 1970), p. 29. Used by permission of Presbyterian and Reformed Publishing Co.

3. *Ibid.*, p. 103.

4. *Ibid.*, p. 126.

5. The recent fall from grace of a famous evangelist, who preached against any need for psychology, and yet was

ensnared in the very sins he so vehemently denounced from the pulpit, is a good example of this.

6. *The Person Reborn*, pp. 34-37 *passim*.

Chapter Twenty

1. An excellent history of prayer for healing and anointing is Morton Kelsey's *Healing and Christianity* (New York: Harper and Row, 1973).

2. Here we should note that the Greek Orthodox Church, far from holding that the sacrament was only to be ministered to the dying or to the seriously ill, held that it was to be ministered to the *healthy* as a preventive against sickness.

3. Study Text II: *Anointing and Pastoral Care of the Sick* (Washington, D.C.: U.S. Catholic Conference, 1973).

Chapter Twenty-One

1. Howard Ervin, who teaches at Oral Roberts University, has made an intensive study of the Greek text of 1 Corinthians 12. He says that the term usually translated in English by the word "gift" is more accurately translated as "manifestation" of the Spirit. This puts the proper emphasis on the Holy Spirit who chooses to manifest knowledge or healing through us at particular times. We are the channels, the instruments, and not the permanent possessors of something which belongs to us. The only accurate translation of the Greek into "gifts" (in the plural) is the one phrase "gifts of healing." Paul does not explain why it is in the plural. Perhaps it is because God chooses to use some people for healing particular sicknesses more than others.

2. In Pentecostal and charismatic circles some of Paul's phrases in 1 Corinthians 12 such as "word of knowledge" and "gift of miracles" have come to have commonly accepted meanings which correspond to our experience of God's

helping us when we minister. We are not sure, however, of exactly what Paul himself meant when he talked, for instance, of a "miracle" as distinct from a "healing."

3. For the encouragement of parents of children who have Down's Syndrome I know of several who have prayed for their child over a period of years. They did not see immediate, instant improvements (which is, of course, always to be hoped for), but over the course of time the child was healed. I think particularly of a boy I met who was in grade school. When this boy was a toddler his doctor recommended that his parents give him up to an institution because he was destined to be like a vegetable. But they took this teaching on constant prayer to heart. Today, not only is their boy still at home, but he is even able to go to school as well.

4. New York: Basic Books, 1977.

5. *Op. cit.*, p. 92.

6. Agnes Sanford, *Sealed Orders*, pp. 153, 154.

POWER HEALING

John Wimber

Healing is high on the agenda in many churches in the eighties. John Wimber tackles this controversial topic by constructing a practical theology of healing.

In particular he
– presents compelling biblical arguments for the practice of a healing ministry, particularly relating to physical healing
– answers difficult questions such as 'Why isn't everybody healed?'
– provides suggestions for equipping Christians to pray effectively for healing.

Power Healing is structured around John Wimber's personal testimony from his calling to a healing ministry, the barren years during which no-one was healed, to his current international ministry.

John Wimber is the charismatic founding pastor of the Vineyard Christian Fellowship. He lectures widely, particularly in Church Growth and Signs and Wonders.

WHEN THE SPIRIT COMES WITH POWER

John White

With the growth of charismatic renewal around the world, more and more Christians are experiencing powerful phenomena:

– uncontrollable shaking
– sudden falls during prayer
– dramatic healings
– prophecy and visions
– unexpected weeping or laughter
– encounters with demons

What are these 'signs and wonders' among God's people? Is it mass hypnosis, demonic deception or genuine revival? Has anything like this happened before in the Church?

John White's experience as a psychiatrist and as a missionary proved invaluable as he travelled the world to interview many people. His research includes the findings of a year spent with John and Carol Wimber and the Vineyard Christian Fellowship. In addition he has thoroughly studied revivals of the past, highlighting the differences and the similarities to what is happening today.

As always John White remains thoroughly biblical, full of practical wisdom and remarkable insights as he comes to fresh and surprising conclusions. He is a prolific author, best known for *Eros Defiled*, *The Fight* and *Flirting with the World*.

THE PRAYER THAT HEALS

Francis MacNutt

'Praying at home is such a beautiful experience, and so easy to learn if people are taught and encouraged to try . . .

'I hope this book meets needs of families that want to learn, as simply as possible, how to pray at home, who especially want to learn to pray for the healing of members of their family. I would like this book to help in a gentle revolution that will get families to pray together. I hope it will show how you can pray for healing with your husband, your wife, your child, or your friend.'

Francis MacNutt, an internationally respected authority on renewal and healing, is the author of *Healing* and *The Power To Heal*, and the joint author, with his wife Judith, of *Praying For Your Unborn Child*.

'Francis MacNutt communicates his faith and awareness of God's love with clarity and simplicity.'

Dr. Ann England, *Renewal*

'Practical guidelines to healing prayer . . . although primarily aimed at prayer in the family, it is applicable to all relationships.'

21st Century Christian